Irish
Lives

Irish Lives

Biographies of fifty famous
Irish men and women

Written by Bernard Share

Designed by William Bolger

ALLEN FIGGIS & CO. LTD. PUBLISHERS
DUBLIN, IRELAND   •   TOTOWA, NEW JERSEY

FIRST PRINTED 1971
SECOND EDITION 1974

342391

MADE AND PRINTED IN THE REPUBLIC OF IRELAND
BY CAHILL & CO. LIMITED, DUBLIN 8.

Contents

Comparative Table: A.D. 1—1900

A.D.	DATE	IRELAND	REST OF EUROPE	REST OF WORLD
1	180		Decline of Rome begins.	
	326			
	350	? Irish raids on Britain.	Constantinople—Seat of Empire.	*Contrived dates*
	360	Earliest writings.	Picts & Scots appear in Britain.	
	364		Empire again divided.	
	432	St. Patrick's mission to Ireland.		
	449		Angles, Saxons & Jutes invade Britain.	
	476		End of dual E & W Roman Empire.	
	484		First Schism, Eastern & Western churches.	
500	500		(Legendary King Arthur of the Round Table).	
	542			Great Plague in East.
	563	St. Columba founds monastery at Iona.		
	569			Mohamet born at Mecca.
	590	St. Columbanus begins Irish mission on Continent.	Pope Gregory the Great.	
	686		Conversion of Britain completed.	
	719		Charles Martel—King of Franks.	
	795	First Norse (Vikings) Raids on Ireland.		
	800	Book of Kells illuminated.	Charlemagne crowned Roman Emperor at St. Peter's.	
	841	Foundation of Dublin by Norse.		
	857		Papacy dispute—Roman & Greek Empires.	
	888		France separated from Empire.	
	980		Viking attacks begin on English coasts.	
1000	1000			Norse discovery of America (Nova Scotia).
	1002	Brian Boru becomes undisputed High King of Ireland.	Massacre of Danes in England.	
	1014	Brian killed at Battle of Clontarf.		
	1016		Canute, King of England.	
	1066		Battle of Hastings—defeat of King Harold by Normans; William of Normandy crowned William I.	
	1086		Domesday Book completed.	
	1095		Peter the Hermit & First Crusade.	
	1099		Knights of St. John instituted.	Capture of Jerusalem.
	1147		Second Crusade.	
	1152	Synod of Kells.		
	1162		à Becket, Archbishop of Canterbury.	
	1169	Anglo-Norman invasion of Ireland.		
	1170		Assassination of à Becket.	
	1171	Henry II comes to Ireland.		
	1172–1250	Gradual Norman settlement.		
	1173		à Becket canonised.	
	1175	Treaty of Windsor (Ruadhrí O'Connor & Henry II).		Saladin, Sultan of Egypt.
	1187		Third Crusade.	Saladin takes Jerusalem.
1200	1202		Fourth Crusade: France & England at war.	
	1209		Franciscan Order established.	
	1215		Magna Carta signed by King John of England.	
	1216		Henry III, King; first Parliament in England.	
	1217		Fifth Crusade.	
	1224	Arrival of Dominicans, first mendicant friars in Ireland.		
	1227		Thomas Aquinas born.	
	1228		Sixth Crusade.	
	1229			Jerusalem ceded to Christians.
	1231c.	Arrival of Franciscans.		
	1248		Seventh Crusade.	
	1270c.	Arrival of Carmelites.		
	1272		Edward I, King of England.	
1300	1306		Robert Bruce, King of Scotland.	
	1307		Edward II, King of England.	
	1315	Bruce Invasion.		
	1318	Edward Bruce's defeat & death.		
	1327		Edward III, King of England.	
	1348		Black Death (plague).	

A.D.	DATE	IRELAND	REST OF EUROPE	REST OF WORLD
	1366	Statutes of Kilkenny.		
	1377		Richard II, King of England.	
	1384		Death of Wycliffe.	
	1399	Second visit of Richard II to Ireland.		
	1399		Richard II deposed, Henry IV King of England.	
1400				
	1413		Henry V, King of England.	
	1424		James I of Scotland liberated and crowned.	
	1431		Joan of Arc burnt at stake.	
	1438		First printing at Haarlem, by Coster.	
	1455		Wars of the Roses commence.	
	1461		Edward IV, King of England.	
	1469		Marriage of Ferdinand of Aragon & Isabella of Castile. Machiavelli born.	
	1475		Michael Angelo born.	
	1476		Caxton begins printing at Westminster.	
	1477–1513	Rule of Garret Mór, the Great Earl of Kildare.		
	1478		Spanish Inquisition begins.	
	1483		Edward IV died and was succeeded by his son Edward V who reigned two months thirteen days—confined to Tower and murdered—Richard III succeeded him.	
	1485		Henry VII, King of England.	
	1492			Columbus sails on his 1st expedition.
	1494–5	Poyning's Parliament.		
	1497			Columbus discovers Jamaica.
	1498			Vasco da Gama doubles Cape of Good Hope.
1500	1500			Vasco da Gama discovers route to India.
	1509		Henry VIII, King of England.	Discovery of Brazil by Portuguese.
	1521		Martin Luther excommunicated.	
	1526		Diet of Worms.	
	1534	Rebellion of Silken Thomas.	Tyndale's New Testament published. Act of Supremacy.	
	1535		Fisher & More executed.	
	1539	The Geraldine League.	Loyola founds Jesuits.	
	1541	Henry VIII declared *"King of Ireland"* by Irish parliament.		
	1542	First Jesuit mission to Ireland.		
	1549		Act of Uniformity.	
	1551		Council of Trent ends.	
	1552		Somerset executed.	
	1553–58	Restoration of Papal authority in Ireland under Queen Mary.	Mary Tudor, Queen of England.	
	1555		Diet of Augsburg.	
	1558		Elizabeth, Queen of England.	
	1560		John Knox—Reformation in Scotland.	
	1564		Shakespeare born.	
	1567	Death of Shane O'Neill.		
	1568		Moors revolt in Spain.	
	1569–73	Desmond Rising, Second Anglo-Irish rebellion of century.		
	1572		Duke of Norfolk executed; massacre of St. Bartholomew; death of John Knox.	
	1577		Drake's first voyage round the world.	
	1587		Mary beheaded.	
	1588		Death of Catherine de Medici ;	Defeat of Spanish Armada.
	1589		Henry IV of Navarre, King of France.	
	1591	Establishment of Trinity College, Dublin.		
	1594	O'Donnell-O'Neill Rising.		
	1598	Nine years' war.		
	1599		Edict of Nantes.	
1600				
	1602	Defeat of Irish & Spanish at Kinsale.	Oliver Cromwell born.	
	1605		Gunpowder plot: Don Quixote published.	
	1607	Flight of the Earls.		
	1609	Ulster Plantation.		
	1610		Henry IV assassinated; Louis XIII King of France.	
	1616		Death of Shakespeare.	
	1618		Raleigh executed; Thirty Years' War begins.	

A.D.	DATE	IRELAND	REST OF EUROPE	REST OF WORLD
	1625		Charles I, King of England; English attack Cadiz.	
	1642	Confederation of Kilkenny.	Death of Richelieu.	
	1643		Louis XIV, King of France.	
	1645	Victory of confederate army under Eoghan Ruadh O'Neill at Benburb.		
	1648		End of Thirty Years' War.	
	1649	Cromwell's campaign in Ireland; Capture of Drogheda & Wexford.		
	1652		England at war with Holland.	
	1657		Cromwell declines English crown.	
	1658		Cromwell's death.	
	1662		Act of Uniformity passed.	
	1665		Great Plague in London.	
	1666		France declares war against England; Great Fire of London.	
	1668		Triple Alliance (England, Holland, Sweden) against France.	
	1672		England & France form treaty.	
	1679		Habeas Corpus Act passed.	
	1680		Strafford executed.	
	1681			William Penn receives grant of Pennsylvania.
	1685		Death of Charles II; James II (Catholic) succeeds.	
	1687	Appointment of Catholic Earl of Tyrconnell as Lord Deputy of Ireland.		
	1689	James lands in Ireland; Jacobite War; Siege of Derry.	William of Orange & Mary (K & Q of England).	
	1690	James II and his Irish French army defeated at the Boyne.		
	1691	Treaty of Limerick.		
	1695–1727	Penal legislation to destroy Catholicism as political force in Ireland.		
	1695	Flight of Wild Geese.		
	1697	Treaty of Limerick *"ratified"* by Irish parliament.	Peter the Great in England.	
	1699	Irish woollen industry crushed by England.		
1700				
	1701		Frederick III King of Prussia; War of Spanish Succession begins.	
	1702		Death of William III; Anne Queen of Britain; England declares war against France and Spain.	
	1704	Protestant dissenters excluded from office by Test Act.		
	1706		Battle of Ramillies.	
	1708		James the Pretender in Scotland.	
	1714		Death of Queen Anne.	
	1717		Triple Alliance—England, France, Holland.	
	1719	Declaratory Act.	France at war with Spain.	
	1724	Swift's *"Drapier's Letters"*.		
	1727		Peter II, Czar of Russia.	
	1739		England at war with Spain.	
	1740		Frederick the Great, King of Prussia.	
	1742		France declares war against Austria, Britain and Holland.	
	1744		Louis XIV declares war against Britain.	
	1748			Afghans invade India.
	1752		G.B. adopts New Style Calendar.	
	1755			Eruption of Mt. Etna.
	1756	Founding of Catholic Committee.	G.B. declares war against France.	*"Black Hole of Calcutta"* atrocity.
	1757		Seven Years' War begins.	British recapture Calcutta.
	1758		Russia invades Prussia.	
	1762		G.B. declares war against Spain.	
	1763		End of Seven Years' War.	
	1767–72	Viceroyalty of Lord Townshend.		
	1770		Lord North, Prime Minister.	
	1771	Relief to Roman Catholics begins with the Bogland Act.		Capt. Cook discovers New South Wales.
	1772	Rise of Patriot Party in Parliament.	Partition of Poland.	
	1773			Strong opposition to tea tax in Boston.
	1774			Boston harbour closed: Warren Hastings made first Governor General of India.

A.D.	DATE	IRELAND	REST OF EUROPE	REST OF WORLD
	1778	Gardiner's Relief Act for Catholics. Organisation of Irish Volunteers.	France declares war against Britain.	
	1779	English concessions on Trade: repeal of most of the Restrictive Acts.	Spain declares war against England.	France recognises American Republic Capt. Cook killed at Owhyhee.
	1780	Repeal of Test Act for Dissenters.		
	1782	Volunteer Convention at Dungannon; Gardiner's 2nd Relief Act; Establishment of Irish parliamentary independence.		
	1782–1800	Grattan's Parliament.		
	1783	Renunciation Act by G.B.		
	1784	Foster's Corn Law.		
	1788		Death of Prince Charles Edward.	Warren Hastings impeached. Mutiny of the Bounty.
	1789	The Regency dispute.	"Times" first published. Trial of Warren Hastings.	
	1790	Wolfe Tone becomes Secretary to the Catholic Committee.	Start of French Revolution.	
	1791	United Irishmen founded.	Death of John Wesley.	
	1793	Hobart's Catholic Relief Bill.	Louis XVI executed; Reign of Terror begins; 2nd Partition of Poland.	
	1795	The Fitzwilliam episode; United Irishmen become revolutionary; Orange Orders founded.	Napoleonic wars till '98.	British take possession of Cape of Good Hope.
	1796	Ireland put under martial law; First French fleet sails to invade Ireland.	Spain declared war against England.	
	1797	The disarming of Ulster by General Lake; Second French attempt against Ireland.	Vaccination introduced by Jenner.	
	1798	Rebellion of '98 breaks out; death of Wolfe Tone.		Battle of Pyramids— Napoleon victorious.
	1799		Napoleon made First Consul following overthrow of French Directory.	Napoleon defeats Turks.
1800	1800	Act of Union becomes law.	First Parliament of U.K.	
	1802		Napoleon appointed First Consul for Life.	
	1803	Rising organised by Robert Emmet.		
	1804		Code Napoleon published	
	1805		Spain declares war on Britain; Napoleon crowned King of Italy; Battle of Trafalgar; Nelson's great victory and death.	
	1807	Daniel O'Connell becomes the leader of Catholic Ireland.		
	1810		Napoleon & Marie Louise married.	
	1812		Napoleon defeats Russians; Burning of Moscow; Napoleon occupies the ruined city Sept. 14–Oct. 19.	U.S. declare war on Britain.
	1813			
	1814		Defeat of Napoleon.	
	1815		Napoleon deposed.	Battle of New Orleans.
	1820	Death of Grattan.	Escape of Napoleon from Elba; Death of George III.	
	1827		Kingdom of Greece founded.	
	1828	The Clare Election.		
	1829	Catholic Emancipation Bill passed; O'Connell takes up "Repeal".		
	1830		Death of George IV, William IV succeeds.	
	1831	National Education System founded.	Gregory XVI, Pope.	
	1834		Houses of Parliament burned; Faraday discovers electric self-induction.	
	1835–40	Administration of Mulgrave Drummond.		
	1837		Death of William IV; Queen Victoria succeeds June, 20; Morse alphabet adopted.	
	1838		Royal Exchange destroyed by fire; National Gallery opened; Coronation of Queen Victoria.	"Great Western" steamer crosses the Atlantic.
	1840		Penny postage instituted.	
	1841		Armoury at Tower of London burnt. Massacre of British troops in retreat from Cabul.	Livingstone discovers Lake Ngami.
	1842–48	The Young Ireland Movement.		
	1844			Joseph Smith, founder of Mormonism, murdered.
	1845	The Queen's Colleges founded.		
	1845–7	The Great Famine.		

	1846	Peel gets the Navigation and Corn Laws repealed.		
	1847	Death of Daniel O'Connell.	British Museum opened.	Gold discovered in California.
	1848	Rising under Smith O'Brien, and others.	General revolutionary movement throughout the Continent.	
	1850	Tenant Right League formed.		
	1860		Submarine telegraph between England and France laid.	
	1863			Battle of Gettysburg.
	1867	Fenian Rising; Execution of "Manchester Martyrs."	Treaty of Commerce between G.B. and France.	
	1869	Disestablishment of the Church of Ireland.		Suez Canal formally opened.
	1870	Gladstone's first Land Act; Home Government Association founded by Isaac Butt.	Death of Dickens.	
	1871		Trade Unions legalised.	
	1873		Death of Napoleon III.	
	1877	Parnell becomes Chairman of Home Rule Confederation.		
	1879	Land League founded by Michael Davitt. Gladstone's first Home Rule Bill; Parnell arrested for conspiracy.		
	1881	Gladstone's second Land Act.		
	1882	Murder of Sir Fred. Cavendish.		
	1883	Phoenix Park murderers arrested—five hanged.	Royal College of Music opened.	
	1884		General Gordon starts for Khartoum.	
	1886	Gladstone's 1st Home Rule Bill defeated; Riots in Belfast.		Gordon rescued by military expedition.
	1887		Queen Victoria's Jubilee Celebration.	
	1889	Parnell made leader of Irish party at Westminster.	Great London dock strike.	
	1890		Opening of Forth Bridge.	
	1891	Death of Parnell.	Education Act passed; free education in England.	United States of Brazil formed.
	1893	Gaelic League founded.		
	1894	Gladstone resigns.		
	1897		Queen Victoria's Diamond Jubilee.	
	1898		Death of Gladstone.	
	1899	Griffith launches his first newspaper.		
	1900			

Introduction

This book describes the lives of fifty famous Irish men and women, from the time of King Brian Boru to that of the first President of Ireland, Dr. Douglas Hyde. Among them are soldiers, politicians, writers, artists, musicians, scholars, teachers, businessmen and scientists, some of whom—though born in Ireland or of Irish parents—spent most or all of their lives abroad.

It was difficult to choose fifty people from the hundreds who are remembered today. For instance, it would have been easy to fill the book with nothing but soldiers and statesmen but this would have produced a very one-sided picture of Irish achievement, so some of them have been left out and other historical figures included who have made their mark in different ways—in the arts or the professions. Thus a complete social and political history comes to light through the lives of the people.

We have tried to produce a book in which is represented every walk of life in which Irish men and women have won fame. Some of these careers figure more numerously than others: every nation has areas of activity in which its people excel, and it would have been misleading to try to include equal numbers from each group. Just as misleading would have been an attempt to include as many women as men. In the past women have not had the opportunities that they have today and we have intentionally avoided including anyone who is still alive.

We have brought together in this book people of all opinions—conservatives and liberals, Catholics and Protestants, nationalists and unionists, rich men and poor men, poets and hard-headed businessmen—because all these people have contributed to the making of history. It is not practicable to include everything that is known about all of them: these short outlines of their careers are intended as introductions. If the reader finds any one of the fifty particularly interesting he will discover fuller biographies in libraries.

If, on the other hand, he finds that for some reason his favourite character from Irish history has not been given a place in this book, he can always hope for a second volume of *Irish Lives*.

Brian Boru
940-1014

A Viking ship—from the Bayeux tapestry

During most of the tenth century the Norsemen were doing their best to conquer the whole of Ireland. They had already built some towns like Dublin, Wexford and Limerick, but now they wanted to occupy the country as well. Things were so bad, with wars going on all the time, that *Aontach Tailteann*, the big fair that used to be held every year in County Meath, could not take place, and it was not until the year 1007 that it started again. Ireland in those days was made up of more than a hundred chieftaincies, and several of these joined with the Northmen to fight their neighbours in the hope of getting some of their land. What was needed more than anything else was a strong man who could put the Northmen (or Norsemen) in their place and make all the Irish chieftains afraid to start wars. In 978 a man of this kind became King of Munster. His name was Brian MacKennedy, later called Boru, or Boroimhe.

Brian was a Dalcassian, born in a small kingdom of that name in East Clare. He became king after his brother Mathgamain had been killed in an ambush. As soon as he was crowned he began to fight the Northmen who lived nearby. He was a very clever fighter—a soldier who worked out exactly what he was going to do before he rushed into battle. This is called *strategy*. He was also the first Irish king to have a navy. The Shannon is a very wide and deep river and it was possible to sail right up it to Carrick-on-Shannon and beyond when the boats were carried overland at the Ardnacrusha Falls. Brian had 300 ships on Loch Derg, near where he lived at Kincora, and he used to take them right up to Loch Ree when he had to fight a battle there. Later on he even sent a navy and army together all the way around the coast to Donegal to fight a rebel king. Nowadays this is called *"combined operations,"* but in Old Irish it was called *"eter muir is tír."*

By the year 984 Brian Boru had fought so well that he had gained the kingship of the whole South of Ireland—Munster, Ossory and Leinster. But in 980 Maelseachlain (or Malachy as he is sometimes called) had become High King at Tara, and he was a very powerful man, too. Each of them was jealous of the other, so they were continually at war to decide who should rule the whole country. No one really won, however—perhaps because the two kings really rather liked one another—and in the year 997 they met at Lough Ree to make peace. They decided to divide Ireland between them, Brian becoming king of all the south and of Dublin and Malachy taking all the rest.

Viking Weapons

After that things should have improved, but they did
not. Malachy's wife Gormflaith, who seems to have
been a very unpleasant person, persuaded her brother
Maelmora to try to seize power in Leinster and join up
with Sitric, the Danish king who still ruled Dublin. She
wanted her brother to overcome both Malachy and Brian
and make himself Ard Rí. Brian heard about the plan
and quickly marched up from Kincora to Glenmama,
which is near Saggart in County Dublin. Here he beat
the Norsemen and the Leinstermen in a big battle.

All this time jealousy had been growing again between
Brian and Malachy, and in 1000 Brian marched to Tara
to claim the High Kingship. Malachy met his cavalry
with a strong army and destroyed them. Brian retreated

to Kincora, but the next year he sailed his ships up the Shannon and in 1002 marched with a big army to Athlone and called on Malachy to surrender. The High King asked for a month in which to get an army together to fight Brian, and Brian very generously agreed. In those days people were polite and courteous to one another even when fighting wars! So Brian went with his army to Tara and pitched his tents while Malachy tried to persuade all his friends to fight on his side. He was not very successful. All the Ulster kings were afraid of Brian Boru and would not take sides. So poor Malachy had to agree to abdicate, that is, to resign and let Brian become Ard Rí. He sadly arrived accompanied by 240 horsemen at Brian's tent to tell him the news. So Brian Boru of

Munster became High King of Ireland at the age of 61, an age when most people are thinking of retiring.

So far Brian's life had been one long series of battles, but when he became High King he began to do his best to make Ireland a better place to live in. In 1004 and 1005 he went north to persuade the kings there to obey him as High King. When he stopped at Armagh, he gave the church there 22 ounces of gold and agreed to recognise the Archbishop as Primate of All Ireland—as he still is today. He was shown the beautiful Book of Armagh (which can now be seen in the library of Trinity College, Dublin) and his secretary Maelsuthain made a note in it which described Brian as *Imperator Scotorum,* or Emperor of the Irish Nation.

In 1005 he made a *Circuit of Ireland,* marching through Connacht, up to the Erne, across to Armagh again and down through Meath and Dublin to Cashel. Now he was really and truly king of all the Irish, and no one dared to raise a finger against him.

For the next seven years Brian was very busy repairing all the damage that the wars had caused. He had to rebuild churches that had been knocked down, and he built many new ones as well. A lot of valuable books had been stolen from the monasteries and libraries, and he sent abroad for new ones. He also awarded scholarships to students to help them go and study in foreign countries. Ireland was so peaceful that when a lady put a gold ring on the end of a rod and carried it all the way from Tory Island in Donegal to Glandore harbour in West Cork nobody attempted to steal it from her. Even the Northmen who still lived in Ireland dared not make Brian angry, and so kept to themselves.

But in 1013 trouble started again. Brian was now 72 and his enemies thought that he was getting too old to notice what they were doing. The Northmen again joined up with the men of Leinster, who had not forgotten their defeat at Glenmama in 997. Gormflaith again started making trouble and tried to persuade Sitric and the Northmen and her brother to attack Malachy, who was still king in the northern half of the country. Brian marched up from Kincora to Malachy's aid and besieged Dublin from September to Christmas, 1013, but had to go home again because he ran short of food. Meanwhile Sitric had been looking for friends to help him, and 2,000 Norsemen arrived from Scotland and the Isle of Man. Brian had gathered men from Munster and Connacht and had Malachy's army standing by. On

The death of Brian Boru

Good Friday, April 23rd, 1014, the two sides met in battle at Clontarf on the north shore of Dublin Bay.

The battle lasted twelve hours and many of the finest princes on both sides were killed. Gormflaith's brother Maelmora was killed, and so were Brian's son Murchad and *his* son Turloch. Brian himself was too old to join the fighting and stayed in his tent waiting for the result. As the Norsemen retreated, trying to get back to their ships, one of them slipped into the tent and killed the High King. Brian was buried in Armagh, and there was not as big a funeral in Ireland again until the death of Daniel O'Connell. So ended the life of the greatest of all Irish High Kings, a very clever man who had to spend too much of his life fighting but who managed to bring peace to the country and to undo much of the damage done by the Norsemen. Though there were Norsemen in Ireland after the Battle of Clontarf, they were never again able to take over or even attempt to take over the country. If Brian had not won, all Ireland might now be speaking Norwegian!

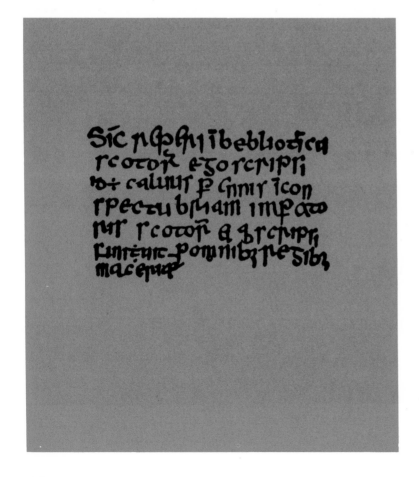

Reference to
Brian Boru in the
Book of Armagh

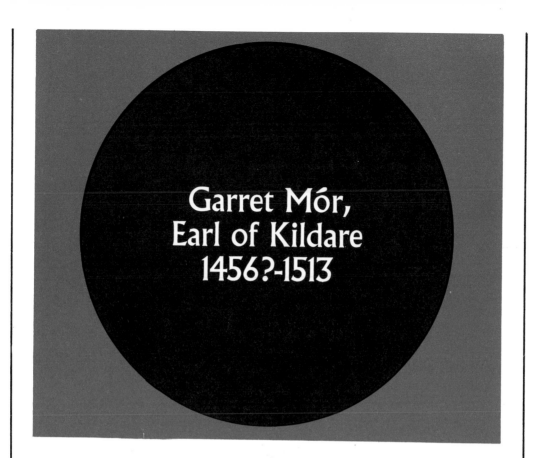

Garret Mór,
Earl of Kildare
1456?-1513

Maps of Ireland as it was about the year 1500 show that most of the country was divided up between different earls and chiefs. The really important earls were Ormond, Desmond and Kildare; throughout most of the fifteenth century one or other of these men held power in Ireland as representative of the English King. This did not mean, however, that they ruled the whole country and that all Ireland was under the control of England—far from it. The English had their own troubles and had not much time or money to spend on the affairs of the remote country that the Pope had granted to Henry II in 1182. The maps also show that the English Pale was a very small piece of Leinster, stretching from Dundalk down to Bray and not stretching even as far west as Trim. This was the only area directly under English rule, but even here more and more people were speaking Irish and going back to Irish ways. Outside the Pale the country was ruled by the great Gaelic chiefs and the great earls.

"Since all Ireland cannot rule this man, this man must rule all Ireland," King Henry VII said of Garret Mór, and the Great Earl came in fact to be the uncrowned king, respected by both the Anglo-Irish and the Gaelic chiefs, related by marriage to all the most important families and with his own army to use as he liked, even though it officially belonged to the English King. At one time, in 1504, he could easily have conquered the English Pale and made himself Ard Rí of an independent Ireland. But he did not and his chance passed, because Garret

The tomb of Piers Butler in St Canice's Cathedral Kilkenny

Ireland about 1500

Mór was not really interested in what we would now call national unity. He wanted power—the power that comes from owning lands and castles; power over smaller chiefs, over the English who had taken up Irish ways; power over the representatives of the English King. He ruled Ireland for more than thirty years, and only once were the English able to get the better of him.

To understand Garret Mór's life it is necessary to know a little of what was happening in England at the time. England ruled part of France, and was not only having to fight wars there but was also trying to deal with people called *pretenders,* who claimed they had a better right to be king than the reigning monarch. These claims led to civil wars—the *Wars of the Roses*—between the supporters of the House of Lancaster and the House of York, and this meant that the King and Parliament had not many soldiers to spare to garrison the Pale in Ireland. They could not forget about Ireland altogether, because the Anglo-Irish interested themselves in what went on across the Channel and often interfered. The Earl of Kildare supported the Yorkists, which made it difficult for him when somebody else was in power.

Garret Mór was born in 1456, perhaps in the huge castle of Maynooth which belonged to his father, Earl Thomas, and later to him. We know very little about him as a boy or a young man, only that he grew up to be *"a mightie man of stature full of honour and courage."* He was Anglo-Irish, which meant that he was descended from the Norman invaders of three centuries before, but like many of the families who had settled in Ireland he had learned Irish ways and the Irish language. His library contained books in Irish, English, French and Latin, and he had many contacts with the great chiefs such as O'Neill and O'Donnell. For most of his life he was warring with the Butler family, who were Earls of Ormond. *"Both these noblemen laboured with tooth and nail to overcrow and consequentlie to overthrow one the other,"* said the English historian Holinshed. *". . . they wrought by hooke and by crooke to be in authoritie superiours."* The Butlers supported the Lancaster party in England.

Edward IV

28

A Norman Warrior

Edward IV became King of England in 1461. In 1472 a parliament was held under Garret Mór's father, Thomas, at Naas, which set up a special army, called *The Guild of Saint George* to defend the Pale against *"Irish Enemies"* and *"English Rebels."* Young Garret was given the command of 24 spearmen. His father died on March 25th, 1477, and Garret became not only Earl of Kildare but Justiciar of Ireland—the King's right-hand man. He called his first parliament together in 1478, at Naas on May 29th, even though the King had sent over another man, Lord Gray, to be his Deputy in Ireland. Garret Mór and his friends refused to have anything to do with him, and after this the Earl was left alone to rule Ireland in his own way and to be elected and re-elected by his friends and relations to the highest position in the land.

Edwards IV and V of England were followed by Richard III, a Yorkist who was killed at the battle of Bosworth on August 21st, 1485. The next man to hold the throne, Henry VII, was a Tudor, but the cause of the White Rose, the badge of the Yorkists, was still supported by the Anglo-Irish. Kildare wondered how long Henry would manage to keep the throne, and whether he was really the next in line for the monarchy. So when, in 1487, a young boy arrived in Ireland who was said to be Edward of Warwick and the real heir to the kingdom of England and France and Lordship of Ireland, many people supported him. If he was the true Edward, then he was the son of a man who had been born in Dublin and who had been very popular. Garret Mór and other important people were ready to believe in him, even though those on the other side said that his real name was Lambert Simnel and that he was a fake.

The Tower of London

Irish Warriors

On May 25th, 1487, 2,000 German soldiers arrived in Dublin, sent over by the Duchess of Burgundy, who was an enemy of Henry VII, and this made the Great Earl decide definitely to support the boy's claim. Lambert Simnel was crowned on May 24th in Christ Church Cathedral, Dublin, as Edward VI of England, and the next step was an invasion of England to try to put him on the throne. A combined force of Germans and Anglo-Irish landed in Lancashire, but were completely defeated in battle on June 16th. Simnel ended his days washing the dishes in Henry VII's kitchen, but Garret Mór stayed where he was—as the King's deputy in Ireland, even though he had plotted against him! He had to swear an oath of loyalty, and the King sent over Sir Richard Edgecombe to arrange this. The Great Earl kept him waiting as long as he could. Poor Edgecombe, who was lodging with the Black Friars in Dublin, wrote in his diary for July 11th, 1488: *"Item the Seyd Sir Richard likewise lay still in the seyd Fryers abyding the comying of the seyd Erle, to the gret costs and chargis of the same Sir Richard."*

Henry VII

For the next few years Garret Mór hosted throughout Ireland, visiting his friends and attacking his enemies. He had his difficulties with the English, but the Gaelic lords respected him more and more. In 1491 he was asked to settle an argument between O'Neill and O'Donnell.

Another pretender to the English throne appeared in 1491, when a young man who said he was one of the two sons of Edward IV landed in Cork. The King's friends said his real name was Perkin Warbeck and that he came from France. Many of the Irish nobles supported him, though this time Garret Mór was more careful. Henry VII, who was a strong, determined man, had decided to try to put an end to the home rule Ireland was enjoying, before it led to complete independence. In 1494 he sent over Sir Edward Poynings to clean up the administration by replacing all the Anglo-Irish government officials with Englishmen. Poynings held a parliament which lasted into 1495, and it passed laws saying that in future the Irish Parliament was only to copy what was done at Westminster. It also ordered a new ditch, or fence, to be put up around the Pale, and it accused Garret Mór of treason. He was tricked into coming to Dublin, was arrested on February 27th, 1495, and on March 5th sent as a prisoner to the Tower of London. *"That was a sad deed!"* said Peregrine O'Clery, the annalist, *"to practice treachery on the man to whom the English and Irish of Erinn submitted and who gave them security . . . a man who suppressed stealth and force and oppression, robbery and violation in his time in Erinn."*

But when Henry VII met Garret Mór he decided that it was better to have the Earl on his side than against him. *"If you can't beat them, join them,"* we might say today—and that is just what Henry did, by arranging for Garret Mór to marry his own first cousin, Elizabeth St. John, and by pardoning him and all his supporters. She was the Earl's second wife, and when he brought her back to Ireland *"joy and exultation seized on the men of Eirinn at his coming."* For the rest of his life Garret Mór was left in charge of Ireland as the King's deputy—but he was far more than that. He was the man whom everyone, Saxon and Gael, respected. In the year 1500 he held a Great Council, like an Irish *"parliament"*, in Kilkenny, without any interference from the English, and in 1503 he again went to England to see the King. On his return he brought back his son whom he had had to leave as a hostage eight years before.

In 1504 a great battle was fought at Cnoc Tuagh near Gaillimh between Garret Mór, O'Donnell, O'Neill and the English of the Pale on one side and the chiefs of Connacht and Ormond on the other. It was really a private Irish fight, but the King was told it was a victory for the English in Ireland and he invested Garret Mór with the Order of the Garter. The Great Earl served in the same office of Deputy under Henry VIII and was finally killed in a fight with the O'Mores of Leix, shot by one of their new muskets. So died a man *"full of honour and courage, open and plain, hardly able to rule himself when he was moved to anger, easily displeased and soon appeased."* *"He succoured and relieved the poets of Ireland,"* said Peregrine O'Clery, which means that though serving the English King he was a man who believed in the old Gaelic way of life and who tried in his own way to treat the Irish and the Anglo-Irish as equals and to rule them as one nation.

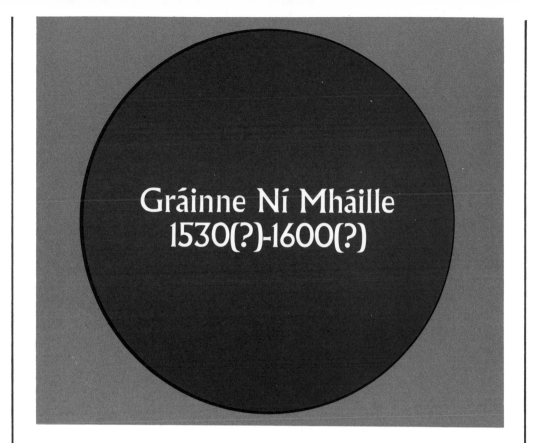

Gráinne Ní Mháille
1530(?)-1600(?)

Gráinne Ní Mháille, Grany O'Mayle, Grany Ne Male, Grany Ny Vale, Grany Ne Malley, Grace O'Malley, Gránuaile . . . those are only some of the ways in which the daughter of Dubhdara Ó Máille, chieftain of Umhaill Uachtrach Uí Máille, was called by people who knew her, and feared her. She was known not only to her own people in Mayo and Galway, and all along the western seaboard, but to the English Government far away in Dublin. In 1593 she was described by Sir Richard Bingham, President of Connacht, as *"a notable traitress and nurse of all the rebellions in the province for forty years."*

Rebellions and rebels were common in Ireland in the second half of the sixteenth century. Henry VIII of England had been crowned King of Ireland and was trying to make the title mean something by bringing all the still independent parts of the country under his

King Henry VIII

control. He met with strong opposition, but none stronger or more determined than that from a woman—and a seafaring woman at that.

In spite of the fact that Ireland is an island with many fine natural harbours, the Irish have never been known as great sailors. Brian Boru commanded a fleet of warships, but he was one of the few leaders to make use of the seas around us—either for peace or for war. The O'Malley clan were an exception. A Latin motto which they used to represent their clan read *"Terra Marique Potens"* (powerful on land and sea), and they were more at home cruising the narrow waters between Inishturk, Inishbofin and Clare Island, than on their lands of Burrishole and Murrisk. They were sea rovers—rather like modern pirates—attacking their enemies both on shore and on the water. These enemies included both rival clans and the representatives and allies of the English forces in Ireland.

16th Century galley as used by Granuaile

There are many stories and legends about Granuaile, as we will call her, but very little is known for certain. Her name may have come from *Gráine mhaol* (cropped hair), meaning that she cut her hair like a boy. Her early years were probably spent on sea-going expeditions with other members of her family. She was married twice, the first time to Domhnall an Chogaidh Ó Flaithearta, of Baile na hInse, Co. Galway. There were two sons of this marriage, Eoghan and Murchadh. Her second husband was a Burke, a member of the De Burgo family who had invaded Ireland with Strongbow and had taken to Irish ways, customs and speech. Richard Burke, who became chief of the Burkes of Mayo in 1582, was known as Risteárd an Iarainn, Richard of the Iron. He and Granuaile had a son, Theobald, who carried on the family tradition and was known as Tióbóid na Long, Theobald of the ships. In later years, however, he sided with the English forces. It is possible that there was also a daughter, because later on we hear of another Richard Burke who was described as Granuaile's son-in-law.

Until the reign of Henry VIII, the powerful men in Ireland, both Gaelic and Anglo-Irish, had been left alone to rule much as they liked in areas remote from the English Pale in the East. In 1568 however, Sir Henry Sydney, the Lord Deputy, arrived in Galway city with an army, and made Sir Edward Fitton the first President of Connacht, ruling directly for the King. This Sir Edward Fitton seems to have been a cruel and violent man, and the *Mac an Earlas,* the sons of the Earl of Clanrickarde, head of the Burke family, broke out in rebellion with many of their supporters. The city and country around it were in a state of turmoil until 1575, when Sir Henry Sydney returned to find the town *"much decayed, and almost desolated, sundery of the good householders having sought new habitations, under MacWilliam Eughter."* MacWilliam Eughter, was the Irish title enjoyed by Granuaile's husband, Burke. When Sydney arrived, several of the rebel leaders, including Richard Burke, were persuaded to submit to royal authority. The King's deputy and Granuaile's husband spoke to one another in Latin, as the latter had no English. Granuaile herself had other ideas, even though she also agreed, for the moment, to stop her warlike activities and submit to the English

Sir Henry Sydney on expedition

Donetto chrcane the messenger

power. This is how Sir Henry Sydney wrote of his meeting with her in 1576:

> "*There came to me a most famous feminine sea-captain, called Grany-I-Mallye, and offered her service unto me, wheresoever I would command her, with three galleys and two hundred fighting men, wither in Ireland or Scotland. She brought with her her husband, for she was, as well by sea as by land, more than master's mate with him . . . This was a notorious woman in all the coasts of Ireland.*"

In spite of her meeting with Sydney, she must have continued in her opposition to the foreign Government, because in 1577 we hear of her being captured by the Earl of Desmond and brought to Dublin. She was released, however, in 1578. In 1579 she was being so troublesome to the Dublin Government that a special body of troops had to be sent from Galway to besiege her castle at Carrig a Chabhlaigh (Carraighooly) near Newport in County Mayo. The expedition sailed on March 8th, but Granuaile put up such a strong defence that they had to raise the siege on the 26th and only just

Queen Elizabeth

avoided being captured. In October, 1582, she was again in trouble—accused of plotting rebellion with the Earl of Thomond and others.

Granuaile was a queen in her own right; she had ignored the claims of her younger brother on the death of her father and had made herself ruler of the whole area around Clew Bay, including the islands. Probably the most famous example of her royal pride is seen in the story of her visit to Queen Elizabeth of England, in London. The date of this visit, if it actually occurred at all, is not known, but Gráinne of the Heroes, as she was called, is said to have refused to be made a countess, saying that she was as much a queen as the English monarch. Elizabeth made Granuaile's son, Tióbóid na Long, who had been born on the way to England, the first Viscount Mayo. It was on the way back from this visit that Granuaile is supposed to have landed at Howth in County Dublin. Instead of a welcome from the St. Lawrence family at the castle she found the gates closed, and was so angry at this that she kidnapped the young heir, who was playing by the sea, and carried him away to County Mayo, refusing to let him return home until the family promised that the gates would never again

Clare Island Castle, an O'Malley stronghold

be shut at mealtimes and that a spare place would always be laid. This tradition has lasted at Howth Castle until the present day.

When Granuaile's first husband, Domhnall Ó Flaithearta, died, she was left without any means of support, as women could not inherit property under the Gaelic law. When she married Richard Burke, it was probably more in the nature of a business arrangement—or at least Granuaile made it so! She is supposed to have taken over many of her husband's castles and to have sent him away not long after their marriage. They must still have been together in 1583, however, because Richard Burke succeeded in calming her down when she threatened to kill a man called Theobald Dillon who had intended to invade her territory. Shortly after this Richard seems to have died, because we learn of Granuaile retiring alone to Carraig an Chabhlaigh with 1,000 cows and mares.

It does not seem that the pirate queen ceased annoying the English forces even then, because we next hear of her obtaining letters of safe conduct from Sir Richard Bingham, the new President of Connacht, in 1586. The letters were not much help to her, for Sir Richard seized her, claiming that she had raided and plundered the Aran Islands, and he was going to execute her. The gallows was built and everything ready when Granuaile was set free after a promise of her good behaviour was made by another Richard Burke, who was probably her son-in-law and who was known to the English as *The Devil's Hook*. The promise of good behaviour was no better than the promise of safe conduct on the other side; Richard rebelled, and Granuaile had to flee northwards to seek protection from O'Neill and O'Donnell in

Stone head from Murrisk Abbey said to represent Granuaile

Ulster and was not able to return for some time because many of her ships had been destroyed.

Very little is certain of Granuaile's actions from then until the end of her life. She was the kind of person who quickly became as much a part of legend as of history, and many, many stories were handed down through the years, telling of her exploits on land and sea. There is scarcely a castle, village or town on the west coast that does not claim some connection with Gráinne Ní Mháille, but stories are one thing and the true facts are another. It was in 1593, some say, that her visit to England took place, and in 1595 she asked Lord Burghley, the Lord High Treasurer of England, for one third of her husband's estates, which had been confiscated, to be restored to her. It does not seem that this was done, because some few years after this she died, probably in great poverty, and was buried, again according to legend, on Clare Island, which had been her home and the headquarters of her naval operations. Granuaile was probably not a beautiful woman, and she was certainly as much of a pirate as were those whom she attacked with her fleet of fast-moving carracks; but she was every inch a queen, and one of the few women of her time to hold power in her own right.

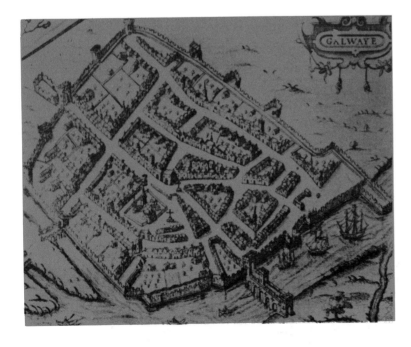

Galway in the 16th century

Hugh O'Neill
1550(?)-1616

"He is the best man of war of his nation"—so said George Carew, Lord President of Munster under Queen Elizabeth I, of Hugh O'Neill, called by the English the Earl of Tyrone, called by his family and followers *The O'Neill,* a descendant of O'Neills who had once kept the High Kingship in the family for 650 years without a break. When on September 14th, 1607, Red Hugh O'Donnell, Hugh O'Neill and 97 of their companions and followers boarded a ship in Loch Swilly and sailed into exile, a civilisation thousands of years old came to an end. The Flight of the Earls marked the end of Gaelic Ireland as an independent nation: the struggle against the Normans, Anglo-Normans and English had been lost. Yet O'Neill came very close indeed to ridding his country of the invader permanently. If he had not listened to the advice of the over-eager O'Donnell before the battle of Kinsale . . . if the Spaniards had sent more help . . . There are so many *"ifs"* in history—and one of the biggest ifs concerns Hugh O'Neill himself.

Ireland in the middle of the sixteenth century was a very complicated place to live in. There was an English government in Dublin, but it only controlled a small

Irish costumes in O'Neill's time

part of the country around the capital, called the Pale, though there were other English cities along the coasts, built with strong walls to keep out the Irish who were always attacking and plundering them. In many parts of the land, particularly in Ulster, the old Gaelic system, with its chiefs, laws, customs, and traditional way of life, still held power. The English were determined to conquer these proud men and make them subjects of the Crown. They found this very difficult, but they would have found it even harder if the Irish had been able to agree among themselves. Instead they fought one another as much as they fought the foreigners. Some joined with the English to destroy their own enemies and were themselves destroyed. People changed sides so often that it was very hard to know who one's friends were. Even brothers fought against one another over lands, cattle, wives and the right to be called Chief. So the English followed a policy of *"divide and rule"*—setting one clan and one chief against another and then seizing their lands and property when their backs were turned. It was into this kind of world that Hugh O'Neill was

Sir Henry Sydney leaving Dublin

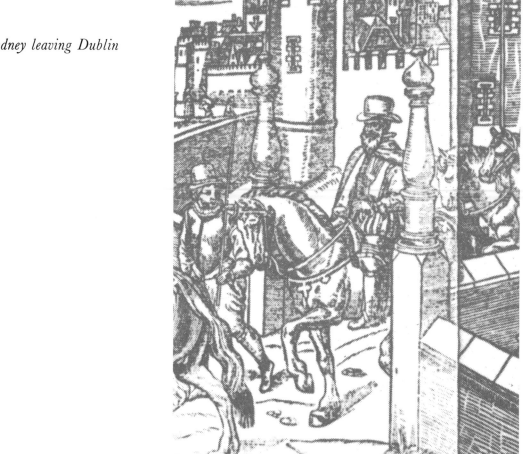

born—a world of treachery, of deceit, of famine, of murder—and in this world the Irish and English were as bad as one another. For much of his life Hugh could not make up his mind about whose side he was on or what he really wanted. It was only when the tide seemed to be turning and there seemed to be some chance of getting rid of the English for good that he threw in his lot completely with his own people—the Irish. Until Hugh O'Neill brought all the anti-English forces together in one great army, people did not really think of themselves as a nation, rather as separate, unassociated units—MacCarthaighs, or O'Flaghartaighs, or O'Neills and others. Hugh taught the Irish pride in their nation-hood, and his lesson nearly brought victory—perhaps because he knew his enemy so well.

Hugh O'Neill was taken to England at the age of nine by Sir Henry Sydney, Queen Elizabeth's Lord Deputy, and brought up as an English gentleman in Ludlow Castle and in other noblemen's houses. The Government's hope in this was to win him over to the English way of thinking and to turn him into what would now be called a "loyalist". They nearly succeeded. O'Neill went back to Ulster at the age of 17, in 1567, full of English ideas and wanting only to gain the leadership of all the O'Neills and rule in his own territory with the agreement of the English Government in Ireland. The family history was very tangled and complicated, and his rival for the chieftainship, Turlogh O'Neill, was certainly not going to give it up without a fight. So for the next few years Hugh spent his time living like a Gaelic leader, raiding his enemies, joining with the English against them, with occasional visits to Dublin to remind the Government that he was loyal to the Crown. He took part in the Desmond rebellion in 1569 on the English side, helped the first Earl of Essex at Carrickfergus in 1573, and altogether did everything he could to persuade the authorities to make him the second Earl of Tyrone. This was not easy, as he was always suspected of playing a double game, of plotting with Spain and of secretly planning to rebel. In 1585, however, he persuaded the Dublin Parliament to grant his request, and it looked as if he was going to give no more trouble to the authorities. But O'Neill was only playing for time. The English intended to wipe out Gaelic civilisation—laws, lands and everything. No title would protect O'Neill against this policy. No title except one: *The O'Neill*, chief of his clan, heir to the High Kings. In 1588 ships of the Spanish Armada, which had been sent to attack England, were wrecked on the Irish coasts. O'Neill helped some of the castaways when the Government's instructions were

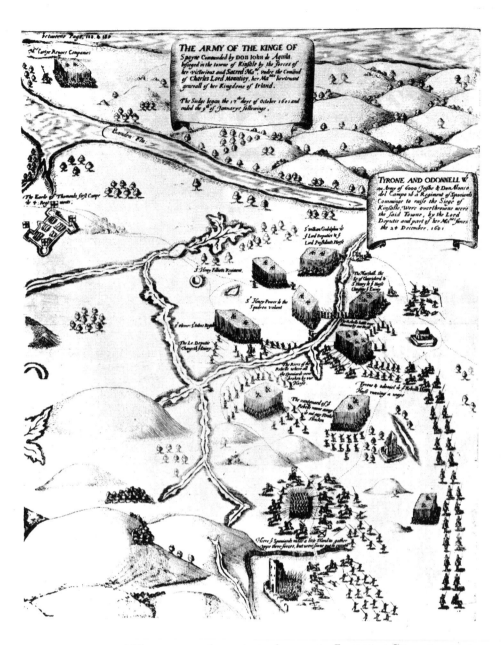

Map of the Battle of Kinsale

to kill any survivors on the spot. In 1590 he was summoned to London over the death of Hugh Gaveloch O'Neill, who had been informing on him. The story was that the angry Earl had personally hanged him. He was kept under house arrest for a few months and then allowed to go home; but before he left London he did some shopping. He bought furniture for his house in Dungannon and lead for the roof. The lead, however, never kept any rain out; when Hugh got it back to Ulster he made it into bullets instead.

In 1591 Hugh married his second wife, Mabel Bagenal, the sister of an English officer who was to become first his ally (against Maguire, in 1593) and then his deadly enemy. He was still running with the hare and hunting with the hounds, but the time was quickly coming when he would have to make up his mind one way or the other. In 1587 the young Red Hugh O'Donnell had been kidnapped and imprisoned in Dublin Castle. In 1592 he escaped, and, after a terrible journey in the snow through the Wicklow mountains, he reached Donegal where he was proclaimed chieftain. Many people believed that Hugh O'Neill had rescued him, and at that time people—particularly the English Government—believed almost every rumour. Certainly Hugh was building up his forces by making treaties with his neighbours and winning them over to his way of thinking. In 1586 he had 6,900 men under him; by 1592 their number had grown to 17,500—a huge army in those days. In 1594 he fought his first battle against the English, which ended in a truce. They were too weak to risk a complete break, but it came in the next year: full-scale war. Hugh was proclaimed *The O'Neill*—which to the English was an illegal title. He had a wonderful secret service organisation and knew what the enemy was going to do almost before they knew it themselves. And he knew the country and knew how to fight in it. The English believed in large, organised armies and pitched battles. The Irish used guerilla warfare, attacking when the enemy least expected it, burning crops, using a "scorched earth" policy to starve them out.

Then something strange happened. In 1595 The O'Neill sued for peace. Did he really want it? Was he waiting for Spanish help? Was he waiting for the many priests who were moving among the people to stir the

The Meeting of the Earls

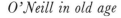
Lord Mountjoy

whole country up into a great religious crusade? The O'Neill was not a fervently religious man—he had been brought up among Protestants and could see good in both sides—but he knew how to use popular opinion to help his cause. There was a truce in 1595–6, during which both sides built up their forces, and Hugh smuggled in arms from wherever he could get them. Then in 1597 the English moved, only to be defeated completely by The O'Neill's forces at Benburb and by Lacy at Tyrellspass. Another truce was arranged and the Queen's pardon was promised for The O'Neill. But in 1598 Sir Henry Bagenal was sent to relieve Portmore with 4,000 infantry and 300 cavalry. O'Neill and O'Donnell collected 8,000 men, and on August 15th completely routed the English at the battle of the Yellow Ford on the Blackwater, killing Bagenal and one third of the enemy forces. The way seemed to be open for complete victory for the Gaelic chiefs.

Then a new force appeared on the scene. In 1599 the second Earl of Essex, sent over to dispose of The O'Neill, had made a truce with him instead and was beheaded for his trouble when he returned to London. The next leader, Lord Mountjoy, was a very different opponent— a tough, ruthless general with a large, well-trained army of 20,000. There were rumours that Spanish aid for O'Neill was on the way, and Mountjoy's task was to break Hugh's power before help could arrive. He tried

O'Neill in old age

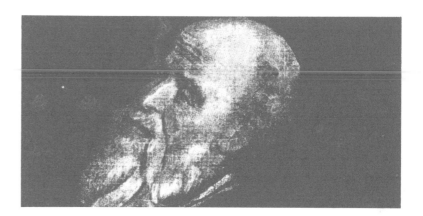

and nearly succeeded through massacre, destruction of crops, and turning one chief against another, but when a disappointing Spanish force finally arrived and occupied Kinsale on September 23rd, 1601, O'Neill and O'Donnell still had powerful forces in the field. Mountjoy besieged Kinsale, but the two chiefs made a swift march from the North and besieged him. The fate of Ireland hung in the balance, for if Mountjoy had been defeated English power in the country would have been completely broken.

The battle of Kinsale took place on December 24th, 1601—a day before Hugh wanted it, and it ended in utter defeat for the Irish and Spanish forces. Within twenty-four hours the whole picture had changed. Hugh was on the run, his forces shattered, his allies gone. Dungannon was occupied and the O'Neill inauguration stone at Tullahogue destroyed. The war went on, but more and more chiefs began to make separate peace, and finally, on March 30th, 1603, The O'Neill laid down his arms at Mellifont and renounced his proud title. Even though when he later visited London some of his lands were restored, the Gaelic system was broken. Ulster was laid open to English settlement and colonisation. O'Neill and O'Donnell came to prefer exile to living in their own country as shadows of their former selves, and so set sail for the Continent, eventually reaching Rome where, on the 20th of July, 1616, The O'Neill died. We know from his letters that even in exile he continually requested the King of Spain and other European rulers to undertake another campaign in Ireland.

O'Neill's tomb

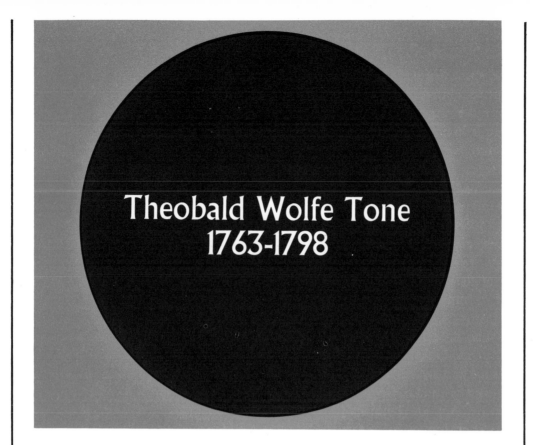

Theobald Wolfe Tone
1763-1798

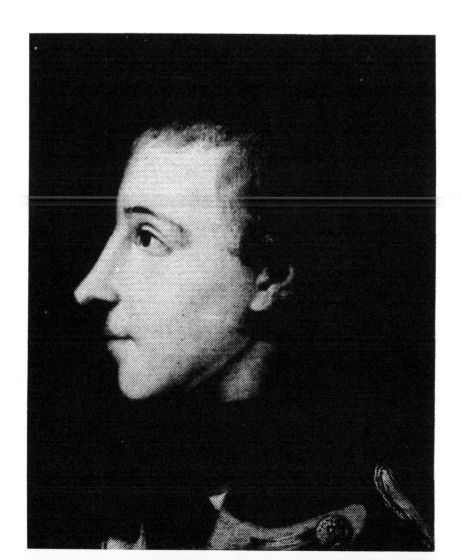

Every year, on a Sunday in June, people make their way to a little churchyard in Bodenstown, County Kildare, where the remains of Theobald Wolfe Tone are said to lie. He is honoured as Ireland's first true republican; as the man who struggled all his life for an understanding between Catholic, Protestant and Non-Conformist; as the patriot who in his speech from the dock just before being sentenced to death for his part in the rebellion of 1798 said: *"From my earliest youth I have regarded the connexion between Ireland and Great Britain as the curse of the Irish nation."* The popular ballad *"Who fears to speak of '98!"* has made us think of that rising as one of the turning points in Irish history, as indeed it was. But history is not quite as simple as all that. Wolfe Tone, who died for the cause of a Republic, had in his earlier years looked for a job under the British Government and had sworn loyalty to the King; and the rising of '98 so frightened the British authorities that they passed the Act of Union and condemned the country to another 120 years of foreign rule. This does not mean that Tone was not a great man and a national hero, or that he was wrong to try to organise a rising. It does mean that we must be careful not to jump to

Mrs. Tone and her sons Theobald Wolfe and Matthew

conclusions about a man whose work for his country was surrounded by so many difficulties.

Tone was born in Dublin, probably in Stafford Street, on the 20th of June, 1763, and was baptised in St. Mary's Church, Mary Street, Dublin. His father, a coachmaker, inherited a small property in Bodenstown and moved there about 1778. After attending a preparatory school run by a Mr. Darling, Theobald, who was a clever boy, was sent to Trinity College in 1781. He had developed a habit of mitching from school with some of his friends, and he did not care for the work in Trinity. *"I began to look on Classical learning as nonsense,"* he said, and was sure that he wanted to be a soldier. But he soon found himself enjoying College society and speaking at the Historical Society's debates, where he won two medals for oratory. His ideas were rather conservative, even though at this time Trinity was very national in feeling. Grattan's Parliament came into being in 1782, and since it met just across College Green and students were allowed into the visitor's gallery, there was great talk about independence and the importance of protecting Irish industry and reducing emigration. Tone's college friends thought he was a brilliant man and marked out for great things, even though he did not pay much attention to his studies. He enjoyed being a man-about-town and acting in plays. In 1785 he ran away to be married—to a girl of 15 named Matilda Witherington. After a few days' honeymoon in Maynooth, the young couple came back to Dublin, and Tone finished his college course, having decided to become a lawyer. He took his B.A. in February, 1786, and that same year went to London to finish his legal studies. He enjoyed the life of London even more than that of Dublin and together with his brother William, who had joined him there, thought up a scheme for turning the Sandwich Islands, which had been discovered by Captain Cook in 1778, into a British colony from where attacks could be made on Spanish ships trading with South America. (The Sandwich Islands are now the 50th state of the U.S.A.). Wolfe Tone wrote to William Pitt, the British Prime Minister, about his idea, but heard nothing in reply. He also tried signing on as a soldier for India, but was too late—all the ships for that year had gone. If he had succeeded in either of these plans the history of Ireland might have been very different.

Tone came back to Dublin at the end of 1788 and moved into lodgings in Clarendon Street. He bought £100 worth of law books and took his LL.B. in Trinity in February, 1789. He did not care much for the law but had to find some way to support his wife and family, though he still hoped to make his way in politics. He was gradually coming to believe in independence for his country and in July, 1790, wrote a pamphlet which suggested that if England declared war against Spain, Ireland could remain neutral. This was the first of his many political writings.

The year 1791 saw the beginnings of the United Irishmen, the movement that was to bring together all the leading political thinkers from all sections of the community. The Volunteers, which had grown up in 1778–9, at the time of the American War of Independence, to defend Ireland against the threat of invasion, had become debating clubs in which nationalist views came to be more and more important, and it was from the Volunteers that the United Irishmen developed. *"We have no national government,"* said a document drawn up by Tone. *"We are ruled by Englishmen and the servants of Englishmen."* This document, though not printed or published, was sent to the British Government by an informer, and from then on Wolfe Tone was a marked man. The Society of United Irishmen was formed in Belfast on the 18th of October, 1791, and Tone and his friend Russell set up a branch in Dublin in the following month. The members included Rowan Hamilton, James Napper Tandy, and two men, Collins and

Napper Tandy

Dublin Castle

Leonard McNally, who were later found out to have been government spies. They met in the Tailor's Hall in Back Lane, and one of their main aims was to try to persuade the government to allow Catholics full rights of citizenship. Many of them were full of the ideas of the French Revolution, which promised equality for all, and a Catholic Committee was set up for which Wolfe Tone began working as Assistant Secretary at a salary of £200 a year. This was in 1792. On November 9th, Tone wrote in his diary: *"Wonderful to see the rapid change in the minds of the Bar on the Catholic question; almost everybody favourable . . . All sorts of men and especially lawyer Plunkett take a pleasure in girding at* (teasing) *Mr. Hutton . . . Sundry barristers apply to him for protection in the approaching rebellion."* *"Mr. Hutton"* was Tone's nickname for himself, but as yet he was not seriously thinking of rebellion. He hoped that all Irishmen could be brought together by peaceful means. Late in 1792 a Catholic delegation went to London to ask the King to grant Catholic emancipation, and Tone went with them as secretary.

The British Government was expecting a war with France and did not want trouble in Ireland, so they persuaded the Dublin Government to pass a Relief Act on the 18th of February, 1793, which gave Catholics the right to vote, though they still could not enter Parliament or become judges. But most of the United Irishmen felt that this was not enough, and when war with France was declared, they tried to get her to send help to their own organisation, which was becoming more and more military. A French agent, William Jackson, visited Dublin in 1794, but the British were following him, and Tone and his friends were in serious danger. Some of them fled the country, and Tone himself was almost arrested and tried for treason. Luckily he had friends who used their influence, and he was exiled instead to America. He sailed from Belfast and reached Philadelphia on August 8th, 1795.

The situation in Ireland was going from bad to worse. Full Catholic emancipation had been turned down by the British; more and more societies of United Irishmen were forming and training on military lines, and on the other side the Orange Order had come into being, leading to a battle between Catholics and Protestants at the Diamond, County Armagh.

As soon as he could, Tone left America for France, arriving at Le Havre on February 1st, 1796, and calling himself Mr. James Smith. His aim was to persuade the French to invade Ireland and drive the British out once and for all. The French were interested, because they saw this as a way of attacking England by controlling the Irish ports, and soon Carnot, one of the directors of the new French Republic, agreed to get a fleet and an army ready. Wolfe Tone was given a commission in the French army, and while he was waiting for action spent some time writing out 30 Irish airs to be played by his regimental band.

At last, on December 2nd, 1796, he embarked on the *Indomitable,* one of a force of 15 ships of the line and 10 frigates, carrying about 14,000 men. This was not as strong as had been hoped, because the French navy was in a poor state following many encounters with the British. It should, however, have been big enough to make a powerful landing in Ireland—if only the wind had blown the other way. The fleet ran into a gale, the ships were scattered—their number had been made up to 43—and Tone waited in terrible weather in Bantry Bay for the force to join up again before the signal was made on December 29th to steer for France again.

What would have happened had they landed? Would the Irish have risen to help them? Many Irishmen were afraid that by inviting the French they would be just changing one set of masters for another; and though the ideas of the French Revolution—liberty, equality and brotherhood—had given the people—particularly the poor—new hope, the Church was against the Republic because of its attitude towards religion. The Bishop of Cork issued a pastoral on Christmas Day which said that *"Loyalty to the Sovereign and respect for the constitutional authorities have always been prominent features of the Christian character."*

The government had arrested many of the leaders of the United Irishmen before the fleet arrived; the organisation was not ready, so there was no attempt at a rising when the French were in the Bay. Wolfe Tone was back in Brest on January 1st, 1797, very miserable. On May 7th he was re-united with his family, which had followed him from America. He waited impatiently in France for another expedition to be prepared, but the French were having their own difficulties and for a long time nothing happened. Tone had an interview with Napoleon on December 21st, and the following April he joined the army at Rouen. Napoleon had decided to strike at Britain through Egypt and India rather than Ireland, and the promised invasion fleet was again held up. But events had been moving fast at home. In March, 1798, the Leinster Directory of the United Irishmen had been betrayed and arrested. Lord Edward Fitzgerald had been captured. The rebellion broke out on May 23rd, but without most of its leaders. When the French fleet did arrive, it was too late.

On August 6th Humbert's expedition sailed and landed at Killala, County Mayo. On September 14th Hardy's expedition sailed from Brest. On board his flag-ship the *Hoche* was Theobald Wolfe Tone. The fleet of the flagship, eight frigates and a schooner, was intercepted by a superior British force off Lough Swilly, and the *Hoche* surrendered after a four-hour fight. Tone was brought ashore, identified by a man who had been at College with him, brought to Dublin and placed on trial. There could be only one verdict. Tone admitted to *"having acted in hostility to the Government of His Britannic Majesty in Ireland."* He was sentenced to death and asked to be allowed to die like a soldier, by shooting. But this was refused and, rather than be hanged like a common criminal, he cut his own throat in jail on Sunday, November 11th, and died on the 19th. *"I have sacrificed all my views in life,"* he said in the dock. *"I have courted poverty; I have left a beloved wife unprotected and children whom I adored fatherless. After such sacrifices in a cause which I have always conscientiously considered as the cause of justice and freedom—it is no real effort at this day to add the sacrifice of my life."*

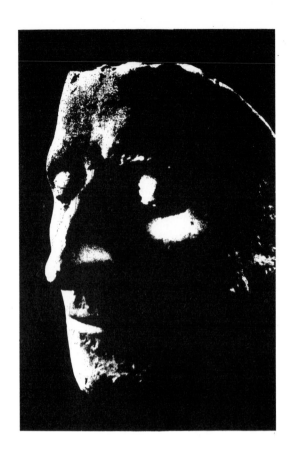

Tone's death mask

Daniel O'Connell
1775-1847

O'Connell's home at Derrynane Abbey

In 1826 Daniel O'Connell set up an organisation called *The Order of Liberators*. To become a member, a person had to do something very special for Ireland, something that would be important in making life better for all her people. Nowadays we remember only one *Liberator*—Daniel O'Connell himself, who earned the title because of the great work he did in getting rid of the Penal Laws against Catholics, and trying to get back for Ireland her own government and her own parliament, which had been taken away by the Act of Union of 1800. These two things are usually described by the words: *Emancipation* and *Repeal*.

When Daniel was born, most Irish people who lived west of a line drawn down the centre of Ireland spoke Irish as their everyday language. O'Connell's first language was Irish, though for most of his adult life he used English and tried to persuade his countrymen to take up that language because he thought it was the language of progress. Throughout his life he was an odd mixture of patriot and what we might now call "West Briton": he believed in some independence for Ireland but still wanted to stay loyal to the British Crown. He was born on August 6th, 1775, at Carhen House, Cahirciveen, County Kerry, and first went to school in 1788 in Cobh. He was a clever boy, and his father wanted him to go on to a university, but at that time Catholics were not allowed to attend the only University in Ireland, Trinity College, Dublin, so he was sent with his brother to the English college at St. Omer, France. This was in January, 1791. The next year he transferred to Douay and two years later went to study at Lincoln's Inn in London. He had decided to become a lawyer.

O'Connell did well in his studies and came home in 1796; two years later he was called to the Irish Bar, which meant that he could start in his profession. Exciting things were happening in 1798 in Ireland, but Daniel O'Connell did not support the cause of the United Irishmen. *"The Irish are not sufficiently enlightened to bear the sun of freedom,"* he said, which meant that he thought his countrymen were not yet ready to run their own affairs. He had seen some unpleasant things in France, which was in the middle of a revolution when he was there, and this made him very suspicious of what we would now call "freedom fighters." He did not believe in bloodshed, even to gain freedom, and this later made him fall out with Thomas Davis and the Young Irelanders. But this was a long way ahead. In 1798 young O'Connell was more interested in doing well in his profession, in hunting, and in enjoying life. He went back to Munster and began to make a great deal of money, for he was a very good lawyer.

Then came the Act of Union. Ireland lost what little independence she had, and O'Connell found himself making his first real political speech, at the Royal Exchange in Dublin (now the City Hall), against the Act. From then until the end of his life he was in the thick of politics. The British had promised that once the two countries were united under one parliament, Irish Catholics would be allowed to vote, to hold public positions and to be educated in the same way as Protestants. O'Connell soon saw that this was not going to happen, and he set about agitating for emancipation in every way that he could. Different British Governments at the time had different ideas about emancipation, but one of the conditions they all laid down was that they should be able to veto the appointment of the Catholic bishops if they wanted to. O'Connell was against this, as were most of the people and clergy in Ireland. They were also against having to pay tithes, or taxes, to the Protestant Church of Ireland and against

The Royal Exchange

all forms of religious discrimination. Wolfe Tone had wanted one Irish nation for all Irishmen—Catholics, Protestants, Presbyterians. O'Connell and his supporters started by trying to get a fair deal for their own people— the Catholics.

There were Irish Protestants and some Englishmen who agreed with them, but most of the Ascendancy, as the Protestants in Ireland were called, did not want any change. In 1808 Henry Grattan, who had gone from the Irish Parliament to Westminster after the Act of Union, presented a petition, or request, for emancipation, but it was turned down. Another Bill, in 1813, was opposed by O'Connell because it did not go far enough and included the veto idea. O'Connell set up several organisations to collect money to help his cause, but they were closed down by the Government. Then, in 1823, he founded the Catholic Association, which anyone could join by paying a penny a week. The money poured in, and O'Connell became a national leader. The Association was suppressed but re-formed again in another way so that the law could not touch it. Wherever he went on his legal business, O'Connell was treated like a hero. In 1828 came his big chance: he was invited to stand for election to Parliament for County Clare, even though as a Catholic he would not be allowed to take his seat. He won, was refused the seat and was elected again. The British Government had changed, and in 1829 an Act granting Catholic Emancipation was passed. His first great aim had been achieved.

This makes it sound much easier than it really was. O'Connell had to spend a great deal of time trying to persuade different British officials and ministers to see his point of view, and he had opposition at home as well. In 1815, on February 1st, he fought a duel at Bishops-court, near Naas, and killed his challenger, d'Esterre. He nearly had to fight another duel with Robert Peel, then Chief Secretary for Ireland, because he was a hot-tempered man who always said what he thought—often in very strong language. He had trouble with money, too, for though he earned a large income from his law practice, he enjoyed entertaining his friends and spending money, and was often in debt.

In 1830 O'Connell started in earnest on his next big project: Repeal. This was going to be much harder to achieve than Emancipation, because Britain looked upon anyone who wanted to undo the Act of Union as a traitor, and many of the Protestants in Ireland at that time felt the same way. In 1834 the vote at Westminster on Repeal was 523 against and 38 in favour, and only one of those in favour was an English Member. In 1833 O'Connell had been elected to Parliament for Dublin City, and in 1841 he became the capital's first Catholic Lord Mayor. But in 1831 he had been arrested, because of his anti-Government activities, and it was easy to see that he was involved in an almost impossible task. *"My struggle has begun,"* he said on April 15th, 1840, *"and I will terminate it only in death or Repeal."*

The trial of O'Connell

As he grew older O'Connell became what we would call now very conservative. He did not agree with ideas being suggested to try to help the poor by giving them public assistance paid by the government, and did not like anything that interfered with private property, even though many of the Irish landlords treated their tenants very badly. There were new ideas being talked about by younger men like Davis, Meagher, and Smith-O'Brien. These young patriots believed in fighting for independence, and though they joined O'Connell in the Repeal Association he did not trust them. The Association, however, was becoming more and more popular, so that a special meeting place had to be built for it. This hall, Conciliation Hall as it was called, was opened at Burgh Quay in 1843. It now forms part of the premises of the *Irish Press* newspaper. This was the year in which Daniel O'Connell organised his famous monster rallies to protest against the Act of Union. The first was at Trim on March 16th; then on August 15th one million people met together on the Hill of Tara. The meetings were peaceful and well organised, but the government was getting nervous. The next protest was arranged for Clontarf on October 16th. At the last minute it was banned by the authorities. What happened? So great was O'Connell's power over the people that when he told them not to carry on with the meeting, they obeyed, and what would surely have been a serious riot was avoided. O'Connell was arrested in January, 1844, and convicted by a Dublin jury made up almost entirely of Protestants. The decision was later reversed by the House of Lords after the Liberator had spent three months in Richmond Jail (May 30th–September 4th), but the experience broke both his health and his spirit. He was no longer the leader whom everyone believed in. In 1846, the Young Irelanders walked out of one of his meetings after a fiery speech by Thomas Francis Meagher. The next year O'Connell, a very sick man, left Ireland for France, hoping to recover his health. He died in Genoa, Italy, on the 15th of May, 1847. His heart was taken to Rome and deposited in the church of St. Agatha; his body was brought home to Ireland and buried in Glasnevin, where a round tower was erected in his memory in 1869.

So O'Connell had failed in his second great aim, but the nation he had brought into being through his successful struggle for Emancipation continued the fight—though in ways he would not have agreed with—until the Irish flag flew over the Post Office in 1916. But perhaps if he had fought for Repeal first and Emancipation second the sad division between Irish Catholics and Protestants might not have been so deep.

O'Connell's return from Richmond jail

Robert Emmet
1778-1803

Two hundred years ago, Dublin was a very different place from the big city of today. Many of the fine, wide streets, such as Merrion Square, were only just being built, and ships could sail right up the river Liffey into the middle of the town. People lived in all the streets where there are now mostly offices and shops. As a boy, Robert Emmet used to enjoy watching ships coming and going when he stayed with friends at Sir John Rogerson's Quay. He watched the canal from Portobello to Ringsend being built, and he tried to make a model of the new Custom House in wood, though he found this rather difficult. He was a clever boy; one of the things he could do was repeat the alphabet backwards without stopping. Robert, or Bob as his friends called him, went to school in Grafton Street and Camden Street, and in October, 1793, when he was only fifteen, he entered Trinity College, Dublin.

Robert Emmet's father was a physician who worked for the Lord Lieutenant. At this time Ireland had her own parliament which met in what is now the Bank of Ireland in College Green, Dublin, but the country was in fact still run by Britain, and very few were allowed to vote. The Lord Lieutenant was the head of the British government in Ireland, and he had a whole army of British soldiers to help him keep order, because many Irishmen wanted their country to be completely free and were always planning to attack the British and drive them out.

Anne Devlin

Robert had many brothers and sisters, and he was particularly fond of his elder brother, who was named Thomas Addis Emmet. Thomas, who was fourteen years older than Robert, had been to Trinity and Edinburgh University, where he had studied to become a doctor. He travelled all over Europe and then came back to Dublin to become a lawyer and joined the United Irishmen who were planning the 1798 rebellion. Robert was only 20 when this rising took place, and his brother was arrested and sent to Scotland. He was never allowed back into Ireland again. This helped to make Robert decide that he, too, would work to help make his country free, and in the year 1802 he set sail for France in order to get aid from the French to fight the British. The French had had their own Revolution in 1789 and since then had

The execution of Robert Emmet

been fighting the British in several wars. Irish soldiers had been fighting on the French side in the Irish Brigades, and when Robert went to France he met some of these soldiers who had been captured, and released when the British and the French made peace in 1801. He wanted them to form an army to come home to Ireland and fight the British there, but, as there were not enough of them, he knew he would need to have French soldiers as well. The leader of France at this time was Napoleon, and Robert Emmet met him to ask him for help, but as this did not appear to be forthcoming, he returned home in 1802 by himself and decided to plan a revolution all on his own. He had to travel in disguise, since the British knew he was up to something and wanted to capture him. He called himself Robert Hammond (he was very friendly with the Hammond family in Dublin) and managed to reach home without being noticed.

He stayed in Dublin all through the winter of the year 1802, only going out when it was dark, or when he thought no one would recognise him. All this time he was secretly planning, collecting as many men as possible and training them for his intended revolution. His brother had told him that the best time would be when Britain and France started fighting again, and Emmet and his friends hoped that revolts would start in several places in Ireland at the same time, and that the British would not have enough soldiers to stop them. He spent most of his own money buying guns and other weapons. At the beginning of 1803 a man named Dowdall arrived from France. He gave Emmet some news of his brother, and told him that war had started again between France and Britain. The two men decided on a date for the rebellion in Dublin and began to set their plans. They did not know whether the French were going to send any soldiers to help them, but they pretended that French ships were already on the way, to keep all the men cheerful and make them believe that they were bound to win.

On July 23rd, 1803, Emmet and his men set out to capture Dublin Castle, which was where the British kept all their guns and ammunition. Some of the men who were supposed to join in the attack never arrived, and some of them only wanted to use the revolution as an excuse to steal things, so Robert Emmet did not have a very good army. As they were marching towards the Castle, some of the men shot and killed Lord Kilwarden, who was the Lord Chief Justice and who just happened to be passing by, not knowing what was going on. Kilwarden was a popular man and his death turned the people of Dublin against Emmet's men. Before long most of the leaders of the rising had been arrested. Robert managed to escape and went into hiding again, but that was the end of the revolution. It was a very small rebellion, but, as we shall see, it soon became very important indeed.

By this time the British knew that Emmet had been the leader, and they did everything they could to locate him. Major Sirr and Major Swann arrested as many of his friends as they could lay hands on, and used to break into houses in the middle of the night looking for him. Even his mother was arrested and put into prison, but none of his friends would tell the soldiers where Emmet was hiding.

There are some people, though, who will do anything for money. These are people called *informers*, who get paid for betraying their friends or their enemies. One of these informers knew where Robert Emmet was hiding and told the soldiers at Dublin Castle, so that in August,

1803, he was arrested at a house in Harold's Cross near Dublin. He was quickly put on trial for treason—that is, plotting to overthrow the government in power—and the punishment for this offence was death. In spite of anything those people defending him could say, he was condemned by Lord Norbury to be hanged in public.

The public was not allowed into the court during the trial, but some of the people in court wrote down what he said, so that now we can read one of the most famous speeches in Irish history. Emmet, though he knew he was going to die, was proud of what he had done for his country, even though the revolution had not been a success. He believed that only in later years would people really understand him and come to believe in his deeds. He said it this way, in the language of nearly two centuries ago: *"Let my character and my motives repose in*

Emmet's arms depot

obscurity and peace, till other times and other men can do them justice:—then shall my character be vindicated; then may my epitaph be written." He wanted no one to write any words on his tombstone until Ireland had won her freedom. Even when he was about to be killed he did not think of himself, but only of his country. He was a very brave man.

On September 20th, 1803, Robert Emmet was taken out of prison and brought to Thomas Street in Dublin, where he was hanged in front of St. Catherine's Church, with all his friends watching. He was only twenty-five, but his memory lived on long after him as an example to all the men and women who wanted Ireland to be ruled by the Irish themselves. His sweetheart Anne Devlin, was kept in prison for three years without a trial because she would not inform on Emmet's friends. His boyhood

The Lying-in-State of Lord Kilwarden

friend Tom Moore, who was at school and at Trinity College with him, wrote a poem about him; and, set to music as one of *Moore's Irish Melodies,* it has kept Emmet's memory green among Irish people all over the world:

> O breathe not his name! let it sleep in the shade
> Where, cold and unhonoured, his relics are laid!
> Sad, silent and dark, be the tears that we shed,
> As the night-dew that falls on the grass o'er his head.
>
> But the night-dew that falls, though in silence it
>   weeps,
> Shall brighten with verdure the grave where he
>   sleeps;
> And the tear that we shed, though in secret it rolls,
> Shall long keep his memory green in our souls.

Thomas Osborne Davis
1814-1845

THE NATION.

VOL. I.---No. 2. DUBLIN, SATURDAY, OCTOBER 22, 1842. PRICE 6*d*.

THE O'CONNELL COMPENSATION FUND

FOR THE PRESENT YEAR, 1842,

WILL BE COLLECTED IN EVERY PARISH OF IRELAND

On SUNDAY, the 30th of THIS MONTH (OCTOBER).

THE PEOPLE are prepared for the call, and feel that to neglect it now would be--practically--to coalesce with the enemies of their country.

It then only remains to enjoin that the Collection be set on foot UNIVERSALLY on the 30th instant, and completed in every possible case within the ensuing month. This is most essential.

JOHN POWER, Bart., CORNELIUS MAC LOGHLIN, } Trustees.
P. VINCENT FITZPATRICK, Secretary.

Office, 44, Dame-street.
Dublin, Oct., 1842. k 7

ST. AUDEON'S PARISH.

DEEPLY impressed with gratitude for the untiring zeal and matchless ability with which Daniel O'Connell continues to guard and improve those political advantages which he has won for his fellow-countrymen, we, the undersigned, request a Meeting of the Inhabitants of this Parish, at Lawler's, UPPER BRIDGE-STREET, on WEDNESDAY EVENING, 26th inst., at EIGHT o'Clock, for the purpose of making such arrangements as shall tend to render the collection for this National Contribution of the 30th instant alike worthy of the object of this noble public compliment, and creditable to the Parishioners.

Thomas Reynolds,	John Carroll,
James Cass,	Nathaniel Halbert,
James Monks, P.P.,	Thomas Berford,
Mathew Lynch, C.C.,	James Egan,
James Corr, C.C.,	John Alcorn,
John Keahan, Alderman,	Nicholas Dawson,
Hugh Duffy,	Thomas Dunne,
Edward Galvin,	P. W. Murphy,
Nicholas Martin and Son,	James M'Evoy,
Mark Malone,	Thomas White,
N. James Caffrey,	James Nugent,
George Atkinson, M.D.,	P. Fitzpatrick,
R. and E. D. Williams,	Thomas Seery,
John and W. Byrne,	James Curren,
John Coyne,	George Faulkner,
John Behan,	John Glennon,
Sylvester Young,	Patrick Doran,
James Reilly,	Francis M'Ardle,
P. and R. Hayes,	Simon Kearney.

k 14

O'CONNELL TRIBUTE.

UNION OF SAINTS MARY, THOMAS, AND GEORGE.

THE SUBSCRIBERS request a MEETING of the inhabitants of this Union, on THURSDAY, the 27th inst., at the hour of ONE o'Clock, p.m., at HAMILTON'S ROOMS, NORTHUMBERLAND BUILDINGS, to make the necessary arrangements for the most effective Collection of the O'CONNELL TRIBUTE, on SUNDAY, the 30th INSTANT, and to evince by acts our grateful appreciation of the untired and untiring services of Ireland's great moral Regenerator, of the PATRIOT CHIEF, of swordless glory, who raised the standard of Civil and Religious Liberty, and by the moral force of open moral combination, peacefully and triumphantly achieved Emancipation, amid the applause of an admiring world, by energetically, judiciously, and perseveringly using the weapons of truth, reason, and argument, in the ways of righteousness and the paths of peace.

Thomas Kirwan,	Charles Brett,
David Lynch,	J. A. Curran,
Charles Meara,	John Smith,
John O'Brien,	Michael Dodd,
John Clarke, T.C.,	R. M'Guinness,
John Joseph Clarke,	Marcus Supple,
Anthony O'Brien,	Walter Casey,
C. Egan, Alderman,	Timothy Green,
Robert M'Kenna, Alderman,	Charles Kennedy,
Daniel M'Nevin,	John Bagnal,
Thomas M'Nevin,	Charles Taaffe,
Robert M'Clelland, T.C.,	Richard Grace, T.C.,
John Hannigan,	Luke Corr,
John Hamilton, R.C., A.D.,	Henry Corr,
Thomas Finn, LL.D.,	J. M'Kenna, T.C.,
John Miley, D.D.,	Patrick Flood,
John Laphen, Clk.,	Patrick Lalor,
Patrick Harkan, M.D.,	Patrick Farrell,
John Gaghran, M.D.,	Thomas Tyrrell,
John Walsh, M.D.,	John Dennan,
James M. Kirwan, M.D., T.C.,	Richard O'Callaghan,
John Dodd,	Thomas Callaghan,
Francis Burke,	Peter Callaghan,
W. P. O'Connor,	N. Drew,
Arthur French,	Hugh Conway,
John Campbell, T.C.,	Thomas Deehan,
Michael Staunton, T.C.,	Peter Martin,
Richard Barrett, E.P.,	T. Morgan,
John Stevenson, E.M.R.,	Thomas Dillon,
John Flanaday, E.F.J.,	Thomas Dillon, jun.,
Martin Crean,	Patrick Sandford,
Stephen Darcy,	T. Byrne,
John Taaffe,	Joseph Neale M'Kenna,
Patrick Nolan,	Michael M'Kenna.
Sylvester Young,	

k 12

O'CONNELL ANNUITY

RATHMINES PARISH.

WE, the Undersigned, request a Meeting of the Inhabitants of Rathmines, Mount Pleasant, Ranelagh, Cullen's Wood, Milltown, and Harold's Cross, on the PAROCHIAL GROUND, near the new Roman Catholic Church, at TWO o'Clock, on SUNDAY, the 23d OCTOBER, 1842, to make effective arrangements for the collection of the O'Connell Annuity for the Present Year. Every Member of the great Community raised by O'Connell from slavery to freedom has benefited by his unequalled exertions, and all should therefore co-operate to compensate and sustain him.

William [illegible], P.P.,	Edward Groves, Clerk,
Nicholas Roche, C.C.,	Christopher Wall,
J. P. Cullinan, C.C.,	Joseph Byrne,
Mathew Collier, C.C.,	Bryan Hackett,
B. M'Dermott, C.C.,	Peter Hayes,
Michael Merriman,	James Lynam,
Thomas Scallan, E.C.S.	John Scally,
Patrick O'Brien,	Daniel Hodgens,
Edward Gallavan,	Charles Denneby
John Murphy,	Terence M'Cabe,
James Berry,	Peter Murphy,
Michael Mangan,	Walter Furlong,
Thomas Pidgeon,	John Mackey,
Francis E. O'Brien,	Patrick Kearney,
Denis Costigan,	John Colclough,
Hugh Duffy,	Edmond Lawless,
J. W. Spain,	John Rooney,
Thomas M'Enery,	John Conlan,
[illegible] Macivor,	Edward Freeman,
[illegible] Murray,	James Fitzsimons.

k 14

THE O'CONNELL TRIBUTE FOR 1842.

THE UNITED PARISHES OF SAINTS ANDREW, MARY PETER, AND ANNE.

WE, the Undersigned, request a Special Meeting of the Liberal Burgesses and Inhabitants of the above Parishes, in the Great Room, CORN-EXCHANGE, on SUNDAY, the 23d instant, at THREE o'Clock, for the purpose of making the necessary arrangements for the effectual Collection of the National Tribute on SUNDAY, the 30th October.

C. Rooney, C.C.,	James Rooney, Alderman,
A. Quinn, C.C.,	Wm. Magennis,
Gregory Lynch, C.C.,	Edward Murphy,
W. V. O'Grady, C.C.,	Walter Doolin and Sons,
T. O'Carroll, C.C.,	Patrick Campbell,
P. E. Farrelly, C.C.,	John Kelsh,
J. Coyle, C.C.,	Mathew M'Grath,
John M'Donough, C.C.	Arthur Barlow, T.C.,
John Pearson, T.C.,	Denis Hayes,
John Murphy, M.D.,	John MacNally,
Joseph Byrne,	John O'Neill,
Wm. Hanlon,	Laurence Lynch,
P. Smith,	John Reilly, T.C.,
Jas. Lynam,	Stephen Murphy, M.D.
Thomas Meagher,	John Nowlan,
William Dillon,	M. Dowling,
William Mooney,	Martin Ayre,
Thomas Ryan,	Joseph Brannan,
John P. Baxter,	James Ford,
B. M'Garry,	Stephen Eustace,
William Rudkin,	C. Reddy,
Christopher Baker	Lewis Moore,
Michael Kennedy,	Stephen Flanagan,
James B. Kennedy	William Burke,
James Murray,	Edward Dowling,
James J. O'Toole,	Thomas Carey,
Bernard O'Carroll	William Brannan,
Charles Cavanagh,	Charles Gavan Duffy,
Edward Clements, Barrister-at-Law,	William Fitzpatrick, T.C.

k 14

O'CONNELL TRIBUTE.

ST. MARY'S PARISH, DONNYBROOK.

WE, the Undersigned, request a Special Meeting of the Inhabitants of the above Parish, in Mr. O'Reilly's GREAT ROOM, DONNYBROOK, on SUNDAY, the 23d OCTOBER, at THREE o'Clock, for the purpose of making the necessary arrangements to render the Collection of the National Tribute in this Parish, on Sunday, the 30th instant, worthy of O'Connell and of Ireland.

T. A. Murphy, C.C.,	John Mooney,
John B. M'Hugh, C.C.,	John Madden, P.L.G.,
Patrick Hurly,	Luke Mooney,
Patrick Costello,	Thomas Murphy,
James Tuite,	Hugh Reilly,
James Nedley,	Patrick Byrne,
Michael Doyle, M.D.,	Michael Dillon,
Wm. Dillon,	Hugh M'Guirk,
Charles M'Dermott,	Denis Donohoe,
Richard Doyle,	Patrick Lawlor,
John Whitty,	James Lawlor,
Thomas O'Reilly,	Mathias Carigan,
A. Connell,	Francis Morgan,
Patrick O'Neill,	Michael Hearn,
William Slattery,	Martin Hearn,
Francis Dillon,	John Collins,
Robert Jordan,	F. Dwyer.

k 21

ST. MICHAN'S PARISH.

O'CONNELL TRIBUTE.

AT a numerous and respectable Meeting of the Parishioners of St. Michan's, held on Monday, the 17th instant, at 25, Ormond-quay, for the purpose of organising the Collection of the O'Connell Tribute for the present year--

Alderman JOHN O'NEILL in the Chair--

It was moved by Bartholomew Andrews--That J. P. Doyle, Esq., be requested to act as Secretary.

Moved by Bartholomew Andrews, T.C.; seconded by J. T. Arkins, Esq.:

Resolved--That we hail with joy the approaching anniversary which gives an opportunity to Ireland of again recording its gratitude to the Right Hon. Daniel O'Connell as her Liberator, and her unbounded confidence as her constitutional champion; who, while his virtue and prudence keep her ill-treated and chivalrous sons from recurring to violence, is able to direct all their energies in the legitimate course for obtaining their just rights.

Moved by the Rev. Mr. Coogan; seconded by Thomas Carroll, Esq.:

Resolved--That, under his direction and with his powerful assistance, in this year the illusion is fast disappearing that Ireland would ever tamely suffer herself to be treated as a conquered province, or ever cease from lawful and vigorous agitation until her independent Legislature be restored on the basis established before the miscalled Union.

Moved by Peter Kelly, Esq.; seconded by E. Hogg, Esq.:

Resolved--That in accepting, in addition to his other onerous duties, that of the head of the Dublin Corporation, humbled and stripped as it was of its powers by a Tory government, when those powers could be made no longer subservient to their own purposes, he has preserved the remaining property of the citizens from total destruction, which the mal-administration of its predecessors was calculated to occasion, and has added another proof that he shall stop at no personal sacrifice which he deems useful to his country.

Moved by Michael Flynn, Esq.; seconded by John Archbold, Esq.:

Resolved--That if any part of Ireland be more particularly indebted to *him*, it is Dublin, and, of that again, the parish of *St. Michan's*, which was the first *parish* in it publicly to call on him and obtain his ready consent to urge his, their, and the nation's wishes, on Repeal, in the British Parliament, as the representative of the City of Dublin; and we trust that the following regulations will give every opportunity to the *parishioners* of evincing their feelings by their annually increasing acknowledgments.

Moved by Mr. M. Hickey; seconded by Mr. F. Byrne:

Resolved--That the following Gentlemen be requested to act as a Committee to wait upon the Parishioners for their Subscriptions, and to act as Collectors at the Parochial Church, North Anne-street, on Sunday, 30th instant, viz.:--

Alderman O'Neill,	Bartholomew Andrews, T.C.
John P. Doyle,	John Archbold,
Thomas Carroll,	Michael Flynn,
Michael Doyle,	John Reilly, T.C.
Richard Morrow.	

JOHN H. O'NEILL, Chairman.
J. P. DOYLE, Secretary.

The following gentlemen handed in their subscriptions:--Peter Kelly, Esq., 5*l*.; Bartholomew Andrews, Town Councillor, 5*l*.; Thomas Arkins, Esq., 5*l*.; John Archbold, Esq., 2*l*.; James Sheridan, Esq., Town Councillor, 1*l*.; Rev. Mr. Coogan, 1*l*.; Thomas Carroll, Esq., 1*l*.; Edward Hogg, Esq., 1*l*.; J. P. Doyle, Esq., 1*l*. k 19

O'CONNELL TRIBUTE.

ST. JAMES'S PARISH.

AT a numerous and highly respectable Meeting of the Inhabitants of the above Parish, held at Carmichael's Great Rooms, James's-gate, on Wednesday Evening, the 19th instant,

F. TUITE, Esq., T.C., in the Chair,
C. P. Shannon, Esq., T.C., P.L.G., Secretary,

The following Resolutions were unanimously adopted:--

Moved by C. P. Gavin, Esq., T.C.; seconded by J. Healy, Esq., Assessor:

Resolved--That we gratefully seize on this opportunity of testifying our undiminished confidence in the integrity and councils of the Liberator; and we consider that each year but adds new claims on us for his untiring exertions in the cause of our common country.

Moved by P. Maguire, Esq.; seconded by T. Kelly, Esq.:

Resolved--That we hail with delight the call made on all Ireland by the Trustees of the National Compensation Fund; and we emphatically request of our fellow-parishioners to assist us in making this year's return equal, if not superior, to any former contribution from St. James's Parish.

Moved by O. Shannon, Esq.; seconded by P. Moore, Esq.:

Resolved--That the following gentlemen be and are hereby nominated to attend on Sunday, the 30th inst., as follows:--

ST. JAMES'S-CHAPEL.

Councillors Tuite, Gavin, and Shannon; J. Healy, Assessor; J. Brennan, P. Maguire, P. Moore, J. Langan, J. Murphy, C. Shannon, jun., T. Kelly, F. Moore, J. Owens, R. White, R. Pigott.

DOLPHIN'S BARN CHAPEL.

Christopher Jones, J. O'Neill, P. Rooney, P. Ledwidge, and J. Byrne, Esqrs.

Moved by J. Tiernan, Esq.; seconded by C. Jones, Esq.:

Resolved--That Michael Powell, Esq., be requested to act as Treasurer to the O'Connell Fund in this Parish.

F. TUITE, Chairman.

F. Tuite, Esq., having left the chair, P. Maguire, Esq., was called thereto, when, by acclamation, the thanks of the meeting were voted to the former chairman.

P. MAGUIRE, Chairman.
k 22 COR. P. SHANNON, Secretary.

O'CONNELL TRIBUTE.

ST. CATHERINE'S PARISH.

AT a highly respectable and influential Meeting of the Parishioners of St. Catherine, held on Wednesday, at Mr. Long's Rooms, No. 1, Thomas-court,

FRANCIS PURCELL, Esq., in the Chair.
Mr. JOHN MOLLOY acted as Secretary.

Moved by James Moran, Esq., T.C., P.L.G.; seconded by John Murphy, Esq., P.L.G.:

Resolved--That we hail with the most heartfelt pleasure the approaching opportunity which the collection of the National Tribute affords us of testifying our gratitude for the services of our distinguished countryman and illustrious Liberator.

Moved by John O'Neill, Esq., T.C.; seconded by Andrew Reilly, Esq.:

Resolved--That we call on our patriotic fellow-parishioners to convince, by their generous zeal and co-operation, his maligners that O'Connell has not only our confidence, but that our confidence is increased and unbounded.

Moved by Doctor White; seconded by Thomas Leech, Esq.:

Resolved--That the gratitude of the citizens of Dublin is particularly due to him for his superhuman exertions during the Revision, by which, notwithstanding the limited time prescribed, and unnecessary delay given, he executed the Herculean task, and afforded the Liberal Burgesses an opportunity of returning to the Corporation representatives of their choice.

Moved by Joseph Duffy, Esq.; seconded by Doctor Carroll:

Resolved--That this meeting, at its rising, do adjourn to Thursday evening, the 27th inst., in order to make final arrangements for the Collection of the National Tribute.

FRANCIS PURCELL, Chairman.
JOHN MOLLOY, Secretary.

On the motion of John O'Neill, Esq., T.C., seconded by James Moran, Esq., T.C., Francis Purcell, Esq., was moved from the chair, and the Rev. J. F. Ennis being called thereto, the marked and especial thanks of the meeting were then voted to Francis Purcell, Esq., for his very dignified and proper conduct in the chair.

k 22 JAMES F. ENNIS, C.C., Chairman.

HYACINTH POTS, &c.

ARRIVED TO CHRISTOPHER SHERROCK, 26, POOLBEG-STREET.

A LOT of NINE-INCH HYACINTH POTS. Also, GARDEN POTS of all sizes; SEA-KALE POTS with Lids; Plant Labels; Chimney Cans, with Barrel Tops; 14 and 16-inch Pots for Green-house Plants, &c.

Note.--A Pair of Large Ornamented Pots, for Orange Trees, on Sale as above. k 15

TO PRINTERS.

WILLIAM HOLDEN, Agent to Messrs. SHACKELL and LYONS, Printing-Ink Manufacturers to her Majesty's Printing Offices in London and Edinburgh, the Universities of Oxford and Cambridge, the Bank of England, &c., &c., &c., has now on Sale a stock at 15*s*., 18*s*., and 24*s*. per dozen, to suit every description of Job Printing, and a Fine Ink for Book Work, at 36*s*. per dozen.

No charge for Kegs.
General Printing Office, 10, Abbey-street. k 15

JOHN B. CALLAN, M.D.,

PHARMACEUTICAL CHEMIST AND APOTHECARY, PROPRIETOR OF

THE MEDICAL ESTABLISHMENT, 2, MERRION-ROW.

THIS ESTABLISHMENT, based on the principle of vending none but Genuine Medicines, embraces the Compounding of Prescriptions and the Sale of every Article connected with the practice of Medicine.

It has ever been the object of the Proprietor to support a character for the supply of Drugs in whose purity and efficacy the most entire reliance may be placed. He is constantly supplied with every Chemical and Medicinal preparation in general use, and begs to recommend a selection of the most approved Family Medicines, Select Perfumery, and other miscellaneous articles, viz.:--

Henry and Moxon's Magnesia, Murray's Fluid ditto, Pure Calcined Magnesia, of superior quality; Acidulated Cayenne Losenges, for relaxed Sore Throat; Genuine Bermuda Arrow Root, particularly recommended for Children and Invalids; Mild Aperient and Family Antibilious Pills, for those complaints arising from a disordered state of the Stomach and Bowels; Aperient Seidlitz, Soda, and Ginger Powders; Essences of Peppermint, Pennyroyal, Cinnamon, &c. &c.; Narbonne and English Honey, of the purest quality; Concentrated Essence of Ginger, superior to anything of the kind hitherto prepared; Preston Salts; Roche's Embrocation; Eau de Cologne (J. B. C. is Agent for this article--it can therefore be relied upon as genuine); with every variety of Medicinal and other preparations, too extensive to enumerate in an advertisement.

AN ASSISTANT WANTED.

Also, a Young Gentleman, properly qualified, will be received as AN APPRENTICE. k 22

LOYAL NATIONAL REPEAL ASSOCIATION.

THE LOYAL NATIONAL REPEAL ASSOCIATION OF IRELAND will meet at the Great Room, CORN EXCHANGE, on MONDAY NEXT, Oct. 24th, at TWO o'Clock,

THE LIBERATOR,

And JOHN O'CONNELL, Esq., M.P., will attend.

*** Each person NOT ENROLLED to pay One Shilling admission.

The Gallery free for Ladies, as usual.

N.B.--More than one-half the Room will be reserved for Associates. Each member, in passing through the Secretary's room, where the Books lie, will have to show that they either paid or collected One Pound.

By Order,
k 22 T. M. RAY, Secretary.

WHOLESALE AND RETAIL STATIONARY WAREHOUSE,

Established for the Sale of

WRITING, BRIEFING, DRAFTING, PRINTING, LETTER, NOTE, AND FANCY PAPERS,

From the Establishments of the First Manufacturers in the United Kingdom.

N. WALSH, Account-Book Manufacturer, Stationer, and Licensed Retailer of Stamps, 24, LOWER SACKVILLE-STREET (opposite the Post-office, Dublin). Engraving, Book-Binding, Copper-Plate, Letter-Press, and Lithographic Printing, expeditiously executed. Printed forms of every description, suited to the different Courts of Law and Equity in Ireland. Receivers' Account-Books, and Printed Rent Receipts, &c. &c. &c.

Agents and Country Gentlemen may have their own Forms for Leases, Rentals, Receipts, &c., printed on "Liberal Terms," and their Orders promptly attended to.

Whatman's Drawing Papers. Mordan's Drawing Pencils. Patent Metallic Memorandum Books in great variety.

k 15

J. FRANKLIN,

No. 12, TRINITY-STREET,

BEGS to announce the arrival, per the "Emerald Isle," and other London vessels, of an extensive assortment of the best Wax, Spermaceti, and Composition Candles, Imperial and Hambro' Wax Candles, genuine Kensington and Cocoa Nut Candles, Price's Composite Candles, Palmer's Candle Lamps and Metallic Wick Candles, Windsor Soap, Lamp Oil, &c. &c.

J. F. has his Warehouse also largely supplied with a Winter Stock of Patent Waxed Wick Mould Candles, superior Plain Mould and Dipt Candles, White, Crown, and Yellow Soap, Starch, Blues, &c.

The Bestonian Candle Lamp, for burning Candles with three wicks, have been received, and are now open for inspection.

The above-mentioned Goods will be offered to public notice on the most Moderate Terms, Wholesale and Retail. k 15

WHITEHALL BOARDING AND DAY SCHOOL,

FOR

YOUNG LADIES,

CARYSFORT AVENUE, BLACK ROCK,

Under the Superintendence of the Misses HUGHES, assisted by Eminent Masters, and a Resident French Governess.

PARENTS and GUARDIANS wishing to place Young Ladies at School, are respectfully requested to visit this Establishment. Combined with an unrivalled locality, where the Pupils enjoy the advantages of Sea-bathing, pure air, and extensive grounds for exercise, is its immediate vicinity to the Railway, which gives an equal facility of access to Masters as if it were situated in the City. The domestic arrangements are under the superintendence of Mrs. HUGHES, who bestows the greatest care on the health and comfort of the Young Ladies.

Since the commencement of this Establishment, it has been the object of the unwearied endeavours of the Principals to unite with graceful and fashionable accomplishments a more solid and useful course of Instruction than has been usual amongst young ladies; to develop the mental powers, and thus to lay a sure foundation for future excellence. That they have already partially realised their aims, is evinced by the increasing support they receive, and by the steady adherence of many attached friends, to whom they now return their sincere and deeply felt acknowledgments.

Professors of the first eminence give lessons on the Pianoforte, Harp, and Guitar; also, in Singing, Drawing, Dancing, Languages, Gymnastics, &c. If preferred, the major part of these accomplishments will be taught at a very moderate expense, by members of the family.

Cards of Terms, which will be found reasonable, may be had at Whitehall, or at No. 2, Merrion-row.

*** No Summer Vacation. k 22

BERNARD TANSEY,

PROPRIETOR OF

THE ANTRIM ARMS HOTEL, LARNE,

BEGS to return his grateful thanks to his Friends and the Public for the support which he has received since he commenced business, and to assure them that his constant exertions are given to make the Hotel the most comfortable and complete in the North of Ireland. His House is fitted up with every attention to elegance and comfort; and families visiting this romantic district will find it their interest to make it their resting point.

*** Excellent POSTING HORSES always ready.
Larne, Oct. 13th, 1842. k 15

BOOKBINDING ESTABLISHMENT.

WHOLESALE AND RETAIL PAPER, STATIONARY, AND ACCOUNT-BOOK WAREHOUSE,

NO. 21, SOUTH KING-STREET, DUBLIN.

G. BELLEW begs respectfully to draw the attention of the Nobility and Gentry to his Establishment, where they can be supplied with an extensive assortment of PAPERS, &c, which he flatters himself, for variety and Prices, can be but rarely met with. He is also supplied with the various descriptions of Account Books used in Mercantile and Professional lines, Imperial, Super Royal, Royal, and Medium Ledgers, with most durable Bindings, manufactured under his own superintendence; and in the execution of miscellaneous BINDING, he pledges himself, in point of WORKMANSHIP, to compete with the best London Houses.

Having had many years' experience as a practical Binder, and having purchased the entire of his stock for Ready Money, he is enabled to compete with any other house in the trade. He is also supplied with all those low-priced papers which are so commonly advertised by puffing establishments, and pledges himself to recommend no article but such as will render satisfaction upon use.

Any Article purchased at his Establishment will be exchanged, or the Money returned, to meet the wishes of his Customers. A variety of Bibles, Prayer Books, Scrap Books, Albums, elegantly bound. An Assortment of Second-hand Works of Literature. Morocco Leather, and every description of Material for Bookbinders. Plain and Enamelled Cards for Engravers, &c., at London Prices. Engraving, Printing, &c., executed with punctuality and dispatch. Account Books to any Pattern, Ruled and Bound on the shortest notice.

Libraries Purchased, Catalogued, and Renovated, in Town and Country. k 15

Thomas Davis was only thirty-one years old when he died. At that age most men are just beginning to make their way in the world, but when Davis died he was the hero of the whole nation. Yet just seven years before, when he came home from a visit to the Continent and to England, nobody outside the circle of his own friends had even heard of him. Now there is a fine new statue of him in College Green in Dublin, and the things he wrote about in his paper *The Nation* are still important to us. This is what he wrote about turf, a hundred years before *Bord na Móna*: "*Our bogs have not been done justice to. The use of turf in a damp state turns it into an inferior fuel. Dried under cover, or broken up and dried under pressure, it is more economical, because far more efficient.*" And in the same essay he suggested that we should use our water power—the same power which now gives us so much of our electricity. No wonder the whole country went into mourning when Thomas Davis died. He was one of those men who could understand what was really important, and who could teach others to think as he did.

Thomas Davis was born in Mallow, Co. Cork, on October 14th, 1814. His father, who had been born in England, had died a month earlier, and Mrs. Davis, who was of an old Co. Cork family, moved to Dublin with her family in 1818. They went to live in a house which is now number 67, Baggot Street, and it was here that Thomas Davis spent the rest of his life. Like many people who were afterwards to become famous, he was not very good at school, and he was just as bad at games. He tried to play both handball and hurling but could not get the knack of either. In the year 1831 he entered Trinity College, Dublin.

Trinity in those days was an interesting place because, for the first time, both Catholic and Protestant students were learning together and playing together. Davis, who was a Protestant, made many Catholic friends, and he also met many people who remembered Wolfe Tone and Robert Emmet, both of whom had been Trinity students. Though most people in the University at this time believed in keeping the connection between Ireland and England, there were others who followed Tone and Emmet and longed for a free and independent Ireland. Davis enjoyed his years as a student and later on wrote: "*Many pleasant hours have I spent within the walls of the merry monastery.*" He said "*monastery*" because Trinity College was built where the monastery of All Hallows used to stand. He graduated in 1835 and thought about becoming a lawyer. First of all he decided to travel instead, and visited London and the Continent, studying and buying books.

He returned in 1838 and, going back to Trinity to finish his law studies, became Auditor of the College Historical Society, which had not very much to do with history but was a debating society where the students met to argue about anything that interested them. The *Hist,* as it is still called, had been founded about a hundred years before by Edmund Burke. In 1840 when he was President of the Society, Davis made a very stirring speech, saying that the most important thing of all was to work to make Ireland independent. After this, the rest of his life was spent working for independence and trying to teach Irishmen about their own country and all the good things that were in it.

At this time Daniel O'Connell was holding meetings all over the country to try to persuade the British government to give Ireland back her own Parliament. Davis joined the *Loyal National Repeal Association,* as O'Connell's people called themselves, in 1839, and always had a great respect for the Liberator. The two men did not always agree. O'Connell did not believe in fighting to win independence, but Davis was sure that independence would never be won without some kind of a fight—and, as it happened, he was right. O'Connell did not see the situation this way, however, and they disagreed about other things, such as the opening of new universities. In spite of this, Davis always tried to help O'Connell in his work.

In 1841 something very important happened. Thomas Davis and his great friend John Blake Dillon met Charles Gavan Duffy, a young man who shared their ideas and was also quite rich. They talked about producing their own newspaper, something that Davis had always wanted to do but could not afford. They went for a walk in the Phoenix Park in Dublin and sat down under an elm

Daniel O'Connell

tree to discuss it. Gavan Duffy said that he would put up the money and that the three of them would run it together. They decided to call the paper *The Nation*, and the first issue, which had a special poem by James Clarence Mangan in it, came out on October 15th, 1842.

Dillon, Duffy and Davis planning THE NATION

From the very beginning *The Nation* was a great success. Soon it was being read by more than a quarter of a million people, and its circulation exceeded that of any other Dublin journal. All over the country people were buying and reading it—and keeping it to read over again.

In the early nineteenth century the "news" that most papers reported consisted of the happenings in the British Parliament, the wars in Europe, and bits of gossip about what was going on in Dublin. *The Nation* was different. It set out to teach Irish people about their own country—its history, literature, famous men and famous places—and about what could be done to make the country strong and independent. There were poems, too, by Mangan, and by Davis himself—for he quickly found out that he could write verses that people enjoyed, though he had never tried it before. He wrote about the

Irish language: *"To lose your native tongue, and learn that of an alien, is the worst badge of conquest—it is the chain on the soul. A people without a language of its own is only half a nation."*

Davis wrote for every issue of *The Nation*, and he wrote far more than anybody else. In the three years he was working with the paper he wrote about fifty songs and ballads, as well as his essays and articles. Gavan Duffy described how Davis wrote: *"A song or ballad was struck off at heat, when a flash of inspiration came—scrawled with a pencil, in a large hand, on a sheet of post-paper, with unfinished lines, perhaps, and blanks for epithets which did not come at once of the right measure or colour."* Many of the poems were

Charles Gavan Duffy

set to music and sung all over the country. The poem *"Who fears to speak of '98?"* by John Kells Ingram was first printed in *The Nation*. Soon people started sending in their own songs and poems, and at the beginning of 1843 the editor was receiving at least twenty poems a week. In the same year a collection was made of the best of the songs that had appeared in the newspaper and they were printed as a paperback with the title, *The Spirit of the Nation, by writers of The Nation newspaper*. In July, 1843, this was selling at the rate of a hundred copies a day, and it was reprinted again and again.

Davis had plans to publish a whole series of cheap paper-backs about Ireland and Irish affairs—a very go-ahead idea because in the 1840's most books were too expensive for ordinary people to buy. Several of these did come out, and were nearly as popular as *The Spirit of the Nation.* Davis's whole scheme, as we have said, was to teach people to know about and take pride in their country, and to persuade them to work to make it *"a nation once again."* He wanted Irish men and women to think for themselves, and his *Library of Ireland,* as he called it, was to help in this. Most people in country places at the time had very little schooling, and of course there was no television to show them what was happening in their own land.

The whole idea was a great success. The Young Irelanders, as Davis and his group came to be called, really seemed to have brought Catholics and Protestants together and to have found a way of talking to all the people of Ireland. But then in 1845 Davis was taken ill. He did not think it was serious, neither did his friends, but in a few days he was dead of scarlet fever. Ireland had lost a great man, but his ideas lived on and on and laid the foundation of the republic of today.

What kind of a person was Davis? He was a hard worker, as you might guess, and his friends knew him as a cheerful, friendly man who was very unselfish but who would always stand up very strongly for his ideas. He enjoyed being with his friends, even those who did not agree with him in politics. He loved reading, talking and going on tour through the countryside to places where great events of the past had happened. He was a simple person, and love of his country was the most important thing in his short life.

Hogan's statue of Davis

Charles Stewart Parnell
1846-1891

In the 1870's there were many people still alive who remembered the Great Famine, and many who thought that it was going to happen all over again. The prices which the farmers had been getting for their crops had been falling, the harvests had not been good, but the rents were still as high as ever. Families were being evicted from their homes all over the country. The Irish members of Parliament at Westminster could not make the Government do anything about it. Then in 1875 a young man who had scarcely been heard of before was elected M.P. for County Meath. His name was Charles Stewart Parnell. Within four years he was being called "the uncrowned king of Ireland." Ten years later he was dead. In that time he changed the whole shape of Irish politics, so that people who before him had thought of Home Rule only as a distant hope began to plan for the events that led up to 1916 and Easter Week. He did this not by starting a revolution or by taking arms, but by

Charles Stewart Parnell

clever debate in the United Kingdom Parliament, by stirring speeches at home, and through the power he possessed of being able to lead others and to set them a noble example to follow. When he began in politics he was a shy speaker and a bad one. *"I am not gifted with the power of expression,"* he said to one of his friends. But he taught himself to speak well, and to speak in a way that people would remember. In a speech in Cork in 1884 he said, *"No man has the right to set a boundary to the march of a nation. No man has the right to say to his country, thus far shalt thou go and no further . . ."* You can read the rest on Parnell's monument at the end of O'Connell Street in Dublin, but the words cut in stone give us little idea of how Parnell was able to stir many thousands of people to action in defence of their homes, their freedom and the right to a decent living in their own country.

For fourteen years Parnell had the ordinary people of Ireland solidly behind him, but his life was very different from theirs. He was born into a rich Protestant family at Avondale in County Wicklow, and for the first thirty years of his life it seemed that he was going to be just another landlord, spending his time shooting and riding with hounds, and remote from the tenants who lived on his land. The Parnells, who were originally an English family, had been in Ireland for a very long time, and

Fenian prisoners being led to Manchester prison

Charles Stewart's great-grandfather had been Chancellor of the Exchequer in Grattan's Parliament and had been strongly against the union with Britain in 1800. His mother was an American, a descendant of Ulster Presbyterian emigrants, and very anti-English. As a boy he listened to memories of '98 and the Young Irelanders, so that when in 1867 he heard of the execution of the *Manchester Martyrs*—three men who had been sentenced to death for their part in a Fenian escape plan in which a policeman was accidentally shot—he woke up to the fact that the country was in a sad state and needed someone to lead it to better things. He decided to be that man.

Parnell did little about that decision for some years, living the life of a country gentleman who had been educated at Cambridge University and who had nothing in particular to occupy him. He went on a trip to America in 1871, and it was not until one evening in 1874 that he really made up his mind to go into politics. He approached Isaac Butt, who was then the leader of the Irish party at Westminster, and was accepted as a candidate for the 1875 election. On April 19th, 1875, he came top of the poll with 1,771 votes as against 902 for his nearest opponent, and on the 22nd took his seat in the London Parliament.

After that things moved very quickly. Under Isaac Butt, the Irish members had been able to get very little done at Westminster; most of the English M.P.'s just ignored them. Parnell decided to change this. He disliked the English almost as much as his mother did, and

Isaac Butt

IN DIFFICULTIES!

DISTRESSED HIBERNIA. "IF YOUR TANDEM LEADER TURNS VICIOUS, AND KICKS OVER THE TRACES,—
WHERE ARE YOU?"

Contemporary Political Cartoon

decided to beat them at their own game. Together with Joseph Biggar, the member for Cavan, he stepped up an *"obstruction"* policy, talking for hour after hour on every Bill and making the House sit all through the night. His idea was to get the British to take the sad state of Ireland more seriously. In 1877 he became chairman of the Home Rule confederation and after Isaac Butt's death was made chairman of the Irish Party in the House of

Commons. In 1879 Michael Davitt founded the Land League and Parnell threw his energy into trying to get better conditions for the poor tenants who, when they had paid the rent to the landlords, had not enough left to live on. At Westport on June 7th, he told them to *"hold a firm grip on your homesteads"* and became a national hero. Here was a landlord fighting against landlords, a Protestant standing up for Catholics and standing out against both the Government and the Catholic clergy, many of whom did not agree with Davitt's League. The British brought in a Coercion Bill and in 1881 Parnell was put into jail at Kilmainham and kept there without trial for seven months. But the land movement became stronger and stronger. Tenants refused to pay unjust rents, and invented the idea of *"boycotting"* harsh landlords. (Captain Boycott was an estate manager in County Mayo). In 1882 a National Tribute—a kind of fighting fund—was organised for Parnell, and, even though the Pope spoke out against it, £40,000 was subscribed, mostly by Catholics. When Parnell came out of jail in April, 1882, it was because he had come to an agreement with the British Liberal party to support them if they would introduce laws making life better for the tenants.

Michael Davitt

Parnell would probably have been happy just to see the farmers in the poorer parts of the country getting a reasonable amount of land and paying a fair rent for it, but he found himself the leader of men whose ideas went much further. Davitt believed that all the land of

Ireland should belong to all the people—what would now be called public ownership or nationalisation; and the Fenians wanted complete political freedom for the country, a complete break-away from Britain. But by 1880 Parnell was firmly on the side of Home Rule. In a speech in Galway on the 24th of October he said: *"I would not have taken off my coat and gone to this work if I had not known that we were laying the foundation in this movement for the regeneration of our legislative independence,"* which meant the repeal of the Act of Union of 1800 and the establishment of Home Rule. This was a point at which Irish politics became very mixed up with British politics. We have seen how the Irish party was able to make a nuisance of itself at Westminster by holding up Bills that the Government wanted to get passed, but there were greater opportunities ahead of it. In the general election of 1885 many more people were given the vote and Parnell's party gained 85 seats—just the difference between the British Liberals and Conservatives. So the Liberal government, headed by Mr. Gladstone, which came into power, depended on the Irish party and had to agree to bring in a law to establish Home Rule in Ireland.

Gladstone introducing the Home Rule Bill

Mr. Gladstone was a fair man who had come to believe that Home Rule should be granted. Not all his party agreed with him. The Home Rule Bill of 1886 would have stopped short of total independence had it been passed, with Westminster still in power to control Irish defence, foreign relations and other important matters. But even so it was too much for some members of the Liberal party to allow. When the vote was taken on June 8th, 1886, it was defeated by 342 votes to 313. Gladstone gave the British people the opportunity to decide by voting at a General Election in July and both the Bill and his government were thoroughly beaten. The Conservatives came to power and stayed in power for the next twenty years. Home Rule seemed to have been forgotten for good.

But the organisation that Parnell had built up went on working. He himself was accused in 1887 by the *Times* newspaper of having had some hand in the assassination of landlords, but the information was proved to have been forged and his popularity was greater than ever. The Land League became the National League, an organisation determined to press for Home Rule, after it had succeeded by the Land Acts of 1881 and 1887 in making things better for the tenant farmers. Even though the Home Rule Bill had been defeated in the British Parliament, Irishmen had been made to see that Home Rule was possible, and they began planning for the future. All this was due to the leadership, the strength and the courage of Charles Stewart Parnell.

On November 17th, 1890, Parnell was judged guilty in a divorce case brought against him by Captain O'Shea, formerly a member of the Irish party. Mrs. O'Shea and Parnell had been living together for many years and he wanted to marry her. Some of Parnell's party turned against him because of this, but many decided to go on supporting him because he was the best leader Ireland had. They believed that a man's private life was his own affair. But Gladstone said that the Liberal party could not continue to support Home Rule as long as Parnell was the leader of the Irish party, and in Ireland also many people criticised him. On December 6th, 1890, at a meeting in Committee Room 15 in the House of Commons, Parnell was defeated by 43 votes to 27. His party had split.

Parnell did not give up. He decided that as long as Irish fortunes depended on any British political party they would come to nothing. He went all over Ireland announcing his new "*Sinn Féin*" policy; but he was no longer the popular leader, the Uncrowned King. He wore himself out holding meetings and making speeches, and died on October 7th, 1891. He was only 45 years old.

His funeral to Glasnevin cemetery was one of the biggest ever seen in Dublin. Friends and enemies paid their respects to the Lost Leader. And his ideas lived on: *Sinn Féin* became the watchword of independence.

Mrs. O'Shea

Edward Carson
1854-1935

Carson addressing an election meeting

Edward Carson's whole life was spent trying to prevent Ireland from getting back her own government, and, after he saw that this was impossible, making sure that Ulster would not form part of a 32-county republic. He wanted all of Ulster's nine counties to remain in the United Kingdom, but when he saw that this, too, was impossible, he sadly agreed to the six counties being set up as a separate political unit. He lived to see Home Rule, a policy he had fought against, tooth and nail, being given to Ulstermen who a few years earlier had raised a volunteer force to fight the British for the right to be allowed to stay in the United Kingdom. If all that sounds like something out of *Alice in Wonderland*, it is because of the fact that the years which led up to the foundation of the Irish Free State were some of the most complicated in Irish history.

The important thing to remember about Edward Carson is that he was not an Ulsterman, and it was not until he was over 50 that he found himself the leader of the Ulster Unionists. He was born in Harcourt Street, Dublin, on February 9th, 1854, and was descended from an eighteenth-century Italian architect called Carsoni, who had settled in Dublin, changed his name, and worked on some fine Georgian houses that were built at the time. His mother was Isabella Lambert, of Castle Ellen, County Galway, whose ancestor, General Lambert, was one of Oliver Cromwell's major-generals. Edward Carson was sent to school at Arlington House, Portarlington, and entered Trinity College, Dublin, in 1871. He was a good student without being brilliant, and spent much of his time debating in the College Historical Society. One of the students he knew slightly was Oscar Wilde, who was afterwards to become famous as a playwright and who was to meet Carson again in less pleasant circumstances when he was on trial and Carson was prosecuting him. Carson's father had always intended him to take up law, though he himself was at first more interested in architecture, and so in 1877 he was called to the Bar and began his legal career. For about nine years after that nothing very exciting happened in Carson's life. He proved to be a good barrister, because although he was not a flowery or dramatic speaker, he was very tall, with piercing eyes that could make witnesses very nervous. At this time he had no ideas of being anything else but a hardworking Irish lawyer, and perhaps becoming a judge after a number of years; but then a new Chief Secretary for Ireland was appointed by the British Government and, in 1887, Carson found himself in the middle of politics—and in great danger of being assassinated.

To understand why, we must know something of what was happening to Ireland at this time. Parnell had been fighting for better conditions for the tenants who could not pay their rents. A very bad harvest had made things even worse. In 1886 the National League formulated a *"Plan of Campaign,"* a scheme to organise the tenants against the landlords, against evictions, and against unfair rents. The British regarded this as contrary to law, and sent Arthur Balfour to Ireland as Chief Secretary with special powers to prosecute and imprison people without trial. He was so tough and ruthless that he was called "Bloody Balfour"—and he chose Edward Carson, or "Coercion Carson," to help him in his work. Carson believed that he was acting quite correctly in prosecuting those who were trying to get a fair livelihood from the big landlords. His one aim in life was to keep Ireland a part of the United Kingdom, and he agreed that the only answer to the nationalists was to enforce *"twenty years of resolute government"*—which meant, in fact, a police state.

It might appear from this that Carson was an inhuman, cruel and unfeeling person, but in fact he was a kind, very fair man who was admired by even his bitterest enemies. Many people would have liked to kill him, but

Unionist Meeting, September 1911

he often travelled alone and laughed at danger. He wanted to see the poor of Ireland made happier—only he wanted to see it done by Britain and not by the Irish themselves. He came of Anglo-Irish ancestors who thought that Ireland's connection with England was important for both countries, and he just could not understand the nationalist idea of independence and a separate Irish Parliament.

In 1889 Carson became a Queen's Counsel—the senior rank in the legal profession—and for the next three years worked at ordinary civil law cases, living in a house in Merrion Square. Then in 1892 Balfour decided to make him Irish Solicitor-General, but to take this office he had first to become a Member of Parliament.

There was a general election in that year, and Carson agreed to stand for the constituency of Dublin University, which was then strongly Unionist and sent two members to Westminster. He was still not very interested in politics and thought that his future lay in the law. The results of the election were: D. R. Plunkett—2,188; E. H. Carson—1,609; Colonel J. C. Lowry—897. So Edward Carson set off for London, became Irish Solicitor-General, and was called to the English Bar, which meant that he was allowed to appear in lawsuits in England as well as Ireland. A new and exciting period in his life had begun.

He soon made a name for himself as a lawyer in the British courts. More and more people asked him to represent them, and in the year 1899 his income was £20,000—which was worth then about ten times as much as it is today! He appeared in many famous trials, and in 1895 had the unpleasant job of prosecuting his former college acquaintance Oscar Wilde, who was in serious trouble. Carson seemed to have started on a long and very successful legal career in England. Then in 1900 Lord Salisbury asked him to join the English Government as Solicitor-General. This meant giving up his private practice and its large income, but he agreed. And so, he became Sir Edward Carson and an important politician.

For the next few years he worked hard, both in the courts, representing the Crown in many cases, and in the Houses of Parliament, where he spoke often on Irish affairs. He was very much in favour of the new Catholic universities which were then being discussed, though

Donegall Place, Belfast 1921

most of the Unionists did not agree with them. *"For my part,"* he said, *"I value so highly a university training that I would make almost any sacrifice which would enable Roman Catholic young men to receive the benefits of such a treasury."* And when the colleges were finally established in Dublin, Cork, Galway and Belfast in 1909 he hoped that it would be *"a step forward in the union of all classes and religions in Ireland for the progress of our country and its education."*

He was determined, however, to prevent Ireland from getting Home Rule. The government changed in 1906 and he was out of office. The election of 1910 gave the Irish Nationalists, led by John Redmond, the balance of power between the Conservatives and the Liberals, so that it seemed very likely they could use pressure to persuade the Liberal Government to bring in a Home Rule Bill. The Ulster Unionists had made up their minds to fight the Bill in every way they could, and to do this they needed a strong leader. In 1910 James Craig, later the first Prime Minister of Northern Ireland, asked Carson to take command. In September, 1911, he spoke to a gathering of 100,000 Unionists in Belfast: *"We will yet defeat the most nefarious conspiracy that has ever been launched against a free people."* The men of the North were preparing to fight the British for the right to stay within the United Kingdom! They planned to set up a government of their own if the Home Rule Bill should be passed, and in January, 1912, started training the Ulster Volunteer Force. On the 28th of September Carson signed the Solemn League and Covenant in Belfast, together with 200,000 Ulstermen. This covenant stated that they would take up arms if necessary to defeat Home Rule. Carson still hoped, however, that the Home Rule Bill would never be passed and that there would be no need to fight, but the Bill was passed in May, 1914. In the meantime arms had been smuggled into the North and everything was ready for battle. Then a much bigger battle began—the Great War. Most of the Ulster Volunteer Force joined the British army, and Carson became Attorney General and then First Lord of the Admiralty in the British Government. In July, 1917, he joined the War Cabinet.

When the war ended, in 1918, the world had changed. Ireland had been changed by the 1916 Rising and what followed. Carson was elected M.P. for the Duncairn division of Belfast in 1918 and in 1920 saw the passing of the Act against which he had fought for so long—the Government of Ireland Act. He resigned as leader of the Ulster Unionists in 1921 and also left the House of Commons, becoming Lord Carson of Duncairn. He attended the opening of Stormont Parliament in 1932 and in the following year a statue of him was erected outside the parliament building. He died on the 22nd of October, 1935.

"*It's only for Ireland that I'm in politics,*" he said; and though his idea of the future of his country did not agree with that held by men like Pearse or Connolly, he was always concerned with the happiness and welfare of Irishmen of all classes and creeds. In a speech in England in 1907 he said, "*If you are not prepared to govern Ireland according to the ordinarily elemental conditions of civilisation that prevail in every country, then go out of Ireland and leave us to govern ourselves.*" He was a life-long Unionist, but a life-long Irishman.

Constance De Markievicz
1868-1927

Most people know one thing about Countess Markievicz—that her name is very difficult to spell! It is a
Polish name: the man she married in the year 1900 was
called Count Casimir Dunin-Markievicz, and he owned
large estates in Poland, just as the Countess's family, the
Gore-Booths, were big landlords in Ireland. Constance
Gore-Booth was born in London but went when very
young to live at Lisadell in Co. Sligo, a beautiful part
of the country which the poet W. B. Yeats was later
to make famous in his poems. As a girl she was very fond
of riding, and would spend hours galloping over her
father's large estates. Sir Henry Gore-Booth was a polar
explorer, like Ernest Shackleton, but he went North, not
South, and was one of the first explorers to visit such
strange places as Novaya Zemblya, the Matochkin Shar
Strait and the Kara Seas. During the famine of 1879–80,
Constance saw people being evicted, forced to leave their
homes because they could not pay the rent, and this
horrible sight first made her concerned with their plight.

All Constance's family and friends supported British
rule in Ireland, and at this time she agreed with them.
Although she had helped to give out food to hungry
people and had been interested in Michael Davitt's plan
to get the landlords to agree to fair rents, she was presented to Queen Victoria in 1887, and used to go to
London for "the Season"—which meant for the most
part going to dances and parties and wearing expensive
clothes.

She lived a gay and happy life, and it looked as if she
would marry and live on a big estate just like her friends
and relations, but then W. B. Yeats came to visit her
parents in Lisadell, in 1894, and talked to her about
fairies and magic and other old Irish stories and legends.
After that Constance began to think for herself as well as

to enjoy herself, and in 1896 she became a suffragette. Suffragettes were women who believed that they should be allowed to vote in elections like men, to go to universities, and even to become members of parliament. Nowadays women can do these things, but in 1894 they could do none of them. Later on Constance de Markievicz was to become the first woman elected to the British Parliament, and the first woman Government Minister in western Europe.

The Countess with her children

That was a long time ahead, however. In 1897 Constance persuaded her father to let her go to Paris to study painting, and it was there that she met her future husband. The Count was a painter, too, and was also interested in books and wrote plays. After they were married, they went to live in Sligo, where Constance's daughter Maeve was born. But in 1903 they moved to Dublin, and began meeting the people who were to make such a difference to Countess Markievicz's later life.

Dublin in the early years of this century was full of writers and artists, some of whom are featured in this book. There was W. B. Yeats and his brother Jack; George Russell, who was known as *"AE"* because that was how he signed one of his articles; J. M. Synge; Percy French, who wrote *"Phil the Fluter's Ball," "The Mountains of Mourne,"* and many other songs which are still sung today; James Stephens, who wrote *"The Crock of Gold"*; James Joyce, and many others. There were politicians, too, anxious to end British rule over Ireland and let the country run her own affairs again. Madame de Markievicz met all these people and liked their ideas, especially their ideas about a free and independent Ireland. She supported Arthur Griffith's *Sinn Féin* party and had the idea of starting *Fianna na hÉireann* to teach boys to fight for the freedom of their country. Of course all these meetings, as well as the parades and camps of the Fianna, were being watched by the police and military, who felt that something big was going on. In 1911 Madame de Markievicz was arrested for the first time and taken to Store Street Police Station in Dublin. This time she was a prisoner only for an afternoon, but in the years to come she went to jail many times for fighting for what she believed to be the most important thing of all—the freedom of her country.

During the General Strike of 1913 in Dublin, Constance set up food kitchens in Liberty Hall (which was exactly where the 16-storey building with the same name is today) to help those who had no money because they were not working. At this time the Citizen Army and the Irish Volunteers were formed, and in 1914 *Cumann na mBan* came into being. Madame de Markievicz was helping with all these important arrangements, travelling all over the country to make speeches, and persuading people to support *Sinn Féin* and work for a free country. During 1915 the Citizen Army drilled and the Countess drilled with them. She had always been brave and did not seem at all afraid of having to fight. She did not have to wait long.

It would take too long here to tell the whole story of the 1916 Rising. Madame de Markievicz fought in Dublin under Michael Mallin, first in St. Stephen's Green, and then in the College of Surgeons. When the surrender was made, she was marched to Dublin Castle with the rest of the Volunteers and put into Kilmainham Jail. For days she waited there, not knowing what was going on outside except that her friends were being shot one by one. At last she was told that her life was to be spared and she was moved to Mountjoy Prison, where she became a Catholic, and then to Aylesbury in England. She was kept there until June, 1917.

The Countess was set free in June; in July she was in Ennis speaking at an election meeting in support of the *Sinn Féin* candidate, who was Eamonn de Valera. Mr. de Valera won, and Irish people started believing

Welcoming the Countess after her release from prison

that soon Ireland would gain her independence. The British, who of course were busy fighting in the Great War, were afraid that there would be more trouble in Ireland and thought that the best way to stop it would be to arrest all the *Sinn Féin* leaders. On May 17th, 1918, Madame de Markievicz found herself arrested again and taken off to an English prison—this time Holloway in London. But the War ended shortly afterwards, and there was a general election. Many of the *Sinn Féin* leaders who were still in jail stood as candidates and nearly all of them were elected. Countess Markievicz was top of the poll in the St. Patrick's Division of Dublin.

The gun which the Countess used in 1916

She got 7,835 votes against 3,742 for William Field and 312 for Alderman J. J. Kelly. She was the first woman Member of Parliament, even though she never took her seat at Westminster.

Sinn Féin had won so many seats that they decided to hold a completely Irish parliament in Ireland, the first *Dáil Éireann*. This met on January 21st, 1919, though the Countess was not released from prison until March 6th. At the second meeting in April she was made Secretary for Labour (which is like being Minister for Labour nowadays). She was soon in jail again, though,

arrested by the British who still ruled Ireland. This time Madame was sent to Cork jail—*"The most comfortable jail I have been in yet!"* she said. She was out again in October and went on working with the Citizen Army and trying to make things better for the workers. She believed that Ireland should be *"a state run by the Irish people for the Irish people"* in which the workers would have just as much power as the rich.

In 1920 Countess Markievicz was in jail again, this time for setting up the *Fianna* (Ireland was still officially under British rule). She fought on the Republican side in the Civil War which followed the Treaty, because she had always believed in a completely independent Ireland, having no connection with Britain. By this time she was an elderly lady; yet she "went on the run" with the young men, hiding both from the British and from the pro-Treaty forces all over Dublin. She even went on a hunger-strike in 1923.

When the Civil War ended and Ireland was at peace again, she was old and tired. She died on July 25th, 1927, and at her funeral Eamonn de Valera said: *"Madame Markievicz is gone from us, Madame, the friend of the toiler, the lover of the poor. . . . She now lies at rest with her fellow-champions of the right—mourned by the people whose liberties she fought for; blessed by the loving prayers of the poor she tried so hard to befriend. The world knew her only as a soldier of Ireland, but we knew her as a colleague and a comrade."*

The Countess

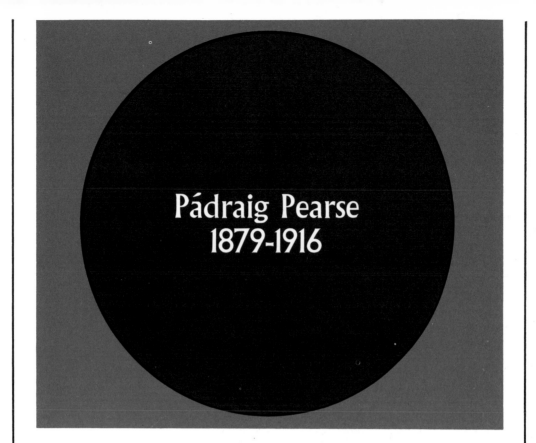

Pádraig Pearse
1879-1916

"If we do nothing else we shall rid Ireland of three bad poets," said Pádraig Pearse in the spring of 1916. He was talking about the coming Easter Rising, and the fact that he himself and two of his friends on the Military Council of the Irish Republican Brotherhood—James Plunkett and Thomas MacDonagh—were writers as well as revolutionaries. This joke is a necessary reminder that Pearse was not always solemn and serious, and that, although he had realised when quite young that he would probably have to die for his country, he enjoyed life very much. In private he was a rather shy, gentle man; only when he was speaking to a large gathering on the freedom of Ireland did he become fierce and angry. That is because he knew what he wanted most of all and was determined to get it—an Ireland, as he said, *"not free merely, but Gaelic as well; not Gaelic merely, but free as well."* For this idea he fought, and for this idea he died.

Pádraig Pearse was shot by the British military in Kilmainham Jail in Dublin at 3.30 a.m. on the morning of May 3rd, 1916. The Easter Rising was over, its leaders captured and most of them about to be executed. Yet Pearse was not sorry about what had happened. *"We have done right,"* he wrote in a letter the night before he died. *"People will say hard things of us now, but later on will praise us."* People certainly said hard things. *"I do not believe this wicked and insane movement will achieve its ends,"* said John Redmond, who was the leader of the Irish Members of Parliament who sat in the British House of Commons. He was wrong. So was the Archbishop of Cashel, who said : *"The people of Ireland do not want any revolutionary measures."* Not everything that Pearse, Connolly and their friends fought for in 1916 came to pass: partition prevented the establishment of a 32-county republic, and social injustice and economic dependence on Britain did not disappear overnight. But on Easter Monday, April 24th, 1916, Dublin was in the hands of the Irish for the first time for 700 years. When Pearse had reached that point he was ready to die a happy man.

To be ready to give up one's life for an idea or a cause, one must be a very special kind of person. Most people want to go on living as long as possible. Pádraig Pearse was only thirty-six years old when he was executed, and he knew beforehand, before he ever began the Rising, that it could only have one ending for him and his

...rse's oration ...the Grave of ...Donovan Rossa

friends. Yet all these brave men went to their deaths calmly and peacefully, spending the night before their executions writing letters and poems explaining how proud they were to die for their country. Most of their fellow Irishmen thought they were wicked rebels who had stabbed England in the back when she was fighting a war to preserve the rights of small nations. They were not ready for the freedom Pearse was trying to give them.

Pádraig Pearse was born on November 10th, 1879, at 27 Great Brunswick Street (now Pearse Street), the son of a stonemason who had emigrated from Devon in England and who had become very interested in the struggle for Irish independence. His mother was Margaret Brady from County Meath, and he had one brother, Willie (who was shot the day after him in Kilmainham Jail), and two sisters. He was taught by the Christian Brothers in Westland Row, but learned far more important things than arithmetic and spelling from an old aunt who used to take him on her knee and tell him stories of the Ireland of long ago, of the Fenians, the

Young Irelanders, and even of Wolfe Tone and '98. Young Pádraig decided he would have to learn Irish, and started to teach himself when he was about eleven, though afterwards he went to Canon O'Leary's classes in Dame Street. When he was older he used to go off to Ros Muc in Connemara, where his cottage is now kept as a national monument. By the time he was a young man he could both write and speak the language, and when he graduated from the Royal University of Ireland (now the National University) he became editor of the magazine of the Gaelic League, *An Claidheamh Soluis*. The League had been founded in 1893 by Douglas Hyde and was attracting people from all walks of life who wanted to learn and use Irish. People wanted to take this idea further by starting a school in which not only Irish would be taught, but other subjects taught through Irish. This does not seem a very original idea today, but in Pearse's time the British educational system, which was used in Ireland, compelled even Irish speakers to learn through English.

Pearse studied law in College but soon found that he had no taste for the legal life. His father died soon after he graduated and for a time Pádraig had to help his brother Willie run the stonemason's business. He lectured in Irish in the University, but in 1908 his dream came true and he founded Scoil Eanna, a school which was, as he said, *"to help as many boys as possible to become good men."* This included being good Irishmen (for you cannot make an Irish boy a good Englishman or a good Frenchman), and *"as my definition of learning as applied to an Irishman includes Irish learning as its basis and fundament, it follows that my school would be an Irish school in a sense not known or dreamt of in Ireland since the Flight of the Earls."* Pearse was trying to stop the *"murder machine,"* as he called the British educational system, and his school was so successful that after two years he had to move it from Cullenstown House in Rathmines to larger premises at The Hermitage, Rathfarnham, which had once been the home of Robert Emmet's brother, Thomas Addis Emmet. Cullenstown House then became a school for girls, St. Ita's, run on the same lines. Pearse believed in as much freedom as possible. The students of Scoil Eanna formed a Council to run their own affairs. *"I would urge that the Irish school system of the future should give freedom,"* said Pearse, *"—freedom to the individual school, freedom to the individual teacher, freedom as far as may be to the individual pupil. Without freedom there can be no right growth."*

Pearse gave up the editorship of *An Claidheamh Soluis* at the end of 1908 because he found the two jobs too much for him, but in 1912 he started a paper of his own, *An Barr Buadh*. He was then becoming more and more

els under arrest
Bachelors Walk, Dublin

The ruins of Sackville St. (now O'Connell St.) Dublin 1916

interested in active politics, and when the Irish Volunteers were formed in November, 1913, he was elected a member of the provisional committee and later the Director of Organisation. The Irish Volunteers had been started in reply to the Ulster Volunteers in the North who were arming to resist Home Rule, which looked as if it was about to be granted by the British Parliament. Home Rule would have given Ireland a very small amount of independence; many things, such as defence, foreign relations and finance would still have been controlled from London. But the Unionists in the North wanted to stay part of the United Kingdom and were prepared to fight the British if necessary. Some of the people who were running the Volunteers were not thinking at this time of a rising, but the Irish Republican Brotherhood, a secret organisation, had members—one of whom was Pearse—on the committee, and they were planning to get arms and rise against British rule.

In 1914 Pearse went to America to try to raise some money for his school, which looked as if it might have to close down for lack of funds. There he met the old Fenians, John Devoy and Joe McGarrity, and they encouraged him to continue planning a rebellion. "*We are about to attempt impossible things,*" he said when he joined the Irish Republican Brotherhood, and as soon as he saw that the Great War was about to begin, he realised that England's difficulty would be Ireland's opportunity.

The political happenings that led up to 1916 are very complicated. There were many different ideas and disagreements among nationalists as to the best course of action to follow, and these lasted right up to the eve of the Rising, so that the number of men who took up arms was far less than it should have been. One thing changed the picture very much, however: when Britain declared war on Germany the leader of the Irish Volunteers, John Redmond, said they would support her. By no means all the Volunteers agreed with him, and the force divided into two. About eleven thousand agreed with Roger Casement: *"Ireland has no blood to give to any land, to any cause but that of Ireland."* These men went on training for the fight that was to come, the rising for which Pearse was planning.

In April, 1916, Pearse was elected President of the Provisional Government and Commandant-General of the Army of the Irish Republic. The plans for the Rising were changed many times, and everything seemed to be

Pearse surrenders

lost when Roger Casement was captured on Banna Strand, County Kerry, on his way from Germany, and all the guns that the *Aud* was bringing were lost. The mobilisation timed for Easter Sunday was postponed, but on the afternoon of Easter Monday a column of men marched from Liberty Hall with Pearse, Connolly and Plunkett at its head. Outside the General Post Office in O'Connell Street, Dublin, Pearse read the proclamation of the Irish Republic to a few bystanders who did not really understand what was happening: *"We declare the right of the people of Ireland to the ownership of Ireland . . ."* The Rising had begun.

Pearse and his men evacuated the Post Office, which was by then in flames, the next Friday night. On Saturday morning the members of the Provisional Government held a council of war in 16 Moore Street and decided to surrender. He signed an order for all the other commandants to lay down their arms. He and they were tried in secret by army court martial and all seven members of the Provisional Government were sentenced to death and shot. They died, as Pearse wrote in a poem the night before his execution:

"In bloody protest for a glorious thing."

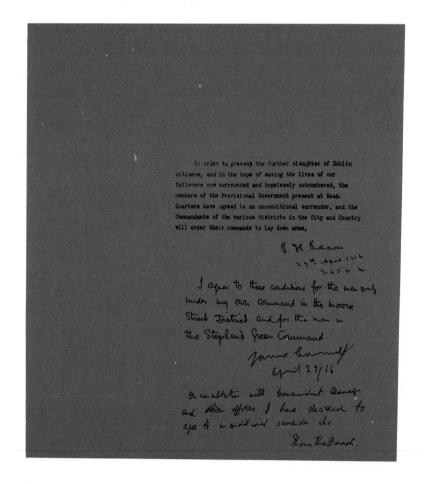

Mícheál Ó Cléirigh
1575(?)-1643

If you want to know what happened on the 15th of August, 1923, what do you do? You can look up old newspapers that are kept in libraries, or you can read *"Year Books"* which tell you all the main events. But supposing you want to know what happened in the year 1023? What do you do then? In those days there were, of course, no newspapers and the only books in existence in Europe were beautiful manuscripts like the *Book of Kells*, made by monks who worked for years on one copy. There were never very many of them, and as Ireland was plunged into wars, most of these were stolen or burnt. It is amazing that we know anything at all about what happened in the days of Niall of the Nine Hostages, St. Patrick and Brian Boru. We would know even less if Brother Mícheál Ó Cléirigh had not been sent from Louvain, now in Belgium, to Donegal in the year 1626.

The Irish Franciscans, many of whom had been driven out of their homeland by the the invading English, founded a College at Louvain in 1606. By 1611 they had their own printing press, and were printing and publishing books in many languages—including Irish. After the Flight of the Earls in 1607 more and more Irishmen began arriving in Louvain and one of these was Mícheál Ó Cléirigh's brother, Maolmhuire. We do not know for sure when Mícheál himself arrived there, although it is recorded that on July 23rd, 1621, someone called Tadeo O Cleri was given a kind of pension of two crowns every month by the Spanish Government (which ruled Holland at the time). This does not appear to have much to do with Mícheál, but we know he was baptised Tadhg and was known in Donegal as *"Tadhg an tSléibhe."* He took

The Flight of the Earls

Luke Wadding

the name Mícheál as his religious name. We are not certain when he was born, though it was probably about 1575. Anyway, we *do* know that by the time he became a lay brother at Louvain he was quite famous as an expert in Irish history, and that two other Franciscans, Father Hugh Ward and Father Patrick Fleming, asked him to help them with the work of making a book about all the Irish Saints.

Now there were manuscripts in libraries all over Europe which had been brought from Ireland by the Irish missionaries hundreds of years before, and when Father Fleming went to Rome he spent as much time as he could in copying them out. He was given a lot of help by Father Luke Wadding. All the more important manuscripts, however, remained in Ireland, so the Franciscans decided to send Brother Ó Cléirigh on what would now be called a fact-finding mission, to travel all over the country and copy down everything that seemed important. He said goodbye to his friends and took a boat which brought him to the Franciscan monastery in Donegal in 1620.

The Franciscan Abbey in Donegal had been founded in 1474, but had been plundered and wrecked in the wars several times—in 1591, 1592, and in 1601 when it was so badly damaged by fire that the monks could live in it no longer. They moved to Bundrowes in Donegal and it was here that Mícheál set up his headquarters. It was here, too, that he spent the winter of each year—copying out the manuscripts he had found in his summer journeys which took him over the length and breadth of Ireland. He probably travelled on horseback, for the roads were far too bad for a man on foot, particularly for a man carrying a heavy bag full of manuscripts written on sheepskin. He stayed in monasteries, with noblemen—anywhere he could find some old document which told the lives of the Irish saints. He went to Dublin in July, 1627, and stayed in the Franciscan monastery in Cook Street. Its guardian was luckily a friend of the Anglican Archbishop of Dublin, James Ussher, who had a very fine library, though Mícheál did not find very much in it that interested him. He went on to Drogheda, and somewhere on his travels came across the famous *Book of Leinster* from which he copied a poem which was probably written by Saint Ciaran.

Mícheál returned to Donegal for the winter, and spent the long, dark months copying out properly all the manuscript poems and stories of the saints he had collected. It must have been about this time that he started a book of his own, because by 1628 he had finished the first copy of *Feilire na Naomh Ereannach*, which became known as the *Martyrology of Donegal*, because that is where it was written. During the years 1628/29, and 1630 he was travelling all over Ireland, "*where he heard there was any book good or bad,*" as he himself said. In 1630, also, he finished a much longer Martyrology of Donegal, based on his first one. For this book he used all the stories he had collected in his four years of wandering. This great work was finished on the 19th of April, 1630, but it was not published until more than two hundred years later—in 1864.

Collecting all the stories about all the Irish saints was a great deal of work for one man, and when Brother Mícheál decided to start another book, he thought it would be a good idea to find some other historians to help him. He also needed a patron—that is, a rich man who would give him food and somewhere to live while

he was working. He soon found someone, Toirdhealbhach Mac Cochlan, and also three learned men to help him. Together they sat down in the Franciscan monastery of Killinure on the shores of Lough Ree near Athlone to write a book with the long name *Reim Rioghraidhe na hEreann agus Senachas na Naomh.* This told of the families of all the old Irish Kings and of the Saints as well. The names of Mícheál's helpers were Fearfeasa Ó Maolchonaire, from County Roscommon; Cuchoigriche Ó Cléirigh, from County Donegal; and Cuchoigriche Ó Duibhgheannain, from County Leitrim. Their names are hard to remember, but everyone knows the three of them and Brother Mícheál as the Four Masters.

These four wise men seem to have been able to work very well together without arguing or wasting time, because they began their first book on October 4th, 1630, and had it finished before the end of the year. Though Mícheál had been sending all the finished manuscripts to Louvain, this one did not get there for some reason until six years later, and after wandering around Europe for a long time, it was sent back from Rome to the Franciscan monastery in Dublin in 1872.

In 1631 the Four Masters rewrote another important history book, *The Book of Invasions of Ireland,* or the *Leabhar Gabhála* as it is called in Irish. They wrote this one very quickly, too; it was begun in Lisgoole on the banks of the Erne on October 22nd and finished on December 22nd, just in time for Christmas. The Four Masters did not take a very long Christmas holiday, though. On January 22nd, they began their biggest and most important book, *Annala Rioghachta Eireann,* that is the *Annals of the Kingdom of Ireland*—now called by everybody the *Annals of the Four Masters.* This book set out to tell the story of Ireland from just after the Flood to the year 1608—a very long time. The Masters used all the old manuscripts, most of which have now disappeared, so that their *Annals* are often the only information we have on the happenings of long ago. In it the Masters wrote down everything they could think of, big things and little things. Here is what happened in 1472: *"A wonderful animal was sent to Ireland by the King of England. She resembled a mare and was of a yellow colour, with the hoofs of a cow, a long neck, a very large head, a large tail, which was ugly and scant of hair. She used to kneel when passing under any doorway, however high, to let her rider mount."* That was a description of a dromedary, a kind of camel! The great book was written at the Franciscan monastery at Bundrowes in Donegal, where one of Mícheál's brothers,

Page of the Annals in Ó Cléirigh's handwriting

Bernardine, was then a Guardian. He also had been trained in Louvain. Another brother, Conaire, helped the Masters with the work, and so did another scholar called Muiris Mac Torna Ó Maolchonaire. There were several interruptions, and Mícheál went off travelling again, but at last on August 10th, 1636, the *Annals* were finished and Mícheál realised that his work in Ireland was over and that it was time to return to Louvain.

First of all, though, he took the book to the best historians in the country to see if they liked what the Masters had done, and then in February, 1637, he brought it to Dublin to get the *imprimatur* of the Archbishop, Thomas Fleming, O.F.M. In July he set sail for Holland and was never seen in his native land again.

A page from the Annals

We do not know much about how Brother Mícheál spent his last years. He must have helped other scholars with their work, particularly those who were writing anything about Ireland. He wrote and printed one book himself—a dictionary of hard words in Irish called *Focloir no Sanasan Nua*—which came out in 1643 and was to help people trying to read the old Irish manuscripts. In the same year he died, but we know neither the date nor where he was buried. Even his great book the *Annals,* was nearly forgotten until it was translated by John O'Donovan in 1847, when everyone realised how important it was.

Luke Wadding
1588-1657

Munster at the end of the sixteenth century was not a pleasant place to live in. English armies sent by Queen Elizabeth were roaming the country, killing and looting. Traditional Irish dress had been forbidden, and Catholics were not allowed to practise their religion in public. The city of Waterford was one of the strongholds of English power and was, for the most part, loyal to the Queen and her governors, who often visited it between their military campaigns. It was in Waterford that Luke Wadding was born on October 16th, 1588.

His father was of Anglo-Irish origin and, though he was a Catholic, owned large estates from which he drew his income. Luke was one of fourteen children, and at the age of six was sent to Mrs. Jane Bardon's school in the city. Here he met two fellow-pupils who were later to become famous—one as Bishop Comerford of Waterford and Lismore, and the other as Archbishop Walsh of Cashel. Luke soon showed that he was a clever child, and in 1602 his parents sent him to Peter White's seminary in Kilkenny, a school which was known throughout Europe. Luke continued to be a good scholar, but he enjoyed life and became a good harpist as well. His teachers noticed that he was very attracted to religion, but they had no time to encourage him in this because in 1604 his mother died and he had to return to Waterford. His father did not live long after his mother, and was perhaps killed by the plague which was then sweeping the country. The school in Kilkenny was closed, and at the end of 1604 Luke Wadding left Ireland with his brother Matthew to continue his education abroad.

At this time there were very close connections between Ireland and Spain, where many men of noble families had gone to live after the O'Donnell-O'Neill rising and the battle of Kinsale in 1602. The Wadding brothers went to Lisbon (Portugal was then a part of Spain) and enrolled in the Irish college at Matozinhos. From there Luke went to the University of Coimbra, where he graduated with honours in 1605. Matthew had married a rich Spanish girl and hoped to find a rich wife for his brother also, when Luke went to live with him after he left college. But Luke met a friend of his, Richard Synott of Wexford, and together they decided to enter the religious life. He was ordained in the Franciscan Order in 1613.

For three years the young priest ministered in the town of Leiria, to the north of Lisbon, but his fame as a scholar and a man of learning spread so much that in 1617 he was appointed Professor of Theology at Salamanca, a

Auro mens Lucæ magis aurea, et aurea penna
alterutrum potuit pingere nulla manus.

Luke Wadding

very old University at which Miguel de Cervantes, the
author of *Don Quixote,* had studied. He stayed in this
position for two years, and then his interest in the cause
of the Immaculate Conception attracted the attention of
the Bishop of Cartagena, Diego de Torres, who was
setting off for Rome to place the case before the Pope.

The argument over the Immaculate Conception had
been going on for centuries, with the Franciscans on one

side and the Dominicans on the other. The Council of Trent in 1546 had tried to bring the matter to a decision, but without success. In the early 1600's the Jesuits and the Franciscans in Spain were strong supporters of the doctrine, and it was the Spanish King Philip III who sent the mission to Rome in which Luke Wadding was included. Once he was in Italy, Luke set to work to prepare the evidence to lay before the Pope, and visited libraries in Naples, Perugia and many other places, collecting information which was put together under the title *Acta Conceptionis Immaculatae*. The doctrine was not finally proclaimed until 1854, more than 200 years later, but Luke Wadding's enthusiasm and scholarship paved the way for its ultimate adoption.

It is not surprising that such a gifted priest decided to remain in Rome. First of all, it was the home of his Church and of his Order; secondly, it was a city rich in books and manuscripts; thirdly, it was quickly becoming a second home for many Irishmen—both those who had come to study and those who had fled Ireland for political or religious reasons. Luke Wadding never again left the Eternal City, except for short visits, and until his death he was regarded as Ireland's unofficial Ambassador at Rome. He became Procurator-General of his Order, but was not a man who was anxious to become mixed up with the politics of the Church. Later in life he stopped a petition that was on its way from Ireland to the Pope asking that he should be made a Cardinal. His main interest was scholarship and the welfare of Irish students for the priesthood, and it was to help them that he founded the College of Saint Isadore on the Pincian hills to the north of the city. The College was called after the patron saint of Madrid, and it was, at first, no more than a simple boarding house. Wadding gradually added to it, building six chapels and cloisters and starting a magnificent library. Some of the finest Italian artists of the time painted pictures for the College, though many of these were stolen in later years by occupying foreign troops. Luke Wadding's Constitution for the College was approved by Pope Urban VIII on June 26th, 1625, and he was appointed guardian and professor of theology.

At the same time he was continuing his scholarly work, and his edition of the writings of Saint Francis was published in 1623. This was followed in 1624 by editions of two volumes of Biblical criticism, and in the years 1626–54 by his most important publication, the *Annals of the Franciscan Order*, or *Annales Minorum Ordinum Franciscanorum* as it is called in Latin. This was a complete history of the Order from its foundation to the time at which he was writing, and covered every country in which there was, or had been, a Franciscan foundation. It was a huge task, and took up eight big volumes. He also wrote a book on the Hebrew language, which he had learned from a Jew in Portugal when he was young, and had planned an ecclesiastical history of Ireland—but he could not find in Rome all the manuscripts he needed.

Though he had left Waterford at the age of 15, he had never lost touch with his country. His friend Comerford had come to Rome for his consecration as Bishop of Waterford and Lismore, and he had met Hugh O'Neill, too, after the Flight of the Earls had taken him into exile. The news from Ireland was bad. The country was

St. Isidore's College

ANNALES
MINORUM
SEU
TRIUM ORDINUM
A S. FRANCISCO INSTITUTORUM
AUCTORE
A. R. P. LUCA WADDINGO HIBERNO
S. T. Lectore Jubilato, & Ordinis Chronologo.
TOMUS XI.
Editio secunda, locupletior, & accuratior
OPERA, ET STUDIO
R.ᴹⁱ P. JOSEPHI MARIÆ FONSECA AB EBORA
S.T.Lect. Jub. S.& U.Inquifit. Confultoris, S.C.Confiftor.Vot. Epifcop. Examinat.
Ord.Min.in Cifmont.Fam.tam Obferv.quam Refor.& Difcalc.Cõmifs.Gen.&c.

ROMÆ Typis Rochi Bernabò MDCCXXXIV.)(*Superiorum permiſſu*.
CUM PRIVILEGIO SUMMI PONTIFICIS.

in turmoil, and the departures of O'Neill and O'Donnell had left the people without a true leader. The political situation was very complicated, with different groups joining with one another and breaking away again, and it was not until the Irish and the "Old English" Catholics —people of English origin whose families had long been living in Ireland—joined together in the rising of 1641 that there seemed any hope for the country. Luke Wadding was first and foremost a priest; he wanted to see the Catholic people of Ireland free to practise their religion, but he also wanted to see the country united and free from outside interference. He began collecting money, weapons and equipment to send to the Confederate armies under Eoghan Rua O'Neill and arranged for exiled Irish soldiers who were living in France and other countries to return home to help in the struggle. He even spoke at public meetings, in Venice and Florence in 1642, asking people to help his countrymen in their fight. When the Pope decided to send his nuncio, Cardinal Rinuccini, to Ireland to help the Confederates, Luke Wadding gave him what we would now call a briefing on what to expect in his homeland. Unfortunately, Rinuccini's journey was not a success, and the Confederates started arguing amongst themselves. In spite of O'Neill's victory at Benburb in 1645, they were later crushed by Oliver Cromwell. This upset Luke Wadding very much, because he could see that it would be a long time before Ireland could again put up a real struggle for independence. Wadding died on the 1st of November, 1657, and was buried in Rome.

Unfortunately not every Irishman understood the part Wadding was trying to play in the future of his country. Then, as now, Irishmen from North and South did not agree, and there were some who thought that Luke Wadding was secretly on the side of the Munstermen against the Ulstermen, or on the side of the English because of his Anglo-Irish background. There were those Irishmen who were prepared to trust France more than Spain for foreign help, and those who thought the other way round. When the Confederate rebellion failed, several people, including priests, believed that Father Wadding had hindered rather than helped the cause. This was unfair, but it was natural at a time of very confused politics. One historian has called the years 1641–51 *"the most complicated decade in the history of Ireland,"* and when one remembers how long it took letters or messengers to reach Rome from Ireland in those days it is not surprising that plots and schemes and suspicions

Handwriting of Luke Wadding

grew up. Luke Wadding loved his religion and his country. We know from his writings that he wanted to see Gael and Gall living together with fairness and freedom, even under an English king. He was not a republican, because the idea of the modern republic had not yet come into being and people saw nothing strange in the king of one country ruling over others. But he was a patriot, a great teacher, and, for all his learning, a humble man of God.

Edmund Ignatius Rice
1762-1844

When Edmund Rice was born in Callan, County Kilkenny, on June 1st, 1762, the Penal Laws which had caused so much suffering in Ireland since 1695 were gradually being relaxed. He spent his childhood on a farm of about 150 acres, which cost his father two sovereigns an acre in rent. The house in which the Rice family continued to live until 1888 can still be seen—in fact it is now kept as a memorial to the great founder of the Christian Brothers. In spite of the fact that life for Catholics was not quite as hard as it had been, there were still no proper primary schools which they could attend, and so the young Edmund went to a hedge-school which was held in the old moat in Callan. The fees were fourpence a week and an extra halfpenny for dancing lessons. He attended this school until he was fifteen, when he was sent to a boarding-school in Kilkenny—Burrells Hall, which was near St. Mary's Cathedral. He only stayed at this school for two years, because in 1779 he was sent to Waterford to join his uncle, Michael Rice, who was in business there.

Waterford at this time was a busy port, with ships coming and going from and to all parts of the world. In 1778 the leading citizens of the town had voted for a *"Buy Irish"* campaign to try to keep home manufacturers going, and passed a resolution saying, *"That we will not deal with any merchant or shopkeeper who shall, at any time hereafter, be detected in imposing any foreign manufacture as the manufacture of this country."* Michael Rice, whose office was at Barron Strand Street, dealt mainly in meat which he exported both to England and to Newfoundland; he also imported fish from Newfoundland. Edmund quickly learnt the business and soon became very successful; he continued in this trade for many years as a respected member of the city's business community. He married when he was twenty-three and had one daughter, though his young wife died a few weeks after the child's birth. Throughout his business career he spent a great deal of time and money visiting and helping the poor, the sick, and those people who had been put in prison, especially those who were gaoled because of debts they could not pay. In fact Edmund Rice often paid these debts so that they could go free.

The more time he spent among the poor sections of the Waterford people, the sorrier he felt for the children who had no chance of going to school to learn the things that would help them to get worth-while jobs. There were very few Catholic schools for poor people in the city,

and Edmund Rice decided to try to do something to help them. In 1796 he and some friends had set up the *Distressed Roomkeepers' Society* to help adults who needed food and money, and now he and his friends planned to help their children as well. Rice had been thinking of retiring from the world and joining an Augustinian monastery in Rome, but he saw that there was work for him to do in Ireland. He was given encouragement by Bishop John Lanigan of Ossory and Bishop Thomas Hussey of Waterford, who themselves had opened a charity school in 1785, and by the year 1800 he was teaching boys in a business premises in the city. In 1802 he rented a stable in New Street and converted it into a schoolroom. The first day the school opened it was packed, but the two paid teachers Edmund Rice had brought in to help him did not like the work and left. Later on, however, he was joined by two of his friends from Callan—Thomas Grosvenor and Patrick Finn— and between them they managed to carry on the school.

The next year, 1803, Rice decided to give up his business completely and to spend all his time teaching. He realised that the stable in New Street was not a very good place for a school, so with four friends and with the help of Bishop Hussey he built a new school at Mount Sion. This was opened on May 1st, 1804—the first of what was to become the great network of Christian Brothers' schools all over Ireland and all over the world.

Of course they were not called Christian Brothers' schools from the beginning. Rice and his four friends were only laymen, though they were all of them very religious people. At first there were many difficulties, because, although Edmund Rice had made a lot of money in business and was spending it on the school, it still needed more financial support. In 1805, Dr. Power, nephew of the new Bishop of Waterford, joined them and gave them a large sum of money which helped to open two new schools the next year—in Clonmel and Dungarvan. Many young men came to Mount Sion to help in the great work, and in 1808 Edmund Rice and his friends met and decided to take religious vows and to wear habits. Each of them took a new name, and Edmund Rice became Edmund Ignatius Rice, the leader of a dedicated band of men who were to change the whole picture of education in Ireland.

In 1811 the first school of the new Order was opened in Cork, and the next year Bishop Daniel Murray of Dublin invited Ignatius Rice to extend his work to the capital. Rice asked him, in turn, to present a memorial to the

Commemorative stamp

Waterford 1824

Pope asking for recognition for their Order, and in 1820 Pope Pius VII sanctioned the establishment of the Order under the name of *Religious Brothers of Christian Schools (Ireland)*. In 1822 Ignatius Rice was unanimously elected the first Superior General, a position he held for sixteen years.

One of the people Edmund Ignatius Rice had helped in earlier years was Charles Bianconi, who had arrived in Waterford with very little money. *"Arriving in Waterford a poor, penniless, desolate Italian boy, I found in Mr. Rice a generous and sympathetic friend,"* he said. The two men remained good friends until Rice's death. Bianconi has left us this description of Rice: *"He was a tall, vigorous, somewhat austere-looking man; grave, practical, businesslike, and eminently respectable, though decidedly plain in appearance and homely in manner."* Bianconi remembered their friendship in his will, and wrote that part of his fortune was to be given to the Christian Brothers should he die without male heirs. Rice was also a good friend of the Liberator, Daniel O'Connell. In June, 1828, when he laid the foundation stone of the C.B.S, North Richmond Street, Dublin, with 100,000 people in attendance, O'Connell in his speech referred to his dear old friend Edmund Ignatius Rice, the *"Patriarch of the Monks of the*

Mount Sion, Waterford

West." On the 19th of March of the same year Ignatius Rice had said goodbye to Mount Sion, because it had been decided to move the headquarters of the Order to Dublin. He was very sad to leave Waterford, where his great idea had been born and where he had begun in such a small way, but the Order was now growing fast. Schools had been opened at Thurles in 1815, at Limerick in 1816, at Mill Street, Dublin in 1818, at James's Street, Dublin, in 1820, at Ennistymon in 1824, and at Ennis in 1827. In the year 1825 the Order went overseas for the first time and opened a school at Preston in Lancashire, to be followed by schools in Manchester (1826), London in the same year, Sunderland in 1836, Liverpool in 1837 and another in London also in 1837. They were also asked to open a school in Gibraltar, and this was done in 1835. All these schools were opened during the lifetime of the Founder, and after his death many more were established—in Ireland, Australia, America, South Africa and other countries.

In 1829 the British Government passed the Catholic Emancipation Act, but there were two clauses in it which seemed to threaten the religious Orders, and to make their future very unsure. The Protestant clergy and ministers of Carrick-on-Suir were so worried about what might happen to the Christian Brothers' schools that they got up a petition, led by the Rector, Standish O'Grady, to ask the Government not to interfere with the Order. People of all beliefs agreed that the Brothers were doing wonderful work in educating the poor of the country, and a British Royal Commission which investigated Irish education in 1837 spoke very highly of them. In 1831 a new educational system had been introduced to Ireland with the idea of making primary education available for everyone. It was known as the *National System,* and aimed at teaching Catholics and Protestants together for all subjects except religion, for which they were to have separate classes. Many people thought that this was a good scheme, but Ignatius Rice believed that religious teaching should play a part in every lesson rather than just having a period to itself. He was persuaded by the Archbishop of Dublin to bring six of his schools into the scheme, but was never very happy about it, and in 1836 he decided to take them out again.

By this time he was an old man, and his health was failing. He had tried to resign from the position of Superior General in 1829 but his friends had encouraged him to stay on, and in 1831 he was again elected and remained as Superior until 1838, when he at last gave up the very tiring job he had held for so long. He retired to Mount Sion, where he spent the last years of his life. He sometimes visited the schools he had founded, but soon he grew too weak to leave the monastery. Ignatius Rice died on August 29th, 1844, and was buried at Mount Sion. In the same year Thomas Francis Meagher, then mayor of Waterford, laid the foundation of a chapel in memory of Rice and, in 1941 his remains were reburied in a special mausoleum at Mount Sion. The cause for Ignatius Rice's beatification was opened in 1963. He was indeed a saintly man, a man who hated to see his fellow-men suffer: but he was also a man of great energy, intelligence and practical knowledge whose work has given millions of boys a wonderful start in life.

George Petrie
1789-1866

A visitor to any of Ireland's really old buildings—round towers, castles, or places like Mellifont or Clonmacnois—will see a little notice telling him that he is looking at a National Monument which is cared for by the State. Not much more than a hundred years ago many of these beautiful and important places were falling down because there was no one to look after them. Farmers were taking stones from them to build walls, weeds were growing over them, and no one seemed to be interested in the buildings in which so many important events in our history took place. George Petrie was one of the first men to try to save them for the nation. He was the man who, more than any other, made Irishmen understand the importance of archaeology.

Archaeology means the study of antiquities and in 1833 Petrie published a book called *The Origin and Uses of the Round Towers of Ireland* which was the first in which anyone seriously tried to explain why they had been built and what they had been used for. Until then everyone had his own idea; some people even thought that they dated back to prehistoric times. Petrie read all the old Irish manuscripts very carefully and decided that they were certainly built in early Christian times and that they were used as fortresses in which the monks could guard their treasures during the Viking raids. Not everybody nowadays agrees with everything that he said about them, but his book made people so interested in our ancient monuments that scholars began

The Petrie Crown *in the National Museum, Dublin*

to study them properly and try to save them from being destroyed, or simply allowed to crumble.

George Petrie was born in Dublin and spent all his life in Ireland. His father, who was from Scotland, was an artist and painted portraits of many of the leaders of the 1798 rising, and one of Robert Emmet. Young George was rather a delicate boy and went to school only for a short time. He attended White's School in Grafton Street, Dublin, where Emmet himself had been educated, but then his father decided to let him go his own way, since he was clearly interested in becoming an artist, too. When he was nineteen he set out on the first of his many journeys around Ireland: to Wicklow from Dublin was quite an adventure in those days. George spent many weeks walking in the Wicklow mountains, making drawings of the scenery and of the many old monuments he found, and he also took down the old songs that were sung to him in the cottages in the evenings. He loved music as much as he did painting, and he did as much for traditional Irish songs as he did for our antiquities and national treasures. He was never a rich man, but he made us all richer by saving things which otherwise would have vanished forever. He was the first man to write down the beautiful tune which is now known as the *"Derry Air"*, and which musicians have called the most perfect melody in the world.

In his young days George Petrie earned his living as an artist, drawing pictures for the guide books which were then becoming popular. Nowadays this kind of book has photographs in full colour, but in the 1820's all the pictures had to be drawn by hand and then engraved on steel plates to be printed. Several of Petrie's pictures are now in the National Gallery, but, as he painted, he began to discover that he was more interested in the history behind the old churches and monuments he drew—who built them, when they were built, what they

One of Petrie's Illustrations

were used for. He went to the Aran Islands in 1821, the same year in which he was married, and drew and described wonderful places like Dun Aonghusa which were then hardly known at all. In 1826 the Royal Hibernian Academy was founded, and he put several pictures into their first exhibition. Two years later he became a member, and two years after that, in 1830, the librarian of the Academy. In 1828 he had become a

member of the Royal Irish Academy, which Rowan Hamilton had joined the year before; and in 1831 he went to an auction of old books and bought for the R.I.A. a manuscript of the second part of the *Annals of the Four Masters*. No one else had realised what it was, and after he had bought it, he was offered much more to sell it again. But George Petrie presented it to the Academy's library and the members were so pleased that they made him a member for life.

One of the most important things he did for the Academy was to build up the museum, going around the country finding precious objects and persuading people to sell them so that they could be properly looked after. Many of our national treasures, such as the Cross of Cong and the beautiful gold torcs, were rescued by Petrie and preserved for the nation. He managed to buy back valuable collections of books which might otherwise have gone outside the country, and he gathered together a wonderful storehouse of knowledge about ancient Ireland, its people and its arts and crafts. He wanted as many people as possible to share this knowledge and to enjoy the treasures, so in 1832 he helped to start a magazine, *The Dublin Penny Journal*, run by the Rev. Caesar Otway, in which he wrote about antiquities and drew pictures of them. The paper lasted for only a year, but it was enough to tell people how important the things of the past are in enabling us to understand our history and traditions.

In 1824 the British House of Commons had decided to start an Ordnance Survey of Ireland, making new maps of the whole country, county by county. In 1833 George Petrie was made head of the Topographical Survey team, which was given the job of collecting all the information it could about the history, monuments, antiquities and place-names, and writing a report to go with each set of maps. Petrie had several clever men to help him: John O'Donovan and Eugene Curry, the finest Gaelic scholars of their day, and James Clarence Mangan who used to fall asleep in the office and made jokes about Conn of the Hundred Bottles (he was very fond of the drink himself). They all worked very hard, and in 1839 the first volume of the Survey, *The County of Derry*, was published. Everyone thought it was a magnificent production, but unfortunately the Government began to worry that the whole idea was going to be too expensive, so they cancelled it then and there. Petrie and his friends were very disappointed, as were many people in Ireland, and he found himself out of a job. The only thing for him to do was to return to his painting, and this he did, working in the meantime at his books on the military architecture of Ireland and on the history and antiquities of the Hill of Tara. The work of the Topographical Survey was not wasted, however; it encouraged people to take a new interest in Ireland's past and in particular to read and study the Irish language and its literature, which at that time were hardly taught at all. Irish began to be taught in Maynooth, in the Queen's Colleges (now the National University of Ireland), and in St. Columba's College. Petrie had designed a special type-face, called *"Round Irish,"* in which to print Irish manuscripts and passages from Irish manuscripts, and his beautiful letters are still admired today.

In 1845 Petrie went on a trip to Scotland to compare the round towers there with those in Ireland, and he went back again the next year, paying a short visit to St. Colmcille's island of Iona. In 1847 he was given an honorary degree of Doctor of Laws by Trinity College, Dublin, and two years later he received a government pension which meant that he had enough money to live on while continuing his important work. He was becoming more and more interested in the ancient music of Ireland, and in 1851 helped to found the Society for the Preservation and Publication of the Melodies of Ireland. In 1855 this society published his important

Ar fada milte óó g-captaó ríor
    Agur ruar an fán,
Ir clanna raoit ar earbaió grinn;
    San cluain gan rcác;
San cancain bíobacta, gan pleag, gan fíon,
    San cruaóar, gan óeópo,
Ag braié apír an Caicilín
    Ní Uallacáin.

Ná mearáigió gur caile críon,
    Ná guaireacán,
Ná cailicín an ainnir thín,
    Caír, buacac, rínáihail;
Ar fada apír ba banalcra h-í,
    Ir bo mór a h-ál,
Dá m-beié mac an rig ag Caicilín
    Ní Uallacáin.

Ba óear a gnaoi, óá mairimír,
    Le ruagairc námaó,
Ir bracaib ríoba ag carraing gaoite,
    'Gur buaó óó'n báib;
Pleaó go groióe ó bacar cinn
    Anuar go ráil,
Ag mac an rig ar Caicilín
    Ní Uallacáin.

N'íl rear ran tír bo glacramaoir
    Do'n rcuaire mná,
Gió caiceann luigo le Saxainín
    'Nar ruar a cnáiha.
Ir fada an thoill ar an b-fararie aoibinn,
    Uaral áro,
Do b'fearra linn 'beié ag Caicilín
    Ní Uallacáin.

Sgreaóamaoió le h-acóuingió
    Cum Uain na n-grár,
Do ceap na ríorta, calah cruím,
    Agur cruacaib áro;
Do rgair na b-címcioll fairrgióe,
    Seal-óuanta ir crága,
Ag cur malairc críce ar Caicilín
    Ní Uallacáin.

An có éarraing Irrael carrna caoibe
    Ruaó, ó'n námaió,
'Soo beacaig baoine óá fióit geithre
    Anuar le h-arán;
Do nearcaig Maoiri 'mearg a náithoe;
    Ag ruargailc crá,
'Sag cabairc bín bo Caicilín
    Ní Uallacáin.

Petrie type face

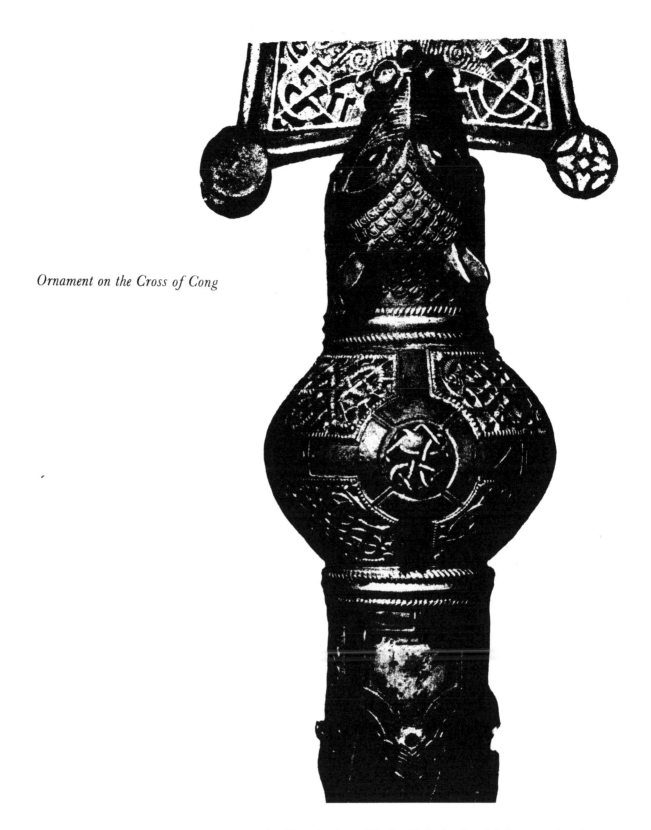

Ornament on the Cross of Cong

book *The Ancient Music of Ireland,* which contained 147 airs, together with many notes about the tunes and where they came from. Petrie realised that the Great Famine had killed many of the old people who alone could remember the traditional songs and stories, and he tried to collect as many as possible before the rest were forgotten. If it had not been for his work, many of the beautiful tunes still sung today might have disappeared without trace.

Petrie was still a member of the Royal Hibernian Academy—in fact he had been made its president—but in 1859 he resigned because the council wanted to adopt a new constitution with which he did not agree. The Academy had decided to stop letting poor people in to the exhibitions at a charge of a penny, whereas he believed that everyone, rich or poor, should have a chance to enjoy painting. He was a very generous man, but could get quite annoyed with people who did not know their job. He was asked to design a monument to Daniel O'Connell, but when it was erected over the grave in Prospect Cemetery it had been so altered by the committee who were looking after the work that he wanted to have nothing more to do with it. He loved animals—he was particularly fond of dogs—and he hated cruel sports such as hunting and coursing. His last years were spent in the study of archaeology all over Ireland and Britain, and he died peacefully in Rathmines, Dublin, on January 17th, 1866.

Petrie's work was important to many artists, writers and scholars. Thomas Moore, J. M. Synge, P. W. Joyce and many others all learned from this modest and generous teacher.

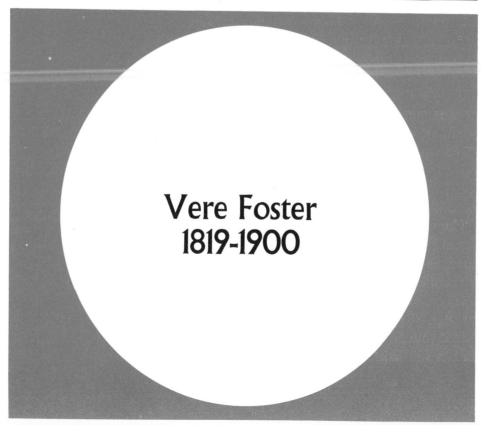

Vere Foster
1819-1900

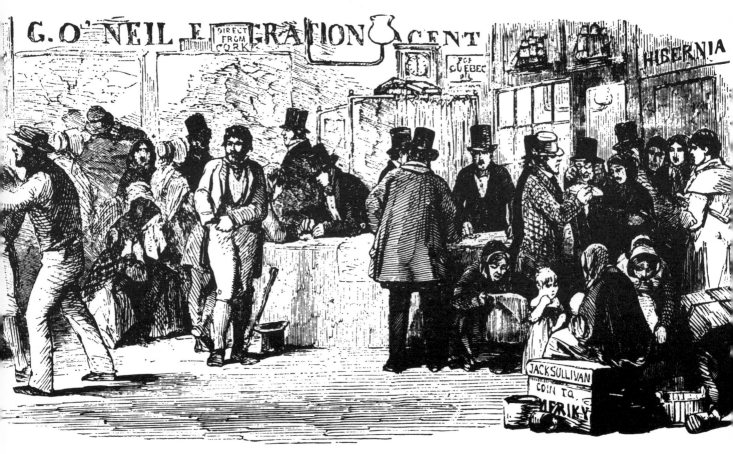

The Emigration Agent's Office—the passage money paid

There was a time when Vere Foster copy books were to be found in every National School in the country. They were used to teach children to write properly, and millions of them were printed in Belfast and paid for by the man who designed them—Vere Henry Foster.

Vere Foster was born in Copenhagen, Denmark, on the 25th of April, 1819. His father was a diplomat who, at that time, was representing Britain in Denmark. The family was related to John Foster, who had been the last Speaker of the Irish House of Commons before the Act of Union, and they owned a large house at Glyde Court, Ardee, County Louth. Vere Foster went to school at Eton in England and then to Oxford University, after which he joined the diplomatic service and was sent abroad, as his father had been. Vere did not go to Denmark, however, but to South America, where he spent the years 1841–1847. We do not know how good he was as a diplomat, but he did make a fine collection of butterflies which is still kept at Glyde Court.

Emigrant Ships

He was back in England in 1847 when he first heard news of the Great Famine that was sweeping Ireland. He went at once to Glyde Court to see the state of affairs for himself. He found that the hunger was even worse than he had thought and immediately decided to give up his diplomatic post to try to do something for the unfortunate people who were starving all around him. Vere Foster's first idea was to organise relief schemes—that is, to find work for the people to do, so that they could earn money to buy the food that they could not grow themselves because of the potato blight. The trouble was that there was just not enough work to be done. You may have heard of a "famine wall"—many of the walls around the big estates were built as relief schemes, but this kind of work soon ran out and the men were to be seen digging holes only to fill them in again, just for something to do. By the year 1849 Vere Foster decided that he would have to find some other answer to the problem, and he came to the conclusion that there

147

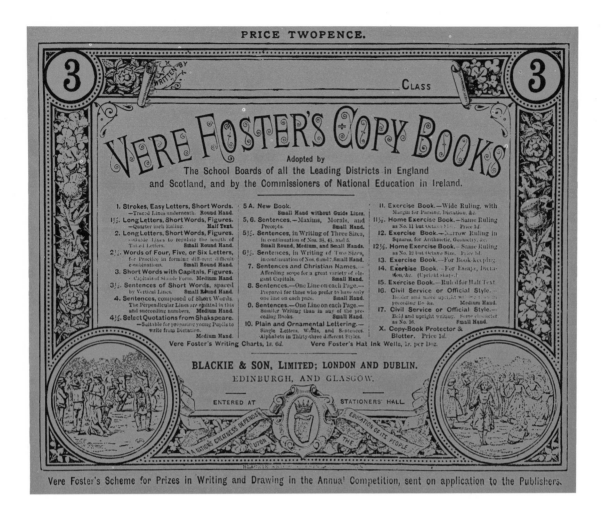

Vere Foster's Scheme for Prizes in Writing and Drawing in the Annual Competition, sent on application to the Publishers.

were far too many people in Ireland for the amount of food that could be produced. The population then was about eight million.

Irishmen had been emigrating to America for a long time, but this was the beginning of the huge emigrations that made such a difference to the make-up of the American population. Often the emigrants had no money and very little hope of a job when they reached the New World. The first thing Vere Foster had to do when he decided to help people leaving Ireland was to make sure that they would really be starting on a better life, and not just exchanging misery in one place for misery in another.

Luckily, Vere Foster was a rich man. There was no aid to be expected from the Union Government, or even from other rich people in Ireland, though there were a few like the Earl of Rosse who did try to do something. Vere Foster paid the fares of many emigrants out of his own pocket, and the first people he sent out were a group of young girls from Ardee for whom he had found

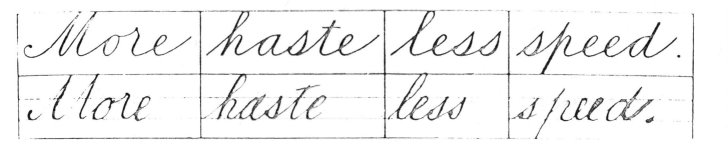

jobs on farms and in big houses in the United States. Often people would go to America who were too old or sick to work. Vere Foster believed in picking people who would have some chance of doing well, and so leaving what food and work there was at home for those who were in no condition to travel. He arranged places in New York where the emigrants would be welcomed and helped. He wrote a special booklet called *Work and Wages, or the Penny Emigrant's Guide to the United States and Canada for Female Servants, Labourers, Mechanics, Farmers, etc*. It described places to live, rates of wages, the cost of board, lodging and rent, the price of land, and very useful information on the cost of travel and what to take on the voyage.

Not everybody was as anxious to help the emigrants as Vere Foster. The ships which took them across the Atlantic were often old, dirty and unsafe, and living conditions on board were dreadful. In those days it might take a month to sail from Cobh to New York, and poor travellers often had to sleep on deck in the cold and wet and to eat food that nowadays we would not give to a dog. Foster decided to travel on an emigrant ship himself to find out what it was really like, and so in October, 1850, he set sail on the *Washington* from Liverpool. He found that conditions were even worse than he had expected, but when he complained to the captain he was told that he was a "damned rogue" and the mate knocked him down. He wrote everything in a diary, however, and later on this was published in parliament. The government then decided to pass laws to put an end to the harsh and cruel treatment of the emigrants. Foster sailed many more times with exiles to America and was helped there by Doctor John Hughes, the Archbishop of New York, and by Abraham Lincoln, who had two immigrants working in his house. When the American Civil War broke out, in 1861, Foster had to stop sending parties from Ireland, but by that time he had paid the passage money for about 25,000 emigrants

—all out of his own pocket! He sent more groups in the years 1879–1883. These were again years of distress, though not so acute as in the previous Great Famine.

Vere Foster was obviously a very generous man. Whenever he saw poverty, unhappiness or bad conditions, he felt he had to try to do something to help, and while he was travelling all over the country making arrangements for his emigration groups, he could not help noticing that most of the schools were in very bad shape. The roofs were leaking, the floors were nothing but mud and there were no means of keeping the boys and girls warm in the winter. He started to make notes of the measurements of the buildings and then sent carpenters and slaters along to put on new roofs and make wooden floors. The Board of Education were very mean about giving grants for improving schools, so Vere Foster paid for all this work himself. Luckily he came into more money when his mother died and left him her fortune, so that he was able to help rebuild more than 2,000 schools, both Catholic and Protestant, all over Ireland. He built new schools, too, and was very particular that the buildings should be well-designed and comfortable to work in.

Teachers at this time were very badly paid—they earned only one third of the salary of teachers in England. They had no way of complaining about this to the government, because there was no union or other organisation which they could join. So Foster persuaded them to get together and form themselves into an organisation, and in 1868 the Irish National Teachers' Association (or Organisation, as it is now called) came into being, with Vere Foster as its first President. After this the government had to take more notice of the teachers' complaints, and conditions gradually improved. The I.N.T.O. still represents teachers, both Catholic and Protestant, in the 32 counties of Ireland, and has over 15,000 members.

While he was busy helping teachers to claim their rights, Vere Foster had another idea. He had noticed the bad standard of writing in the schools he visited and planned his series of Copy Books which, as usual, he paid for himself. He had them designed by experts, printed on very good paper and they were sold to the schools for a penny each, which was less than they cost to print. Even Vere Foster, however, was surprised by their popularity. Over one million were sold in the first year— the first series came out in 1864—and he went on adding new ones which taught different kinds of writing as well as other subjects such as drawing, painting and book-keeping. There were no typewriters at this time in use in offices, so handwriting was very important, especially in the Civil Service. Soon Vere Foster copybooks were being used not only in Ireland but in Britain and America as well. Foster should have become a rich man, but instead he went on giving his money away to help people. In 1870 he moved to Belfast, where his books were printed, and lived very simply, scarcely spending anything on himself.

He lived for the rest of his life in Belfast, overseeing his printers and helping many charities. He was one of the people who founded the Belfast School of Art, and he paid the fees of many young people who otherwise would have been too poor to go to Queen's University (or Queen's College, as it was then called). He gave money to the Royal Victoria Hospital, Belfast, and even collected in the streets on what we would now call "flag days." This good and generous man died in an attic on Great Victoria Street on December 21st, 1900, and there were scarcely a dozen people at his funeral. Today we think of him as one of the finest Irishmen who ever lived—doing as much in one lifetime as countless ordinary men, spending all his time and money to help those whom nobody else would help.

A National School at Carberry, Co. Kildare in 1870.

Douglas Hyde
1860-1949

In the year 1937 a new Irish Constitution came into being, which created for the first time the office of *Uachtarán na hÉireann*—President of Ireland. The man chosen to fill the highest position in the land was a 77-year old scholar and poet, and no one disagreed with the choice. Douglas Hyde, known everywhere by his nickname *An Craoibhín Aoibhinn,* had done more than any other man to save the Irish language from disappearing forever.

Douglas Hyde by Sarah Purser

Douglas Hyde was born at Frenchpark, County Roscommon, on January 12th, 1860. His father, who came of Connacht stock, was Rector there and instead of sending him to school decided to teach him at home. Douglas did attend a school in Dublin for a short time, but most of his childhood was spent roaming the Roscommon hills in company with an old Fenian called Johnny Lavin and a gamekeeper called Seamus O'Hart, both of whom were native Irish speakers. At this time Irish was still spoken as the everyday language in large areas of the country, and Douglas listened for hours to the stories told by the old people and the songs they sang, so that when later on he went to Trinity College, Dublin, he said to one of the professors that he always dreamt in Irish! His father sent him to Dublin University in 1880, and he must have taught him well at home because Douglas excelled in his studies, winning prizes for English verse and English prose, and graduating in 1884 with a Large Gold Medal. He did not like Trinity very much, however; he found that no one there loved Irish as much as he did and that the professors thought that Greek, Latin and English literature were far more important than that of their own country. Even though he was popular in the College, he always felt that he was in a hostile place.

Douglas Hyde planned to follow his father into the Church of Ireland ministry, but after some time spent studying divinity, he decided he had not a vocation and chose to carry on instead with the study of Irish and with his efforts to help more people to learn it. He had joined the Society for the Preservation of the Irish Language in 1878 and in the same year helped to start the Gaelic Union, which later published a monthly magazine called the *Gaelic Journal*.

Hyde went to Canada in 1891, to teach English in the State University of New Brunswick. He spent a year there, and when he came home he was married and set up house at Ratra Park, County Roscommon. He then threw himself into the movement for the revival of the language. He had already published his first book, a collection of folk tales, in 1889, and was one of the first men to realise the importance of taking down stories that had been told in Ireland, perhaps for centuries, before they were lost forever with the increasing loss of the language from many parts of the country. He produced another book of tales in English translation in

1890, and the Irish version, *Cois na Tine,* in the following year. His famous *Love Songs of Connacht* appeared, a collection of poems both in Irish and English, some translations, some originals, and this book showed Hyde to be a very fine poet as well as a scholar. Here are a few lines from one of his Irish poems:

> Is dorcha anocht í an oiche, ní fheicim aon réalt
>   amhain,
> Agus is dorcha trom atá smaointe mo chroí-se tá
>   sgaoilte ar fán.
> Níl torran air bith ann no thimchioll, ach na
>   héanlaith dul-thart os mo ceann
> Na filbání ag bualadh na spéire le buille fad-
>   tharraingthe fann.

And, his English version of a prayer from Roscommon:

> A fragrant prayer upon the air
> My child taught me
> Awaken there, the morn is fair,
> The birds sing free.
> Now dawns the day, awake and pray
> And bend the knee,
> The Lamb who lay beneath the clay
> Was slain for thee.

Fr. Eugene O'Growney, sometime editor of 'The Gaelic Journal'

President Hyde in 1939

There had been several societies founded in the second half of the century with the aim of restoring the language, but none of them had come forward with any really practical ideas. Douglas Hyde brought his great powers of leadership to the whole movement, encouraged it with his enthusiasm, directed it with his scholarship, and made ordinary English-speaking Irish people understand for the first time the importance of their own culture and traditions. In an important speech to the National Literary Society in 1892 he said: *"When we speak of 'The Necessity for De-Anglicising the Irish Nation,' we mean it, not as a protest against imitating what is* best *in the English people, for that would be absurd, but rather to show the folly of neglecting what is Irish, and hastening to adopt, pell-mell, and indiscriminately, everything that is English, simply because it is English."* Hyde went on to say that we had lost our language, traditions, music, genius and ideas, and that we had ceased to be Irish without becoming English. To try to turn the tide before it was too late, Douglas Hyde and his friends set up a new body in 1893: the Gaelic League.

Eoin MacNeill co-founder of
The Gaelic League

The League was from the very beginning independent
of political parties and open to people of any religion or
none. As well as its work for the language, it encouraged
an interest in Irish music, dancing and games, and in the
setting up of Irish industries (at this time Ireland was
almost entirely an agricultural country and nearly
everything had to be imported). Branches of the League
were opened all over the country—by 1905 there were
five hundred and fifty of them—and people of all ages
and of all walks of life began to learn and speak Irish.
Douglas Hyde, who was President of the League from the
beginning, travelled the country, helping the new
branches and trying to persuade school managers to
teach the language as part of the day's lessons. The
National Board, which at that time controlled primary
education, was persuaded to provide money for the
teaching of Irish, and in 1900 a Commission was set up
to look into secondary education. Hyde spoke before this
Commission, arguing the importance of Irish against
people like Dr. Mahaffy, then Provost of Trinity College.
He fought another battle, too, a few years later: the
battle to have Irish accepted as a compulsory subject

for matriculation in the new National University. There were many people against it, including Cardinal Mannix and other prominent churchmen—though there were also many priests who supported Hyde. In 1908 the President of the Gaelic League addressed a large public meeting in the Rotunda in Dublin: *"There will be a fight,"* he said, *"as there was a fight in the days of the Confederation of Kilkenny between the old Irish and the new Irish, between the Marquis of Ormond and Owen Roe O'Neill; and if anyone wants to know on which side I shall be, I'll be on the side of Owen Roe."* On St. Patrick's Day, 1909, a procession was organised in the city to support the League's campaign for the language. It was so big that it took three hours to pass and ended with a big meeting in Sackville Street (now O'Connell Street).

Douglas Hyde went on writing books—*The Story of Early Gaelic Literature; A Literary History of Ireland* and several plays for the Abbey including *Casadh an tSúgáin*—as well as organising and leading the language movement. In 1905 he set off on a tour of the United States to collect money for the League. He spoke in towns and cities from New York to San Francisco and came back with more than £11,000—a large sum at that time. He was a man of great strength and energy. An American newspaper wrote of him: *"Dr. Hyde is a man of sturdy build and countenance. His voice is fine and mellow, his manner quick and alert . . . He is Gaelic head and heels. No other language is spoken in his household, though his English is prime. He is genial, gentle, and withal tireless."*

When the League was growing in strength, attracting men such as Pádraig Pearse and The O'Rahilly, political events were moving fast. The *Sinn Féin* party had been founded and was working for full independence, and many of its members were also active members of the

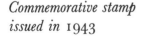

Commemorative stamp issued in 1943

League. Douglas Hyde tried to keep politics out of the League's affairs, but with the growing excitement following the formation of the Ulster Volunteer Force and the Irish Volunteers, this soon proved to be impossible. In 1915 the *Árd Fheis* of the League was held at Dundalk, and a motion was put before it to add a clause saying that *Conradh na Gaeilge* was *"working for a free Ireland."* This divided those who were for and those who were against political action, and Douglas Hyde resigned the presidency that he had held for more than twenty years.

This was a great blow to his friends, but Ireland had changed greatly since he began the movement in which he hoped to bring together Catholic and Protestant, Nationalist and Unionist in a common love of their country and its traditions. Things were to change even more. Douglas Hyde became a member of the Senate of the Irish Free State in 1925 and again in 1937, and was professor of Modern Irish in University College, Dublin, until 1932. In 1937 the new Constitution was adopted, and Ireland paid tribute to the man who had devoted his life to strengthening the roots of her nationhood by electing him *an chéad Uachtarán*, the first President. Though by now an old man, Dr. Douglas Hyde served his full term of seven years as President, from 1937 to 1945, and died on July 12th, 1949, in a house in Phoenix Park, Dublin, provided for him by the Government. *"With the death of Dr. Douglas Hyde,"* the *Irish Press* said the next day, *"there passes away one of the greatest Irishmen, not merely of our time, but of all time."*

Jonathan Swift
1667-1745

Jonathan Swift was born at Hoey's Court, Dublin, almost under the shadow of St. Patrick's Cathedral, on November 30th, 1667. He often told people quite angrily that he was not Irish and even pretended that he had been born in England, and he was certainly disappointed when he was made Dean of St. Patrick's in 1713, because he had been hoping to be a bishop of the Church of England. He was a very strange man, however, and it is impossible to believe everything that he said about himself. He enjoyed mysteries and keeping people in the dark, and he enjoyed saying one thing and doing another. So, although he sometimes said that he hated Ireland, he was very upset by the cruel way in which the English were ruling the country at the time, and did everything he could to help the poor people of Dublin. He was one of the first people to suggest a *"Buy Irish"* campaign—in a pamphlet he wrote in 1720: *A Proposal for the Universal Use of Irish Manufactures*, and some people say he could speak, or at least understand, Irish, and that his most famous book, *Gulliver's Travels*, is partly based on an old Irish story called *Imtheachta Tuaithe Luchra agus Aideadh Fherghusa*. There are stories of his friendship with the bard, Turlough O'Carolan; in fact, there are so many stories about Swift—some, there is little doubt, invented by himself—that people have been arguing about him for more than 200 years. Was he ever married? Who was his real father? Was he mad? These are the kind of questions that have been asked, and not all of them have found answers. Everybody agrees, however, about Swift's importance as a writer and about his kindness and goodness, in spite of his crotchety ways. When he died, his friend Dr. Delaney, who knew him very well, said of him: *"A steady, persevering, inflexible friend; a wise, a watchful and a faithful counsellor, under many severe trials and bitter persecutions . . . He lived a blessing, died a benefactor, and his name will ever live in honour to Ireland."* And so it has. When he wrote verses on his own death in 1731 (a good time before he actually died) he said:

> *"He gave what little wealth he had*
> *To build a house for fools and mad."*

And St. Patrick's Hospital (sometimes called "Swift's Hospital"), which he endowed, is there to this day in Dublin. In Swift's time people who were what we would now call "mentally retarded" were laughed at and treated very cruelly, but he wished them to be treated like human beings and cared for properly.

His father had died before Swift was born, and he was brought up by an uncle who sent him to Kilkenny College in 1673, where one of his schoolmates was the playwright, Congreve. In 1682 he entered Trinity

St. Patrick's Cathedral in the 17th century

College, Dublin, where he seems to have done very badly. Not only did he neglect his studies, but his general conduct was very wild. In 1686 he was given a B.A. degree *speciali gratia,* which meant that it was only awarded as a favour and not because he had earned it. The future Dean never forgot this, and made rude remarks about Trinity for the rest of his life.

His mother had gone to England after the death of his father, and in 1689, after graduating, he went to see her in Leicester, and then found a job as secretary with Sir William Temple, a distant relation, who lived at Moor Park in Surrey. He stayed for only a few months, and then came back to Ireland. He was once again at Moor Park in 1691, and in the next year took his M.A. degree at Oxford: but he had an argument with Sir William Temple, and decided to return to Ireland and take Holy Orders. When he reached Dublin again he could find no bishop who would ordain him without a reference, and he had to write to Temple—which he

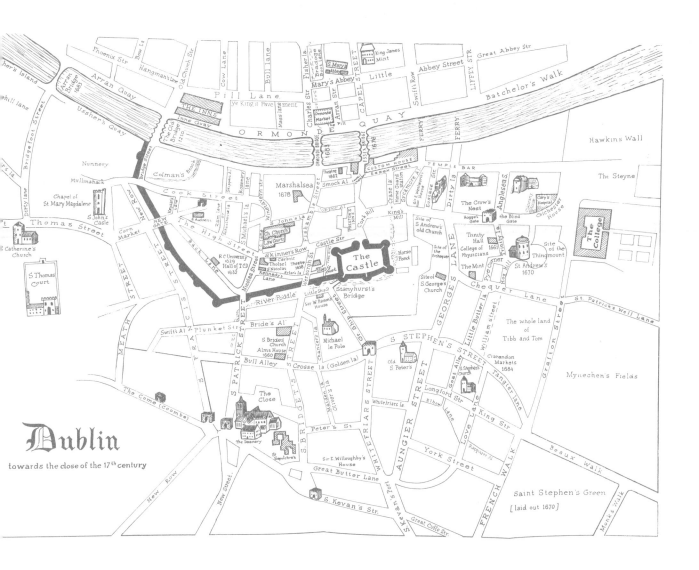

Dublin

towards the close of the 17th century

hated doing—and ask him for one. In 1694 he was ordained and appointed to the parish of Kilroot, which is on the shores of Belfast Lough. He did not stay there very long, however; in 1696 he was back working with Sir William Temple, and stayed at Moor Park until his employer died in 1699.

Monument to Swift
in St. Patrick's Cathedral, Dublin

Sir William had been very much involved in British politics, and not only did young Swift learn a good deal at Moor Park about political problems, but he also started writing. Most of his writings can be described as *satire*, that is something which by making fun of people tries to make them change their ways. It is a kind of serious joke, and can sometimes be very cruel. Most of the characters in *Gulliver's Travels,* for instance, are portraits of politicians whom Swift did not like and whom he wanted to make fun of. One does not have to know this to enjoy the story, but the readers of 1726 would have recognised most of them and so laughed at the book twice over.

Vanessa

Swift's first satires *A Tale of a Tub* and *The Battle of the Books* were published in 1704. From then on he was continuously writing, mostly about English politics, even though he had returned to Ireland in 1700 and had been appointed vicar of Laracor, County Meath. For the next ten years or so he travelled often to London, sometimes on Church business, and became friendly with the leading writers of the day, who included Addison and Steele, of *The Spectator* and *The Tatler*, to which Swift also contributed. He himself ran a paper called *The Examiner* in 1710, which was more or less the official publication of the Tory party, which had just come to power. For this work he was rewarded by being made Dean of St. Patrick's Cathedral, Dublin, though after his installation in 1713 he was again in London, a member of the Scriblerus Club, and a friend of the writers John Gay, William Congreve and Alexander Pope.

Queen Anne died in 1714 and the government changed, so that Swift found himself back again in Dublin, where he lived (apart from two short visits to England) for the rest of his life, shut up in the Deanery of St. Patrick's, but taking more and more interest in Irish affairs as the years went by. He became good friends with Thomas Sheridan, Richard Brinsley's grandfather and often visited him at his house at Quilca, County Cavan, which seemed to cheer him up, because he wrote verses like this one on *"The Plagues of a Country Life"*:

> *"A companion with News*
> *A great want of shoes*
> *Eat Lean Meat or chuse*
> *A church without pews*
> *Our horses astray*
> *No Straw, Oats or Hay;*
> *December in May.*
> *Our boys run away.*
> *All servants at play."*

In 1720 Swift produced his first important pamphlet on Irish affairs, in which he suggested a *"sinn féin"* economic policy. He was in advance of his time in realising that there could be no true political freedom without economic freedom, and as long as Ireland's economy remained tied to England there would be little chance of the country being left alone to run her own affairs. Not that Swift was a real nationalist in the way that Wolfe Tone and Pearse were: he was so angry with England for, as he thought, not recognising his value, and he hated the Whig government so much, that he could hardly help becoming an Irish patriot. In his famous *Drapier's Letters* of 1724 he attacked a plan of the British

Government to flood Ireland with copper halfpennies from which a certain Mr. William Wood was hoping to make a big profit (in those days not all coinage was produced directly by the State). Swift, pretending to be a humble draper, stirred up public feelings so strongly that the plan had to be abandoned. In 1729 his *Modest Proposal* appeared, a savage pamphlet which suggested fattening up Irish children to be eaten in order to solve the country's economic problems! This was satire at its most bitter, but it had far more effect than a speech in Parliament or a letter to the papers. Most of Swift's work was published anonymously, though everyone knew who wrote it. His printer, George Faulkner, was even put into jail for something the angry Dean had written!

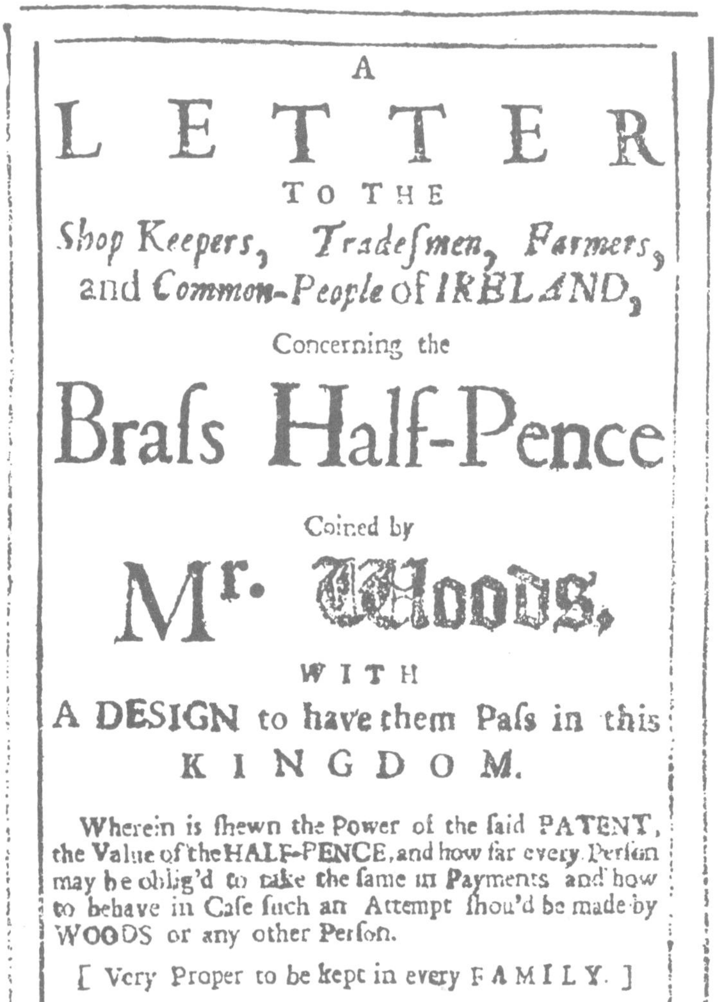

A

LETTER

TO THE

Shop Keepers, Tradesmen, Farmers, and Common-People of IRELAND,

Concerning the

Brass Half-Pence

Coined by

Mr. Woods,

WITH

A DESIGN to have them Pass in this KINGDOM.

Wherein is shewn the Power of the said PATENT, the Value of the HALF-PENCE, and how far every Person may be oblig'd to take the same in Payments and how to behave in Case such an Attempt shou'd be made by WOODS or any other Person.

[Very Proper to be kept in every FAMILY.]

By M. B. Drapier.

Dublin : Printed by *J Harding* in *Molesworth's-Court.*

Stella and Vanessa were the names of the two ladies who played an important part in Swift's life. He was very mysterious about them, and people are still arguing as to whether he was in love with either or both of them, or if they were just friends. He wrote poems and letters to each of them, and his *Journal to Stella,* a kind of diary, gives us a vivid picture of his life in London around 1714 when he was meeting important people and moving in high society. Vanessa, whose real name was Esther Vanhomrigh, died in Celbridge in 1723. Hester Johnson,

Stella

whom he had met at Moor Park in 1689 and whom he called Stella in his writings, died on the evening of Sunday, 28th January, 1728, and is buried near the Dean in St. Patrick's Cathedral.

In 1726–27 Swift paid his last visit to London, to see his friends Pope and Arbuthnot, and to arrange about the publication in England of *Gulliver's Travels*. This was to be his final journey outside Ireland. Though he continued writing and attending to the affairs of the cathedral, he was troubled more and more by a disease which brought on fits of giddiness and vomiting— something rather like very bad seasickness. He wrote of himself:

DEAF, giddy, helpleſs, left alone,
 To all my Friends a Burthen grown
No more I hear my Church's Bell,
Than if it rang out for my Knell:
At Thunder now no more I ſtart,
Than at the rumbling of a Cart:
Nay, what's incredible, alack!
I hardly hear a Woman's Clack.

Jonathan Swift died on October 19th, 1745, old and sick but certainly not mad, and was buried in the cathedral he had come to love so well. His famous epitaph, which he wrote himself, tells us that he lies where savage indignation can no longer rend his heart. To many Dubliners he is as real today as when he bequeathed to them *"what little wealth he had"*, and to the world he is still the finest satirist ever to write in English, a man who often hated life but who loved liberty.

Turlough O'Carolan
1670-1738

It is difficult to imagine Ireland without good roads, without radio, television, trains and buses. But when Turlough O'Carolan was alive, there were none of these things. The roads were no better than muddy tracks, especially in the winter. And in the evenings people had to make their own fun and entertainment—or get somebody else to do it for them. Rich people might afford to ask a harper to stay with them for a fortnight and play and sing songs every evening for their family and visitors. This was the way Carolan lived—travelling from house to house on horseback and composing songs and tunes for the people with whom he stayed. He was the last of the great Irish harpers who had been playing the same kind of tunes on the same kind of instrument since the days of Brian Boru. He lived at a time when the whole of Ireland was changing—when the old Gaelic culture was being destroyed by wars, by the Flight of the Wild Geese, and by the Penal Laws.

Carolan was born in Newtown, near Nobber, County Meath, in 1670. We do not know much about his family; though his father may have been a blacksmith. He used to work for some people called MacDermott Roe, and when they moved to County Roscommon, he followed them, settling down in Alderford near Carrick-on-Shannon. This was about the year 1684, when young Carolan would have been 14. Four years later he caught smallpox and went completely blind.

In those days there were no schools for blind people or anything like that, and life would have been very hard for Turlough if he had not found a good friend. Mrs. MacDermott Roe decided to help him and arranged for him to be taught the harp for three years by a very good harper. Three years seems like a long time learning to play the harp, but so young a man had to work very hard to be invited to the big houses. A lot of people thought that 18 was too old to begin—because one's fingers are usually too stiff by then to play really well! Since Carolan was already 18 his teacher thought he should learn to write tunes—and the words for them—as well as play them, just to be on the safe side. So after three years Carolan was ready to go and earn his living as a poet, a composer and a player—except that he was blind and could not travel long distances by himself through every kind of weather.

A Carolan composition

Carolan entertains

Here again Mrs. MacDermott was able to help him. She gave him a horse and found him a guide who would go with him on his journeys and look after him. And so the two of them set out to travel the four provinces, making music wherever they went.

Although he had lost his sight, Carolan was not a sad person—far from it. Though he could not see, he was good at the game of backgammon. *"My eyes are transplanted into my ears,"* he said. He loved a joke and the good things of life—particularly a glass of whiskey. Some

people have said that he drank too much, but it must be remembered that at this time people—particularly those who lived in the big houses—drank more than we do today, largely because drinking was all a part of entertaining their friends and passing the long winter evenings. A doctor once told Carolan to give up the drink, but it made him very miserable, and it was not long before he went back to his whiskey again. He wrote a little poem about it:

Is duine leamh do thréigfeadh an t-ól,
Bheir sé beós do dhuine gan chroidhe,
Eineach don té bhíos cruaidh,
Meisneach is stuaim don daoi . . .

Yes, Carolan always wrote, as he talked, in Irish, and was often teased by his friends because he had so little English—and even less Latin! In case you find his Irish verse difficult, here is a translation: *"He who gives up drink is a foolish person. It gives strength to the faint-hearted, generosity to one who is mean, encouragement and ability to the dunce . . ."* He was said to have made up this poem on the spur of the moment when the doctor gave him permission to take drink again. Part of the training of the poet and harper was to be able to make up tunes and words for them straight away without having to write anything down. Of course Carolan could not write them down in any case, but even so he seems to have been very quick at what we would now call *extemporisation*, that is, the art of inventing speech, music, dance, etc., on the spur of the moment.

An early Irish harpist entertaining at a feast

When we said that Carolan was working for his living that is not quite accurate. He was not paid, like somebody who appears on a television show. He went to the big houses as a guest, and would receive his board and lodging in return for singing and playing. Sometimes the man of the house would give him gifts of money, but this did not always happen. He depended on the kindness of his friends—and most of the people he visited were very friendly with him. He would go back to some places again and again, and because he was such a good composer and musician, and such entertaining company, he was always welcome.

Carolan was a devout Catholic, and played his harp in church on special occasions. But the people he visited were Protestant as well as Catholic, old Irish families and the families of people who had come from England. He wrote and played for both Gael and Gall and, though this was a very difficult time politically, he did not show any interest in the battles that were being fought all over the country. He once went on a pilgrimage to Loch Derg, but he often stood up for his Protestant friends when they were criticised by his own people. He was a fair minded man who enjoyed life and wanted others to enjoy it too. It is a pity that we know so little about how Carolan spent his days. We know that he married Mary Maguire and that they lived very happily until she died in 1733. He wrote a lament for her:

> Fuar mé seal i n-Eirinn go h-aerach is go
>   sóghamhuil,
> Ag ól le gach tréinfhear bhí éifeachtach ceólmhar;
> Fágadh 'na ndéidh sin liom féin mé go brónach
> I ndeireadh mo shaoghail 's gan mo chéile bheith
>   beó agam.

(*I spent a time in Ireland happily and contented, drinking with every strong man who was a real lover of music. When they had gone I was left sorrowing, at the end of my days, without my wife alive with me.*)

He also met several of the most famous poets and musicians of his day. Mac Cuarta, the Ulster poet, composed a poem of welcome for Carolan when they met, probably at Ballymascanlon, County Louth. He had a great "*scolding match*" with his friend MacCabe. The two of them had had a drinking competition and Carolan had tied MacCabe up in a sack when he had fallen asleep. When he woke up he was very upset and didn't see the joke, so Carolan composed a poem scolding him for not having a sense of humour and MacCabe replied suitably!

It is quite possible that at some time or another Carolan met the great Jonathan Swift. Swift was rector at Laracor, not far from where Carolan lived, from 1701–1710, and even after he went to Dublin and became Dean of St. Patrick's, he used to come back to visit his great friend Dr. Patrick Delany, who was also a friend of Carolan's. It is not known for certain whether the Dean and the Harper ever met, but there are many stories that suggest they did. If they did meet they almost certainly got on well together. Swift translated a poem *"Pléaráca na Ruarcach"* by Hugh MacGauran, for which Carolan had written the music.

Carolan died at Alderford on the 25th of March, 1738, and is buried in the old church of Kilronan. One of his friends wrote in his diary: *"Trócaire go bhfagha a anam, óir bu fiaghalta agus bu cráifeach."* (*"May his soul find mercy, for he was a moral and a religious man."*)

Ancient Irish Harp

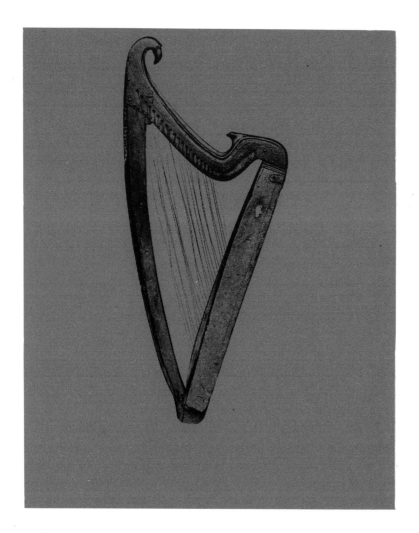

Aodhagán Ó Rathaille
1670(?)-1726(?)

Muckross Abbey

It is not often that we come across an important figure in Irish history about whom we know so little. Not even the dates of Aodhagán Ó Rathaille's birth and death are certain. He probably never left his native Munster in his whole life, yet there are hardly any records which tell us how he spent his days, where he lived, or whom he married. Some traditions say that his family came from Cavan, but others insist that he was a Kerryman born and bred, and this seems more likely to be true. He was probably born in the Sliabh Luachra district which lies to the west of Killarney, but in what village or townland is not recorded. Neither do we know where he died—nor when—though he is buried, again according to legend, in the nave of Muckross Abbey. There is little more that we can say about his life, except that it was a hard one and that he died in great poverty. All the rest that is known about him must be learned from his poems. Aodhagán Ó Rathaille was one of the last poets to write in the great Gaelic tradition, and before he died the Gaelic world as he knew it in his young days had almost passed away.

The seventeenth century marked the beginning of the end for the old Gaelic civilisation that had ruled in Ireland for countless hundreds of years. The defeat of the battle of Kinsale began it; this was followed by the arrival of Cromwell in 1649 and in 1690 by the battle of the Boyne. In 1691, Patrick Sarsfield and the Wild Geese sailed from Cork, leaving Ireland leaderless and at the mercy of the English forces. The ancient Gaelic families were split up, and the big houses demolished or taken away and given to English settlers, together with their lands and forests. The Penal Laws, which were introduced in 1695, made it impossible for the Catholic Irish to own property or to become members of any of the professions. The Gaelic aristocrats who were left had either to change their religion or learn to live as peasants —so the poets, who depended on them, no longer had anyone to pay them in cattle for their poems, to listen to their elegies, or to give them a roof over their heads. The profession of poet, which had been one of the most important in Gaelic Ireland, disappeared. One of the oldest traditions in Europe was wiped out.

Oliver Cromwell

This did not happen all at once, even after the battles of the Boyne, Aughrim and Limerick. Ireland was still a country of small "states," ruled very often by the family in the Big House, and for some time English law did not take effect everywhere. But it was only in the districts a long way from Dublin that the old system managed to resist the new. Munster, and the western districts in particular, became the last stronghold of the Gaelic world; a few families still held on to their houses and lands and a few poets still made verses for them as they had done since long before Saint Patrick. It was in this dying world that Ó Rathaille lived; it is small wonder that most of his poems are sad and bitter, comparing Ireland of the olden days with the sad state of the country in his own time:

> Tír bhocht bhuaidheartha, is uaigneach céasta!
> Tír gan fear, gan mac, gan chéile!
> Tír gan lúth, gan fonn, gan éisteacht!
> Tír gan chomhthrom do bhochtaibh le déanamh!
> (A land poor, lonely and tortured!
> A land without a husband, without a son,
>   without a spouse!
> A land without energy, without spirit, without
>   hearing!
> A land in which no justice is to be done
>   to the poor!)

The battle of the Boyne

James lands at Kinsale

From having been a province which could raise a warlike army to fight the invaders, Munster became powerless without leaders. The ancient family of MacCarthaigh Mór were no longer in power in the land, and their estates and the earldom of Kenmare had passed to the Browns, people of English origin but Catholic and Irish-speaking. A poet needed a patron, a powerful man who would pay him for his writing and give him what might now be called a subsidy on which to live, but men like Ó Rathaille felt themselves to be every bit as good as the noble lords and a good deal better than the upstarts the English were putting in their places. When he moved his home to Duibhneacha, near Tonn Tóime, he wrote:

Dá maireadh an rí díonmhar ó bhruach na
  Leamhan
'S an ghasra bhí ag roinn leis ler thruagh mo chall,
I gceannus na gcríoch gcaoin gcluthair gcuanach
  gcam,
Go dealbh i dtír Dhuibhneach níor bhuan mo
  chlann.

(If the protecting prince from the bank of the
    Laune (MacCarthaigh) were alive
  And the band who shared with him who would
    pity my misfortune—
  Ruling over the fair, sheltered regions, rich in
    havens, and curved,
  My children would not long remain in poverty
  in Duibhneach-territory

Ó Rathaille tried to make the best of it by giving his
loyalty to the Browns, but Nicholas, the second Viscount,
was deprived of his estates for having supported King
James in the wars, and the property was given to
Englishmen. First it went to John Blennerhasset and
George Rogers and later to a man named John Asgill,
who bought it on April 13th, 1703, for £1,000 and
started cutting down the great forests and selling them
for sixpence a tree. So the appearance of the land
changed as well as the ownership; the great woods
which had sheltered men "on the run" for hundreds of
years were disappearing: *"Is díth-chreach bhúr gcoillte ar
feochadh!"* wrote Aodhagán—*"It is a deep loss, your woods
fading away."* Nicholas's son, Valentine Brown spent his
youth as an outlaw, and by the time he was restored to
favour the old world had gone forever. The Big House was
no longer a centre of Gaelic culture and civilisation, but it
was the only place to which a poet like Ó Rathaille could
turn:

Do leathnaigh an ciach diacrach fám sheana-
  chroidhe dúr
Ar dtaisteal na ndiabhal iasachta i bhfearann
  Chuinn chughainn;
Scamall ar ghriain iarthair dár cheartas ríoghacht
  Mumhan
Fá ndeara dham triall riamh ort, a Bhailintín Brún.

(A distressing sorrow has spread over my old
    hardened heart
  Since the foreign demons have come amongst us
    in the land of Conn,
  A cloud upon the sun of the west to whom the
    kingship of Munster was due;
  It is this which has caused me ever to have
    recourse to you, Valentine Brown.)

Patrick Sarsfield

All the poems of Aodhagán Ó Rathaille which we can read today have come down to us in manuscripts or from father to son; the Gaelic poets wrote their verses to be sung or spoken, not read, and they had no means of having them printed or collected into books. Before Aodhagán's time the poets used to travel Ireland, meeting others of their profession, exchanging poems, and creating a national literature, but Ó Rathaille, as we have seen, did not leave his native Munster and in his own time very few people outside his area could have heard of him. He was in a strange position—a poor peasant but part of an aristocratic tradition, with the skill to make great verses but with hardly anyone left who would appreciate them and pay him for his trouble. It is no wonder that he despaired of the future of Ireland and that many of his poems are bitter and tragic. He did not despair completely, however. The Gaelic world had weathered many a storm and it had seemed to come to life again for a few brief years following the coming to the throne of James II of England and before the disaster of the Boyne. Aodhagán wrote many "*Aisling*" poems in which he tells of his visions, of what will happen in the future. His most famous one, *Gile na Gile,* described the sad state of Ireland, who appears as a beautiful young maiden:

Mo threighid! Mo thubaist! Mo thurrainn! Mo
    bhrón! Mo dhíth!
An soillseach muirneach miochair-gheal beol-tais
    caoin
Ag adharcach fuireann-dubh mioscaiseach
    cóirneach buidhe;
'S gan leigheas n-a goire go bhfillid na leoghain
    tar tuinn.
(O my sickness, my misfortune, my fall, my
    sorrow, my loss!
The bright, fond, kind, fair, soft-lipped, gentle
    maiden,
Held by a horned, malicious, croaking, yellow
    clown, with a black troop!
While no relief can reach her until the heroes
    come back across the main.)

Stories have come down to us which show that Aodhagán Ó Rathaille was by no means always a miserable and complaining man. He had a sense of humour and seems to have enjoyed playing practical jokes. He was certainly a learned man who could speak Irish and English and probably Latin, and who was knowledgeable about current affairs on the continent of Europe where so many Wild Geese made their home. He died a sad and disappointed man, however: a poet who had seen his calling fall into neglect from being one of the proudest in the land, and the society into which he had been born changed beyond recognition. His last poem, written on his death-bed, says that he will not cry for help because there is no one left to listen to him!

Stadfad-sa feasta, is gar dam éag gan maill,
Ó treascradh dreagain Leamhan, Léin, is Laoi,
Rachad-sa a haithle searc na laoch don chill,
Na flatha fá raibh mo shean roimh éag do Chríost.
(I will cease now; death is close to me without delay;
Since the warriors of the Laune, the Lein and of
    the Lee are laid low.
I will follow the beloved among heroes to the
    grave,
Those princes yonder who were my ancestors
    before the death of Christ.)

Margaret Woffington
1714(?)-1760

Nobody ever called her Margaret; she was known as Peg, or, in the fashion of the time, "Mrs. Woffington," though she never married. People stood in the streets of London to see her go past and fought for standing room when she was acting in Thomas Sheridan's theatre in Smock Alley, Dublin.

> *"With her a cottage would delight,*
> *All's happy when she's in my sight,*
> *But when she's gone 'tis endless night.*
> *All's dark without my Peggy."*

was what one of her admirers wrote in 1743. She was accused of having love affairs with every man she met, because she was beautiful, clever and spoke her mind at a time when women were thought of as ornaments and little more. She was elected President of Dublin's *Beefsteak Club,* a debating society which until then had been open to men only. She became rich and famous, what we would now call a "star," but she could not forget that as a little girl she had sold watercress on the Dublin streets, barefoot in the depth of winter.

There were no fan magazines in the eighteenth century but people were just as eager to read about the lives of their favourite actors and actresses. What they did not

Smock Alley

Thomas Sheridan as 'Oedipus'

know they made up, so that it is very hard to know which of the stories about Peg Woffington are true and which were invented by her friends—or her enemies. We do not know for sure when she was born, but it was somewhere between 1714 and 1718. Her father was a Dublin bricklayer, who perhaps ran his own building business, but he died in 1720, leaving a wife, two children and money owing to all kinds of people. Peg's mother tried to run a shop on Ormond Quay, but she had no head for business, so her daughters had to become street traders, selling fruit and vegetables to passers-by. In the Dublin of those days there was a very great difference between the rich and the poor; the rich rode in carriages to attend the splendid receptions at Dublin Castle while the poor lived in miserable rooms and tried to earn a living as best they could. It was very difficult indeed for a poor person to get a chance to do anything but the most unpleasant and badly-paid jobs. Somehow or other Peg Woffington was given that chance, and in 1751 rode in triumph through the same Dublin streets in which she must have been so cold and hungry years before. Again we do not know for sure how she managed to get a start as an actress, but at the age of ten she was playing a part in a "lilliput" production of *The Beggar's Opera*, an eighteenth century musical, and went on to sing and dance between the acts and play some parts at the theatre in Aungier Street. In 1737 she acted Ophelia in the production of *Hamlet* at Smock Alley Theatre and was truly on the way to stardom.

Nowadays actors and actresses become world famous and are often better paid than Presidents or government ministers, but in the middle of the eighteenth century they were not considered respectable and theatres were regarded as dens of vice. This was sometimes true: the playgoers would join in the performance by throwing things at actors or actresses they did not like, by stopping the play if it did not please them, or even—as happened to poor Thomas Sheridan's theatre in Dublin in 1754—wrecking the building. Theatres were used to spread political ideas that were against governments and were very often the scene for all kinds of scandal. Yet they were a very popular form of entertainment and theatrical managers and performers could make a good living if they managed to succeed—then, as now—in giving the public what it wanted. Peg could do this better than any other actress of her day. She could play all the favourite comic parts, both as herself and dressed as a man; and in her later years she proved that she was just as effective in the serious roles, even though some critics did not like her voice.

After three years professional experience in Dublin she first went to London in 1740, and opened at Covent Garden on November 6th in *The Recruiting Officer,* by the Irish playwright George Farquhar. She was an immediate success, and the next year acted in the rival theatre, Drury Lane, playing Shakespearean roles such as Nerissa and Rosalind as well as the leading parts in all the modern plays. Not that she always played the lead: Peg did not give herself airs as an actress and was always ready to give as good a performance in a small part as in the most important one. The style of acting was very different from the kind of thing we see on the stage or on television today; it was very artificial, nothing like the way people naturally behave. The public liked it, however, and went on liking it until an actor called David Garrick showed them that there was another way of doing things. David Garrick became Peg's friend; in fact, they lived together for some time with Charles Macklin, another Irish playwright, and many people thought that they would get married. Garrick, however, seemed to change his mind at the last minute, though they remained on good terms for the rest of Peg's life.

Peg Woffington was back in Dublin in 1742, and took the town by storm. It was only a short season, for in the same year she was again acting at Drury Lane with Garrick. At this time plays might only run for a few nights, as the audiences, who were largely made up of the aristocracy and other people with money, always wanted something new, or at least a new production of an old favourite. The list of the parts played by Peg in any one season would be a very long one, because she was a real professional and never let anyone down at the last minute by pretending to be ill; in fact, she often took over other people's parts at very short notice. In 1751 she again went to Dublin and stayed for three seasons, returning to England in 1754 with her manager Thomas Sheridan, father of the dramatist Richard Brinsley.

One of the reasons for Peg's return to Dublin was that she had fallen out with David Garrick at Drury Lane. She was highly offended that he had given some of her parts to other actresses, and acted at this theatre for the last time on April 25th, 1748. Her return to her native city was a triumph, however. On leaving Drury Lane she had gone again to Covent Garden, had spent some time in France studying the theatre there, and when she

Peg Woffington in 'The Female Volun

THE
FEMALE VOLUNTEER:
OR,
an Attempt to make our Men STAND.

An EPILOGUE *intended to be spoken by* Mrs. Woffington *in the Habit of a Volunteer, upon reading the* Gazette *containing an Account of the late Action at* FALKIRK.

appeared again at Smock Alley she was at the height of her powers and the height of her fame. Swift's printer and publisher, George Faulkner, recorded in his *Dublin Journal*: "*The celebrated Mrs. Woffington's performance in Smock Alley Theatre continues to draw the most crowded audiences hitherto known.*" And it went on to describe her performance in the rather high-flown language of the time: "*Her correct pronunciation is accompanied by the most just and graceful action. Her unaffected ease and vivacity in comedy, her majestic pathos in tragedy, show her to be an exact imitation of Nature . . ."*

Peg Woffington had been reared a Catholic, the religion of her mother, though her father's family had been Protestant. Owen McSwiny, who had been a friend for a long time and had helped her at difficult times, told her during this Dublin season that he would leave her all his property if she would go back to the religion of her father. Peg agreed to do this, and drove off into the country with Thomas Sheridan to have the ceremony performed. She wanted to keep it secret because there was strong feeling in Dublin at the time between the largely Catholic population and the Protestants as represented by the Castle. The news leaked out, however, and the people began to turn against Peg, accusing her of having a love affair with Thomas Sheridan, of changing her religion to keep in with her rich friends in government circles, and many other things. Most of the women were jealous of her, both because she was beautiful and talented and because she had a freedom which they were not allowed as wives in "high society." Thomas Sheridan's theatre was wrecked by an angry audience in a political demonstration, and shortly afterwards Peg went again to London for what were to be her last three years of acting life. She acted once more at Covent Garden: *"The return of such a favourite actress as Mrs. Woffington and one so well acquainted with persons in high life drew a great house,"* said the actor Tate Wilkinson, who was later well-known for imitations of Peg.

On May 3rd, 1757, Peg Woffington was appearing in the part of Rosalind in Shakespeare's *As You Like It.* When she was speaking the epilogue: *"If I were among you I would kiss as many of you as had beards that pleased me,"* her voice broke and she could not go on. She staggered from the stage and collapsed. For a long time she was near death, but though she recovered and lived for another three years, she never appeared on the stage again. We know little of how she spent her closing days: she may have paid a last visit to see her mother who was still alive and whom she had supported ever since she had become rich. She died in London on March 28th, 1760, and was buried at Teddington on the river Thames where she had lived. Her early death saddened many, for the stage both in Ireland and England lost one of its finest actresses and most fascinating personalities. John Hoole wrote of her:

> *"Nor was thy worth to public scenes confined,*
> *Thou knewest all the noblest feelings of the mind.*
> *Thy ears were ever open to distress,*
> *Thy ready hand was ever stretched to bless,*
> *Thy breast humane, for each unhappy felt,*
> *Thy heart for others' sorrows prone to melt."*

Not very good poetry, but a warm tribute to a poor Dublin girl who went from rags to riches without ever forgetting those who were less fortunate than herself.

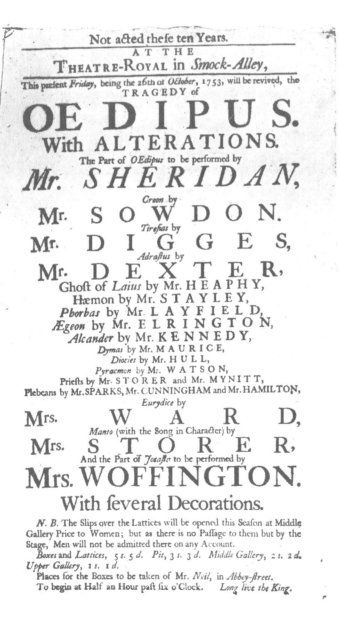

Oliver Goldsmith
1728-1774

Anyone passing through College Green in Dublin
will probably notice the statues of Burke and Goldsmith
outside Trinity College. They were two of the most
famous Irishmen of the eighteenth century. Burke was
a member of Parliament and rather a grand person.
But Goldsmith was just the opposite. He was a country
boy, born in Pallas, County Longford, and brought up at
Lissoy in County Westmeath. Throughout his life he
always preferred the company of ordinary people and
the life of the village to that of the big city and its lords
and ladies, and though he went to Trinity, he was never
very good at his studies. In spite of that, he wrote a book
called *The Vicar of Wakefield*, which people still enjoy and
laugh over today, and a poem, *The Deserted Village*,

Dr. Johnson reads The Vicar of Wakefield

which described the sadness of an Irish village from which everybody had to emigrate. Goldsmith hardly ever had any money—he spent it as fast as he earned it—but he seems to have been a very generous and friendly person who always had something to give a beggar or anybody poorer than himself. When he died in London all his friends were very sad indeed. The epitaph on his tombstone is in Latin and ends: *"Nullum quod tetigit, non ornavit,"* which means that whatever he tried to do, he did very well. It was written by the great Dr. Johnson.

Oliver Goldsmith was the son of a Church of Ireland parson. He went to the village school in Lissoy where the schoolmaster, who was an old soldier, used to tell

The Parsonage

wonderful tales of the wars and make up poetry in Irish.
Oliver loved songs and ballads. He learned to play the
flute, and listened to the great O'Carolan play his harp.
He went to other schools later on, but he never forgot the
place where "*The village master taught his little school,*" as
he wrote in his poem *The Deserted Village*. Oliver was not
very happy at school, because he was a small, rather
ugly boy and the others used to tease him, and because
he was not good at his lessons. When he was 17, he went
to Trinity College as a *sizar*—which meant that, in return
for being taught, he had to do various jobs around the
college. But again he did not bother with his books, and
used to hold parties and play the flute instead of studying.
So when he was given his B.A. degree four years later, he
did not really know enough to get a good job. He went
home to the country and wondered what to do next.

His father, the parson, was dead by now, so Oliver
lived with his mother. He tried one thing after another
but could not settle down. He went off to Cork to get a

Oliver Goldsmith M.B.

boat to America but spent all the money for his fare before the boat sailed. He thought about trying to become a lawyer. And then he decided what he really wanted to be was a doctor. So he managed to get enough money together to go off to Edinburgh. He stayed there for eighteen months and the same thing happened—or rather, nothing happened! He did no work, and left without a degree or even a diploma, and went to the University of Leyden in Holland for another try. He left there when he was 27, still with no doctor's degree or any way of earning a living except playing his flute. And this is just what he did. He wandered all over western Europe earning his keep by playing and entertaining people. He saw a lot of interesting things, and he wrote about them later on in a poem called *The Traveller*. But he had hardly enough to live on, and when he arrived in England in 1756, he had no money at all.

What was he to do? He tried all kinds of jobs: working for a chemist, being an usher (that is, a junior teacher) at a school, and working for booksellers (who, in those days, were usually publishers as well). Then he started writing—not the poems and plays that were later to make him famous, but articles for magazines on a variety of subjects, books for children and other kinds of writing which earned very little money. He lived in a kind of tenement at the top of Breakneck Steps (they were called that because they were so steep and dangerous), and he hardly knew where his next meal was coming from. But then he had the luck to meet Dr. Johnson and his friends, who were very important people in London, particularly among writers, publishers and painters. One of the group was Edmund Burke. In 1763 Dr. Johnson asked Goldsmith to join a Club they were starting for artists

The ruins of "The Three Pigeons" Inn

Lissoy Mill

and writers, and he enjoyed the company of these clever men, even though he could never think of the right witty remark to make when he was talking to them. David Garrick, who was a famous actor, said that Goldsmith *"wrote like an angel but talked like poor Poll"* (by which he meant a parrot!).

In 1764 Goldsmith was about to be put out of his rooms for not paying the rent when Dr. Johnson called to see him. The Doctor asked him if he had written anything he could sell to a publisher, and Goldsmith replied that he had just finished writing a novel. He gave the book to Johnson who rushed round to a publisher and came back with £60, which would be worth about £600 in our money! The book was *The Vicar of Wakefield,* but before it could be published Goldsmith's poem *The Traveller* appeared. Everybody liked this so much that the poor Irishman became famous all at once. He moved to a better house and went on writing all kinds of books, since he was always ready to try his hand at anything. He even wrote a book about all the animals of the world called *Animated Nature,* but Dr. Johnson did not think much of this. *"If he can tell a horse from a cow, that's as much as he knows about it,"* he said.

Though Goldsmith was then doing very well in London, he never forgot Lissoy and always wanted to go back there. *"I sit and sigh for the Lissoy fireside,"* he wrote; and in *The Deserted Village,* which was published in 1770, he remembered all the places he knew when he was young, places like the village pub,

> Where broken tea cups, wisely kept for show
> Ranged o'er the chimney, glistened in a row.

In 1773 his play *She Stoops to Conquer* was produced. Though it is set in England, many people believe that Goldsmith was really thinking of Longford and West-meath when he wrote it. He was then making quite a lot of money—about £400 a year, which would be equal to nearly ten times as much money nowadays—but he spent all of it enjoying himself, and making up for the years when he had been poor and unhappy. He planned to come home on a visit to Ireland, and perhaps to stay:

> I still had hopes, my long vexations passed,
> Here to return—and die at home at last,

he wrote in *The Deserted Village,* but in April, 1774, he

died suddenly and was buried in a grave in the Temple churchyard in London which has now been lost. He was upset by riches and fame in his later years, and must have longed to be sitting telling stories again by the fireside at Lissoy, because when someone asked him just before he died if his mind was at ease, he replied: *"No, it is not."* And that was the last thing he ever said.

Oliver Goldsmith wrote in the language of his time, which one may find a little hard to understand until one gets used to it. But he was a simple, friendly person, and he wrote in a simple, friendly way of the people and places he knew and the funny things that happened to them—or the funny things that he pretended happened to them, for he was a great storyteller, and it didn't do to believe everything he said! For all his gaiety and fun, however, Goldsmith wrote seriously about things which interest everyone, then or now. As Dr. Johnson said in his rather pompous way: *"No man was more foolish when he had not a pen in his hand, or more wise when he had."*

Richard Brinsley Sheridan
1751-1816

Mrs. Malaprop, a lady in Sheridan's play *The Rivals* was always getting her words mixed up. She tried to use hard words like *"comparisons"* but said *"caparisons"* instead, and said *"an allegory on the banks of the Nile,"* instead of *"an alligator"*! It could be that Sheridan put her into his play because he remembered a book his grandfather had written about puns and other diversions with words. Thomas Sheridan, Richard's grandfather, was a great friend of Jonathan Swift, and the Dean of St. Patrick's often stayed with him at his house at Quilca, County Cavan. He is supposed to have been one of the few people who could cheer up that rather gloomy prelate.

The Sheridans were a clever family. Richard's father, who was also called Thomas, went to Trinity College and then took up acting, becoming manager of the Theatre Royal in Smock Alley in Dublin. His mother wrote two

Thomas Sheridan

Elizabeth Linley and her brother

novels which were famous in their day, though not many people read them now. Richard Brinsley was born at 12 Dorset Street, Dublin, in 1751, and at first did not seem to be half as clever as either his father or his grandfather. Thomas Sheridan (Richard's father) had modern ideas about education, and was very interested in getting people to speak properly—this is called *elocution*. He had a new idea for teaching children and tried to persuade the Government to take an interest in it; but when things began to go rather badly at the theatre and he could see no hope of having his teaching ideas accepted, he decided to emigrate with his family. So in 1762 Richard Brinsley Sheridan was sent to school at Harrow, near London, and nearly all the rest of his life was spent in England.

He did not do very well at school, though the rest of the boys liked him. He left when he was seventeen, and his father hoped that Richard would help him in promoting his teaching ideas, which he was now trying to persuade the British Government to accept. In 1771 the family moved to the city of Bath, which at that time was a very fashionable place. Many lords and ladies of England went there to "take the waters," as it was a *spa*, a place where the water which bubbles out of the ground is very good for all kinds of illnesses. Of course they did not spend all of their time "taking the waters," and had plenty of spare hours in which to enjoy themselves. They published newspapers and magazines about what was going on in the city, and it was in one of these that Richard Brinsley Sheridan first appeared as a writer. His poems were not very good, but they were clever and amusing, and many people thought that he would write very well when he was older.

At this time he fell in love with a very beautiful girl named Elizabeth Linley and ran away with her to France to save her from marrying someone whom she did not like. When they both came back, Sheridan had to fight two duels with the original suitor and was badly hurt. When he recovered, he married Miss Linley and

Drury Lane Theatre

Above: Smock Alley

*Below: Richard Sheridan
as a Member of Parliament*

took her to London. This was in 1773 when Sheridan was only twenty-two and had no job and very little money. His wife was quite a famous singer, but he did not want her to go on working after they were married. So the two of them had a difficult time until Richard's play *The Rivals* was put on at the Drury Lane Theatre in 1775.

The first performance was not a success, but Sheridan altered the play somewhat and the next time it went on, about a week later, everyone clapped loudly, and it was performed again and again. One of the funniest characters is Sir Lucius O'Trigger, who was played in the second performance by an actor named Clinch. Sheridan also used his Irish background in his next play, *St. Patrick's Day,* which is a short, funny piece written just to make people laugh. By now he had become really interested in the theatre, and he next wrote an opera, *The Duenna,* with music composed by his father-in-law. This ran at Drury Lane throughout the winter of 1775–6. At this time there were only two proper theatres in London, Drury Lane and Covent Garden, and they were very jealous of one another. In 1776 Sheridan became manager of Drury Lane, so that he had to choose plays and produce them as well as write them! Luckily he had the help of his father who knew a lot about theatre from his days at Smock Alley in Dublin.

Even though he was very busy looking after actors, scenery and costumes, as well as having all the other worries of running a theatre, Sheridan went on writing. In 1777 his play *The School for Scandal* was put on. Most people think that this is the best play he ever wrote. His last real play, *The Critic,* was produced in 1779, and by then he was more interested in politics than in the theatre. He went on being manager of Drury Lane for thirty years, even though the building was burnt down twice, but from 1780 until 1812 he was a member of the British Parliament, and most of his time was spent in making speeches in the House of Commons.

At this time nearly everybody in politics was very rich. Sheridan had very little money all through his life, first of all because his father was only a Dublin teacher and actor and not a great lord, and also because he was very bad at looking after his money. He spent it as soon as he earned it—sometimes before! Making the theatre pay was very difficult at times, and Sheridan always hoped that if he did well in politics it would give him the money he needed to get away from his financial worries. He was very unlucky, however. He belonged to a party (the Whigs) which, in those days, spent most of its time in

opposition to the Government, so that he never became a cabinet minister; on top of that, he had to pay large amounts of money to get himself elected each time. In those days you had to bribe the electors with presents of money to vote for you, and of course if you were rich that was much easier. Most of his friends and fellow-politicians were much better off than he was; he tried to keep up with them and in this way ran himself into debt. You could be put in prison if you did not pay your bills, unless you were a Member of Parliament. It was lucky for Sheridan that he stayed in Parliament as long as he did!

Richard Brinsley Sheridan made many fine speeches in the House of Commons—only we would find them dull today because they were about people and things which do not interest us any more. We have not even complete copies of them, because there were no secretaries to take down the speakers' words and the reports in the papers were not very reliable. We know, though, from what his friends said about him, that Sheridan was a very good speaker—perhaps because his father was an actor and he himself a playwright and the manager of a theatre. His friends also thought that he was not cunning

A peep behind the curtain at Drury Lane

enough as a politician—in other words, that he was too honest. Even when he was very short of money he would never take anything for nothing—even though everybody else was doing it.

After Sheridan lost his seat in Parliament in the election of 1812, he had very little money left to live on and his last few years were spent in misery. He drank too much, and though he talked about writing another play, he could never bring himself to do it. His first wife had died and he had married again. He was trying to persuade his friends to let him help run the new Drury Lane Theatre which was being rebuilt after the fire of 1809, but they did not trust him any more. Sheridan died in 1816 with many debts and hardly a penny to his name, but in spite of that he was buried in Westminster Abbey and all the important friends of his happier years went to his funeral. He was a man with many faults, but he was also a man who was unlucky and had to struggle very hard to keep up with people much richer and more fortunate than he. And he was, most people say, the finest dramatist in the English language since Shakespeare, even though he stopped writing when he was only twenty-eight!

Thomas Moore
1779-1852

One can scarcely imagine a poet being given a civic reception like a politician or a cosmonaut today. That is what happened to Tom Moore when he went to Wexford in 1835 to visit the house where his grandparents had lived. By then he was known as *the poet of the people of Ireland* and had made more money out of one of his poems *Lalla Rookh* than any other poet had ever made before. Nobody reads *Lalla Rookh* today: but *Moore's Irish Melodies,* poems which he wrote to be sung to old Irish tunes, are known and loved all over the world, particularly where Irish people are living. Thomas Moore's poetry made him both rich and famous: he was the friend of lords and princes and his books were "bestsellers" from the moment they came out. But success did not spoil him; wherever his travels took him, he never missed writing to his mother in Dublin twice a week; he was so trusting and kindly that swindlers took advantage of him; and though he spent much of his life away from Ireland, the troubles and problems of his own country were always on his mind.

An illustration from Lalla Rookh

Thomas Moore was born at 12 Aungier Street, Dublin, on 28th May, 1779. His father, a Kerryman, was a spirit grocer, who sold everything from bottles of stout to bootlaces, and made a good living out of it. Tom was the eldest son and his parents rather spoiled him, perhaps to make up for the conduct of his first school-master, a Mr. Malone, whom Moore later described as *"a wild, odd fellow, of whose cocked hat I still have a clear remembrance, and who used to pass the greater part of his nights in drinking at public-houses, and was hardly ever able to make his appearance in the school before noon. He would then generally whip the boys all round for disturbing his slumbers."* Tom was later sent to Samuel Whyte's school (where Sheridan had been a pupil) and at the age of eleven was already taking part in amateur theatricals. He published his first poem at the age of fifteen, and at about the same time taught himself to play the piano; altogether he seems to have had a very happy childhood. The family used to go on holidays to Sandymount, Dublin, which was at that time a seaside village, and sometimes his father used to take Tom to meet his political friends. He was once taken to a dinner given in honour of Napper Tandy, the secretary of the United Irish Society.

These were exciting times. The organisation of the United Irishmen was just beginning and in the year 1793 Catholics were first allowed to enter Trinity College, Dublin, though they could not qualify for all the prizes and scholarships. Tom went to Trinity in 1794 and quickly made friends with Robert Emmet who was one of the best debaters in the College Historical Society. The British Government in Ireland was very suspicious of what was going on in Trinity, and tried to discover who were members of the United Irishmen and other secret societies. Moore did not join any of these societies, because, as he explained, he was *"tied to his mother's apron strings"* and could not get out of the house to attend the meetings, but he agreed with their republican ideas. One of the committee of the United Irishmen, Edward Hudson, was a great friend of his and first made him interested in traditional Irish music. Though he spent much of his time debating, writing poetry and singing at parties, Moore worked quite hard in College: he won a scholarship in 1797 and graduated in 1798. The Provost of Trinity encouraged him to go on with his translation from the Greek of the *Odes of Anacreon*, his first important book. He was a great reader, and used to spend hours in Marsh's Library, near Saint Patrick's Cathedral, study-

Left: Robert Emmet
Right: Sloperton Cottage, the residence of Thomas Moore

ing old books that very few of his friends had ever heard of.

In the year 1799 after the failure of the '98 rising in which so many of his fellow-students had been involved, Tom Moore decided to go to London. His mother sent him off with some golden guineas and a scapular sewn inside his trousers, and at first he was very homesick. He was supposed to be studying law at the Middle Temple, but spent most of his time writing poetry and

enjoying parties and a gay social life. He had an intro-
duction to Lord Moira who in 1800 presented him to the
Prince Regent, who had read and enjoyed some of his
poems. *"Is not all this very fine,"* he wrote to his mother.
At the big houses to which he was invited he used to sing
his songs to his own piano accompaniment and it was
his singing and playing as much as his poetry that made
him popular. One lady with whom he shook hands would
not let anyone else touch her hand for the rest of the
evening.

In 1801 he published a book of poems called *Poetical
Works of the late Thomas Little Esq*—his own poetry, of
course, under a *nom de plume*—but he was not yet making
enough money from his writing to live on, so he had to
find a job. In 1803 there was some talk of making him
Poet Laureate of Ireland, but he realised that this would
mean that he would have to support what the British
Government was doing there, so he decided against the
idea. Then through his friend Lord Moira he was given

a post as registrar of a naval prize court in Bermuda—
a strange job for a poet! Naval prize courts met to deal
with goods and money which had been seized from
enemy ships or pirates, but at this time England was not
at war with anybody so the court had very little to do.
Moore sailed for Bermuda on September 25th, 1803, in
the frigate *Phaeton,* but he only stayed on the island for
14 months. He did, however, get the chance to see something of America, and did not like it very much. Here
is what he said about the U.S.A., which of course had not
been in existence very long:

> Already in this free, this virtuous State
> Which, Frenchmen tell us, was ordained by fate
> To show the world what high perfection springs
> From rabble senators and merchant kings—
> Even here already patriots learn to steal
> Their private perquisites from public weal.

The meeting of the waters, Avoca

He was, however, welcomed in several places, including Philadelphia, by people who had read his poems, and this cheered him. He went up to see Niagara Falls (a journey of "*1,700 miles of rattling and tossing, through woods, lakes, rivers, etc*") but was back in England by November 12th, 1804, and the following year came to Dublin. In 1806 he published another book of *Epistles, Odes and Other Poems* which was attacked as immoral in the *Edinburgh Review*. This unfair criticism so annoyed Moore that he challenged the Review's editor to a duel. Someone had told the police, however, and they jumped out from behind some bushes and stopped the fight before it began: in any case only one of the pistols was loaded! Moore and Jeffrey, the editor, afterwards became good friends, but Lord Byron made fun of the duel in his poem *English Bards and Scots Reviewers* and this annoyed Moore even more. Byron and he ended up by getting on very well together, though, and *The Corsair* was dedicated to Moore, whom Byron called "*the poet of all circles and the idol of his own.*"

The year 1807 was probably the most important in Moore's life. He was back in Dublin, and the publisher William Power suggested that he should write poems to traditional Irish tunes in collaboration with Sir John Stevenson. Tom Moore liked the idea, and wrote to Stevenson: "*Our National Music has never been properly collected . . . our airs, like too many of our countrymen, have for want of protection at home, passed into the service of foreigners.*" So began the famous *Moore's Irish Melodies*, the first volume appearing in 1807, the tenth in 1834. Some of the poems have become so well known that it might seem they are traditional themselves: *The Harp that once*

From Moore's Melodies

through Tara's Halls, The Meeting of the Waters, The Last Rose of Summer, and the poem which Moore wrote in memory of Sara Curran, the sweetheart of his dear friend Robert Emmet:

> She is far from the land where her young hero sleeps,
> And lovers around her sighing;
> But coldly she turns from their gaze, and weeps,
> For her heart in his grave is lying,
>
> He had lived for his love, for his country he died,
> They were all that to life had entwined him;
> Nor soon shall the tears of his country be dried,
> Nor long will his love stay behind him. . . .

Moore always remembered that his words must be suitable for setting to music (*"The poet must write, not to the eye, but to the ear"*) and they need the accompaniment of the music to sound their best.

In 1808 Moore took up theatricals again, acting at Richard Power's theatre in Kilkenny. Here he met the girl who was to be his wife, a young actress called Bessie Dyke. They went back to England in December, 1810, and Moore wrote and wrote at his long Eastern poem, *Lalla Rookh.* In 1819 he had to go to France to escape being put into prison for debt, because the man he had left in charge of his post in Bermuda had disappeared with £6,000, which Moore had somehow to replace. He managed it with the help of friends and was able to return to England after three and a half years. He toured Ireland in 1823 with his friend Lord Lansdowne, wrote a life of Byron, and one of Lord Edward Fitzgerald, and spent most of the years between 1835 and 1846 on a long and dull history of Ireland which he never really wanted to write. In 1832 he was asked to stand for Parliament, both in Limerick and for the Dublin University seat, but he disagreed so much with British Government policy towards Ireland that he refused.

He became more and more interested in Irish affairs, however, and though he did not entirely agree with Daniel O'Connell's methods, he sympathised with what the Liberator was trying to achieve.

Tom Moore and Bessie had five children, but they all died before him, making his last years very sad. He died and is buried in the little village of Sloperton, near Devizes, in Wiltshire, where he had lived since 1817. This is what his famous friend Byron said of him: *"Moore has a peculiarity of talent—poetry, music, voice—all his own; and an expression in each, which never was, nor will be, possessed by another."*

John Field
1782-1837

ROTUNDA.

SIGNOR GIORDANI's

FIRST SPIRITUAL CONCERT,

Will be this present Saturday, the 24th of March, 1792.

ACT THE FIRST.

New Overture,	-	Haydn.
Song by Mr. Weyman,	-	Handell.
Qurtetto, by the musical Children,	-	Pleyel.
Song by Mr. Small,	-	Pasfiello.

Madam Kumpholtz difficult Pedal Harp Concerto, will be performed on the Grand Piano Forte, by Master Field, a child of eight years of age.

ACT SECOND.

Concerto Violin, by the celebrated Madam Gautherot, being her first performance this season.

After which Signor Giordani's new KYRIE and GLORIA, will conclude the Concert.—Tickets, at seven British shillings each, to be had of Signor Giordani, at his house, No. 9, Pitt-street, and all the Music-shops.—To begin at eight o'clock.

On the 4th of April, 1792, there was a large and excited audience in the Rotunda Concert Rooms in Dublin. The advertisements had announced that *"the young Master Field, a youth of eight years of age, will perform on the pianoforte a new concerto composed by Signor Giordani."* Master Field had already played at the Rotunda a month before, and so great had been his success that now all Dublin wanted to hear him. The advertisement was not quite truthful—for John Field had been born on July 26th, 1782, and so was nearer ten than eight, but there was no doubting that he was a real musician, and already a superb pianist.

Field was born in Golden Lane, Dublin, which was then a fashionable and elegant street. His father was a violinist in the orchestra at the Theatre Royal, Crow Street, and his grandfather had been an organist in one of the city churches, so that young John had music in his blood. Both his father and his grandfather were determined that he should follow in their footsteps, and they made him practise all hours of the day until he became so tired of it that he ran away from home. He soon came back though—he had nothing to live on—and found that he really did like music, and particularly the piano. The piano was at this time quite a new instrument, the first one having been made by Bartolomeo Cristófori in Florence early in the century. Field's father sent him to study under Tommaso Giordani, who was conductor of State Music in Dublin, and not only did he play in public at the age of nine, but he also began composing little tunes. Then in 1793 the Field family left Dublin,

John's father having been offered a job in England. They moved to London, where Mr. Field paid a hundred guineas to have his son apprenticed to the composer and pianist Muzio Clementi, who also ran a firm that made pianos. For the next few years young John had to work very hard indeed, playing Clementi's pianos for the people who came to buy them, to show how good they were. Of course this gave him plenty of practice, and he also went on with his composing. He gave concerts which were very much enjoyed, and on February 9th, 1799, the London *Morning Chronicle* wrote about him: *"This young gentleman, though only 15 years of age, has been esteemed by the best judges one of the finest performers in this kingdom."* At that concert he played a concerto which he had written himself.

He went on selling pianos for Clementi until he was twenty-one, and then, in 1802, the two pianists set off for the Continent on a concert tour—during which, of course, Clementi hoped to sell a good number of his pianos! They went to Paris and Vienna, and then, in 1803, to Russia, to the city of St. Petersburg (now Leningrad). The concerts were very popular, but

Cristófori's Piano

Clementi was a mean man and gave his young pupil hardly enough to live on out of the money they made. They met the composer Spohr in Russia, and he later wrote about John: *"When Field, who had outgrown his clothes, placed himself at the piano, stretched out his arms over the keyboard, so that the sleeves shrunk up nearly to his elbows, his whole figure appeared awkward and stiff in the highest degree; but as soon as his touching instrumentation began, everything else was forgotten, and one became all ear."*

The years between 1804 and 1807 were probably the happiest of Field's life. He decided to stay in Russia, in St. Petersburg, to teach the piano, and because he was such a good musician, he always had plenty of pupils. He learned French, German and Russian and he began to make money. But he began to spend it, too. He was odd in his ways, very absent-minded, and fell in love over and over again. He married a French actress, Mademoiselle Percheron, in 1808. He had published a book of sonatas in 1803, and he went on composing mostly for the piano, as well as teaching. One of his students was Michael Glinka, who afterwards became an important composer and founder of modern Russian National music. After the exciting events of the year 1812, when Napoleon's invading armies were finally destroyed on the great retreat from Moscow, Field wrote a March in Honour of the Victories of General Count von Witgenstein, who commanded the Russian forces.

Frédéric Chopin, the Polish-French composer of piano music, wrote a whole collection of pieces called *Nocturnes*, which means "night-pieces"—rather sad, dreamy music, usually with a beautiful melody. People copied Chopin in this kind of music, but Chopin himself had copied John Field, who invented the Nocturne and wrote nearly twenty of them. Chopin's nocturnes have become more famous, but if you play or get someone to play you a nocturne by Field and then one by Chopin you will see how one composer learned from the other. John Field published his first three nocturnes in 1814, and they were an immediate success. In fact all his music—his sonatas, nocturnes and his seven concertos for piano and orchestra—was very popular in its day, although not much of it is played now. You may sometimes hear *A John Field Suite*, which is an arrangement of some of his music by another Irish composer, Hamilton Harty. One music critic has said, however, that the world of music without John Field would be like the world of flowers without the daisy. His music is delicate and pretty, not noisy or dramatic, and it needs a pianist as good as Field to play it.

St. Petersburg

John Field

In 1822 John Field moved from St. Petersburg to Moscow, and gave another series of successful concerts, playing his own works. One of his friends in Moscow was Dr. Quinlan of Kilkenny, who was Head Physician to the Royal Hospital there for 35 years. Field was now beginning to drink more than was good for him, and would disappear from sight for days at a time. Twice when this happened, people began to think that he was dead, and once an obituary notice actually appeared in one of the Moscow papers! Field wrote a rather funny letter explaining that he was still very much alive, but he went on with his bad drinking habits. His drinking was not really interfering with his music, however, because when he went to London in 1822 he gave a concert and played as well as ever—perhaps even better. One of the artists on the same programme, another famous pianist named Moscheles, was very enthusiastic about John Field's *"enchanting legato, his tenderness and elegance, and his beautiful touch"*.

Chopin

Field was so pleased with his concert in London that he decided to set off on another tour of the Continent. He went to France, Belgium, Italy and Switzerland, but he found that he was not as well received as he had been twenty years before. His way of life was beginning to tell on him; he was not quite the performer he thought he was, and his tunes that had once been so popular were popular no longer. In Italy he became very ill, and was taken to hospital in Naples where he lay for nine months without any visitors. He had no friends in the city and almost no money, and was too proud to write to people he knew in Moscow asking for help. Then, luckily, a Russian family, the Rachmanoffs, who happened to be travelling in Italy, heard of his condition and offered to help him, provided he would go back to Moscow with them. John Field promised to do this, so he left hospital and set off for Russia, giving one or two concerts along the way.

He reached home safely, but it was not long before he once again became very ill, and this time no one could do anything to help him. His many friends had not deserted him, and four days after he died on January 11th, 1837, they followed his coffin in a large public funeral to the Wedensky cemetery on the outskirts of Moscow, and put up a simple but beautiful memorial over his grave which can still be seen today. On it is written, in English:

JOHN FIELD

Born in Ireland in 1782
Died in Moscow in 1837
Erected to his Memory
By his Grateful Friends and Scholars.

We hear little of this strange Dubliner in this part of the world, but in Russia he is very well known, his music is played, and many books have been written about him. He was a friend of all the most important composers of his day, and several of them, including Liszt and Schumann, knew his music and thought very highly of it. Field, the pioneer of the piano, the inventor of the nocturne, the teacher of Glinka, is a man with a sure place in musical history.

Field's Grave

James Clarence Mangan
1803-1849

Most people are very pleased with themselves if they can write and read two languages. Here is a list of some of the languages from which James Clarence Mangan translated poems: Irish, German, Latin, Greek, Italian, French, Spanish, Welsh, Persian, Turkish, Arabic, Coptic, Serbian, Czech, Swedish, Danish, Russian, Moldavian, Roumanian and Portuguese! Anyone who claimed that he could read all those languages must have been an unusual person, and Mangan was a very unusual person indeed. This is what one of his friends said about the way he dressed: *"His coat was of an indescribable fashion, both in cut and colour; it appeared to have been a kind of drab. Out of doors he wore a tight little cloak, and his hat exactly resembled those which broomstick-riding witches are usually represented with. Sometimes, even in the most settled weather, he might be seen parading the streets with a very voluminous umbrella under each arm."* Yet this very odd

person was the author of that wonderful poem about
Ireland which begins:

> O my dark Rosaleen,
> Do not sigh, do not weep!
> The priests are on the ocean green,
> They march along the deep.
> There's wine . . . from the Royal Pope,
> Upon the ocean green;
> And Spanish ale shall give you hope,
> My dark Rosaleen!
> My own Rosaleen!
> Shall glad your heart, shall give you hope,
> Shall give you health, and help, and hope,
> My dark Rosaleen!

Mangan was born in 1803 at 3 Fishamble Street,
Dublin—the same street in which Handel's *Messiah* was

Fishamble Street

performed for the first time in 1741. He was baptised James, and he himself added the name Clarence later in life. His father came from Limerick and had been a schoolteacher, but had gone into the grocery trade later, not very successfully. James had two brothers and a sister, and they and their mother found it hard to live on what was left after their father had had all his friends in for meals; so old Mangan tried his hand at buying and selling houses. Young Mangan was sent to Saul's Court School, run by Father Graham, and to several others, but he soon had to go out to work for his living to help keep his mother. Even before he left school, though, he had taken up writing, and used to send poems to magazines such as *Grant's Almanack* and the *New Ladies' Almanack,* which were rather like the comic books we have today. They were full of funny poems, puns and other kinds of not very serious writing. Mangan enjoyed this kind of composition. Here is a poem about a friend of his who borrowed some money and did not give it back. (The word *"shiners"* in the second line means shining coins, probably golden sovereigns.)

My friend, Tom Bentley, borrowed from me lately
A score of yellow shiners. Subsequently
I met the cove, and dunned him rather gently;
Immediately he stood extremely stately,
And swore, 'pon honour, that he wondered greatly.
We parted coolly. Well! (exclaimed I ment'lly)
I calculate this isn't acting straightly;
You're what slangwhangers call a scamp, Tom
    Bentley.

In sooth, I thought his impudence prodigious,
And so I told Jack Spratt a few days after;
But Jack burst into such a fit of laughter.
"Fact is," said he, "poor Tom has turned religious."
I stared, and asked him what he meant—
"Why, don't you see," quoth Jack, *"he keeps the
    Lent."*

When he was fifteen, Mangan went to work in a scrivener's office—a scrivener was a man who copied out legal documents by hand. He did not like the work at all, and to take his mind off it he started to drink. His apprenticeship ended in 1825, and he began to work for various solicitors in Dublin. In his spare time he studied languages, and he certainly taught himself German and French and quite a bit of Irish, whatever about the

Persian and Coptic and Welsh! He went on writing and, in 1831, joined the Comet Club, which was formed by a group of young men all of whom were interested in humorous writing. The poem about the borrowed money was written for their paper, *The Comet*, which was published from 1830 until 1833, when the government shut it down. In 1834 Mangan gave up the legal profession and tried to earn his living by doing translations, by teaching, and by writing for newspapers and magazines. This kind of work was not very well paid, and he found it hard to make ends meet. The first issue of *The Dublin University Magazine* came out later in the year. This was not just a

paper for the College, but used to print the work of many writers who afterwards became famous. It printed Mangan's poems, and paid him a little better than did other magazines.

In 1838 Clarence Mangan (as he was now calling himself) was given a job in the Ordnance Survey Office, where the maps of Ireland were made. He was not a very reliable worker, but he stayed there until 1842 when he became a clerk in the library of Trinity College. This suited him much better, because he could read strange volumes all day. He was paid £60 a year, which was quite a good salary in those days, but this went down instead of up because he was not attending to his work and was spending too much time in writing. He wrote a huge number of poems, some of them for the new paper, *The Nation*, which had been started by Thomas Davis and his friends in the Young Ireland movement. He became interested in politics, and the nationalist movement, and wrote poems with Irish titles like *Kathleen Ny Houlahan*, and this one called *Lament for the Princes of Tyrone and Tyrconnell*:

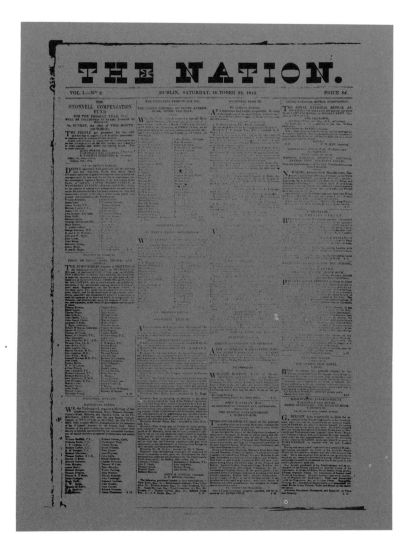

Two princes of the line of Conn
Sleep in their cells of clay beside
O'Donnell Roe:
Three royal youths, alas! are gone,
Who lived for Erin's weal, but died
For Erin's woe!
Ah! could the men of Ireland read
The names these noteless burial-stones
Display to view,
Their wounded hearts afresh would bleed,
Their tears gush forth again, their groans
Resound anew!

In 1848 Mangan lost his job in the library. All his life he had been drinking too much and perhaps taking opium, and this began to have a bad effect on his health. He went to St. Vincent's Hospital but left before he was entirely cured, and was later found lying in the foundations of a new house into which he had fallen. At this time he had almost no money and used to move from place to place, living in cellars and other unpleasant habitations. Very often he would just disappear for weeks at a time, and his friends had no idea where to find him. This was

Bust of Mangan in St. Stephen's Green

the time of the Great Famine, and in the year 1849 many people in Dublin caught cholera. Clarence Mangan was one of them, and he was taken to the Meath Hospital in Dublin, where, although he was dying, he asked for pen and paper and began writing furiously. But the nurse who was looking after him took away all his papers and burnt them, so that we shall never know what he was writing. Mangan died on the 20th of June, 1849, at the age of 45. He is buried in Glasnevin cemetery in Dublin, and there is a monument to him in St. Stephen's Green.

His best monument, though, is his poetry. He wrote humorous poetry, patriotic poetry, love poetry, and poems like *Dark Rosaleen* which will always be remembered. He liked mystery and magic, and perhaps he never knew half the languages he said he did. He had an unhappy life—an unhappy home, bad health, and bad habits which made his health worse—but he has left us some of the most exciting verse that any Irish poet has written.

A drawing of Mangan done after his death, by Sir Frederic Burton

Sarah Purser
1848-1943

The art of making stained glass—of filling the windows of churches and cathedrals with beautiful designs and colours—is one that dates back a very long way. Ireland's places of worship had some of the finest stained glass in Europe, until Cromwell's soldiers were let loose to loot and destroy. These magnificent windows could not be taken away and hidden like gold or silver objects and so they were lost forever. The skills needed to make them vanished as well, so that in the later centuries most of the ornamental windows that were put into our churches were made in Germany or England. Nowadays stained glass designed and made by Irish artists can be seen all over the country and in many places abroad—largely because of Sarah Purser, and one of her good ideas that were to make so much difference to the future of art in Ireland.

Sarah Purser was born in Dun Laoghaire (then known as Kingstown) on March 22nd, 1848. The family came from Dungarvan, County Waterford, where Sarah's father was a flour miller. His father had been a partner in Arthur Guinness's brewery; Sarah's two brothers became professors in Trinity College, Dublin. Sarah also was clever, but at this time women were not admitted to universities (though when Trinity became the first in Ireland or Britain to accept them, her niece, Olive, was the first girl to win a gold medal and take first class honours). Sarah had to be content with going to a good school in Switzerland and studying music and painting on her own. Her family had plenty of money, and there was no need for her to think about having to earn her living. It was thought that she would probably get married, rear her own family, and forget all about her artistic interests.

Things happened rather differently. In 1873, Mr. Purser's flour mills went out of business quite suddenly. It seems that Sarah's father had not been as good a businessman as some of the other members of the family, and he felt the disgrace so strongly that he emigrated to America and died there in 1899. Sarah and her mother moved to a small house in Dublin and lived very quietly with the help of money from her two brothers. Sarah realised that she would, after all, have to earn her living, and she decided to try to become a portrait painter. In the days before photography many people had portraits of themselves or of their families painted by people who, though not great artists, could produce a good likeness.

Stained Glass by Michael Healy

234

Sarah Purser Painting by John Butler Yeats

Sarah started going to classes in Dublin's School of Art, but decided that she needed some proper training. At this time the centre of the art world, and the city where the best painters of the day lived and worked, was Paris. So she borrowed a few pounds from her brothers and in 1878 set off for France.

She attended Monsieur Julien's art school for a few months only, but she stayed long enough to learn her trade. When she returned to Dublin she was good enough to start out professionally on her own, and so she set up a studio at No. 2 Leinster Street, and began painting pictures for a living. In 1880 she exhibited for the first time at the Royal Hibernian Academy. She painted many of the important people of her time, including the young Constance Gore-Booth, later to become Countess

Markievicz. As a result of introductions made when she was invited to the Vice-Regal Lodge (now *Árus an Uachtaráin*) she was asked to paint some portraits in London. Some of these were shown at the Royal Academy there. This brought her work to the notice of a wider public, and soon a great many people wanted their portraits painted by Miss Purser. She began to make quite a lot of money, and in 1886 invested as much as she could in the firm of Guinness when it became a public company in 1886. From then on she had no more financial worries, and could concentrate entirely on her art.

At this time the Yeats family were living in Rathgar, Dublin, and Sarah came to know them well. The father, John Butler Yeats, was a portrait painter like herself, and in 1901 she arranged for an exhibition of his work, together with the pictures of Nathaniel Hone. She always took a particular interest in one of the sons, Jack Yeats, and had kept in touch with him when the family moved to London, in 1887. One of her visitors who saw and admired Jack's work was Lady Gregory's nephew, Hugh Lane. At this time Lane was a dealer in Old Masters, but—partly through Sarah's influence— he decided to make a collection of modern art and present it to Dublin, if the city would build a gallery for it. Sarah gave him support in his efforts and, later, took part in the quarrel over the Lane pictures, though she did not see eye to eye with Lady Gregory. "*Sarah Purser, who has, in our eleventh year of the picture fight, come in to help, and has been useful in collecting Resolutions, came to see me and very rudely attacked me . . .*", Augusta Gregory wrote in 1927. The two ladies were rather fierce and rather jealous of one another.

For some years Sarah had been thinking about stained glass and wondering if the craft could be brought to life again. She was encouraged by Edward Martyn, a friend of Yeats and Lady Gregory, who wanted Irish stained glass to be used in the new Catholic cathedral which was being built at Loughrea. To set up a studio with the necessary equipment would be expensive, but she managed to interest the Secretary of the Department of Agriculture in the idea. This Department was, for some odd reason, in charge of the Dublin School of Art, and its Secretary, T. P. Gill, liked the idea of adding to the School's interests. A bargain was reached by which a stained-glass designer, brought in from England, would both teach at the art school and manage Sarah's workshop, and premises were found at 24 Upper Pembroke Street. In January, 1903, it opened under the name of *An Túr Gloine*, The Tower of Glass.

Stained Glass by Evie Hone

Soon the idea began to attract Irish artists and craftsmen, and Sarah Purser had her hands full trying to keep
all of them at work to complete windows that had been
promised for a certain date. She did not produce any
glass herself, though she did do a few drawings, or
cartoons as they are called, for others to work from, and
she was often very cross with her staff for not coming to
work until half-way through the day! *An Túr Gloine*
never made any money for her, but it made a wonderful

difference to church art and architecture in Ireland. Artists like Michael Healy and Evie Hone in particular became famous far beyond our shores, though Evie Hone's work did not attract Sarah at first and she did not join *An Túr* until 1933. Sarah loved travel and spent as much time as she could spare on the Continent and on journeys to see her friends in different parts of Ireland. She told everyone she met about her craftsmen and her workshop, and often came back to Dublin with a new order. She also paid her glassmakers to go abroad to study French and Italian ideas, though *An Túr Gloine* went back to early Celtic and Norman art for its designs.

Sarah had been living in a house in Harcourt Terrace since 1901, but in 1911 she decided that she needed more space to entertain her friends and to hold her parties, which were becoming famous. So she and her brother John, who was Professor of Medicine in Trinity and who was not married, took a lease of Mespil House, a magnificent mansion near the Grand Canal. She loved to talk, and was famous for her witty and clever remarks, and here on her "Second Tuesdays," as they were called, you could meet all the wittiest and most fashionable people in Dublin. Sarah Purser was not interested in politics, but she knew all the people in power, first under the British administration and later, after the War of Independence, in the first Free State Government. She took an interest in the young artists and tried to find work for them, and to the end of her life was familiar with the most recent artistic ideas on the Continent. A gallery in Harcourt Street had been opened in 1908 to show Hugh Lane's pictures while a permanent home for them was being built, and she never lost interest in this idea even after he was drowned in 1915. The gallery as Lane imagined it was never built, but Sarah Purser played a large part in obtaining for the city what is now the Municipal Gallery of Modern Art. This was opened in 1934 when she was well over eighty years old.

Before this, in 1924, she had another good idea. Pictures by famous artists were expensive, and there were no funds available to buy them for the galleries when they were offered for sale. So a society called *Friends of the National Collections of Ireland* was formed with Sarah as the director, and to this day it continues to buy pictures and give them to galleries in Ireland, both north and south.

Through all these exciting and important events Sarah went on painting, and she was still getting her

'*Le Petit Déjeuner*' *by Sarah Purser*

friends to sit for portraits when she was 85 years old! In her long life she painted nearly everybody of importance in Ireland, and you can see many of her pictures in the galleries today. She loved life, loved people, loved talking to them, and loved trying to make them come alive on canvas. At the age of 89 she went up in an aeroplane to see if she could see what was wrong with the roof of her house. She was on her way to spend a holiday in Mayo when she suffered a stroke and died two weeks later on August 7th, 1943.

Sarah Purser did a great deal for her country as a portrait painter, but more particularly as an encourager of others, a helper, an organiser, a planner. She put an important Irish craft back on its feet again; she added to our wealth of pictures and places to display them; and after the *"terrible beauty"* of 1916 she helped to bring a different kind of beauty into our churches and our lives.

Edward Martyn by Sarah Purser

Augusta Gregory
1852-1932

Coole Park

One day in 1897, Edward Martyn, who lived near Lady Gregory in County Galway, called to see his neighbour and brought with him the poet W. B. Yeats, whom she had met in London two years before. The weather was wet, and they sat all the afternoon talking about theatres and plays. *"I said it was a pity we had no Irish theatre where such plays could be given,"* Lady Gregory wrote later. *"Mr. Yeats said that had always been a dream of his, but he had of late thought it an impossible one . . . We went on talking, and things seemed to grow possible as we talked, before the end of the afternoon we had made our plan. We said we would collect money, or rather ask to have a certain sum of money guaranteed. We would then take a Dublin theatre and give a performance of Mr. Martyn's* Heather Field *and one of Mr. Yeats's own plays,* The Countess Kathleen.*"*

This was the beginning of the Abbey Theatre, and also of a friendship between Yeats and Lady Gregory that was to last until she died. The poet stayed many times at Coole Park, her beautiful home near Gort, and he put the house and the countryside around it into his poems. She was the friend and adviser of other Irish writers as well—George Bernard Shaw, Douglas Hyde, Synge and particularly Sean O'Casey, whom she helped from the beginning of his work for the Abbey Theatre with advice and encouragement. She learned Irish when she was nearly fifty, and wrote a book about Cuchulain and the Red Branch heroes for the Kiltartan branch of the Gaelic League, which she founded. Besides being an authoress of distinction, she was an actress, a traveller, and a collector of folk stories. She was a remarkable woman.

Augusta Persse was born on March 15th, 1852, at Roxborough House, County Galway. Her father had married twice and Augusta was the twelfth of sixteen children, and the youngest girl. Her mother was Frances Barry, who was related to Standish O'Grady. She was looked after by a nurse called Mary Sheridan, who had also been with Rowan Hamilton and who was a walking library of fairytales and folklore. Mary was a good speaker of Irish, and Augusta wanted to learn it too, but was told that *"Irish is not a lady's language,"* and was something that only the servants spoke. She wanted to read, too, but there were not many books at Roxborough, so she had to borrow them from the village schoolmaster. Augusta was taught at home, and spent a quiet childhood and girlhood, until in 1879 she went on a holiday to Nice with her mother and one of her brothers. In the same year she met Sir William Gregory, a widower who lived nearby at Coole Park. He was 63 and she was 28 when they were married, a year later, in St. Matthias' Church, Dublin, on March 4th, 1880.

During the early years of her marriage Lady Gregory travelled with her husband to many countries—Ceylon, India, Spain and Egypt. Her son, Robert, was born in 1881, and in 1892 her husband died. Lady Gregory had

Lady Gregory

already become interested in the activities of the Land League and had always loved the old stories told by the local people, but when she read *The Celtic Twilight* by W. B. Yeats and *Love Songs of Connacht* by Douglas Hyde, she knew she had found her life's interest in the traditions of her own country. She discovered the grave of the poet Raftery in Killeenan churchyard and had a stone put up to mark it. In 1895 she had first met Yeats in London. In 1898 she met Douglas Hyde, joined the Gaelic League, and went to Aran where she began to learn Irish. In 1899 she founded the Kiltartan branch of the League and began to collect the stories of the gods and fighting men which she published in 1902 as *"Cuchulain of Muirthemne"* and which Yeats called *"the best book that has ever come out of Ireland."*

These were busy years, preparing for the launching of the National Theatre, writing herself, and helping Yeats with his own plays. *"In these first years of the theatre,"* the poet wrote later, *"we all helped one another with plots, ideas and dialogue, but certainly I was the most indebted as I had no mastery of speech that purported to be of real life."* Lady Gregory's own first plays were written in 1902, and for the next ten years she was hard at work both writing for and helping to run the Abbey Theatre, which opened in 1904.

Yeats and Edward Martyn and Lady Gregory, together with the Fay brothers, had formed the National Dramatic Society and later the Irish National Theatre Society and had been putting on plays in various halls in Dublin. After a performance in the Molesworth Hall in 1903, Yeats came on to the stage and asked for subscriptions to help them continue. A rich English lady named Miss A. E. F. Horniman, who had been helping with productions, said *"I will give you a theatre,"* and this is exactly what she did. A building in Marlborough Street was bought, and Lady Gregory took out the Patent which all theatres had to have at the time to be allowed to put on plays. The curtain rose for the first time on December 27th, 1904, with two plays: *On Baile's Strand,* by W. B. Yeats, and *Spreading the News,* by Lady Gregory, the first of several good comedies which she was to write. In the years that followed, Lady Gregory *"was the Abbey Theatre,"* as one of her co-directors, Lennox Robinson, put it. She worked hard at nearly everything: writing plays, directing them, criticising actors and playwrights and helping them, even doing the office work. The company went on tour both in Ireland and abroad, and many plays were produced which have since become known and acted all over the world. In

1907 the production of Synge's *The Playboy of the Western World* caused a riot, and in 1910 Miss Horniman broke her connection with the Abbey because it had put on a performance on the day of the death of King Edward VII, even though Lady Gregory had sent a telegram from Coole saying *"should close through courtesy."* There had been trouble the year before when the Abbey put on Shaw's *The Shewing up of Blanco Posnet*, which had been banned by the Censor in England. Lady Gregory went to see the Lord Lieutenant and insisted on producing it in Dublin, and Shaw became a firm friend of the theatre.

By 1910 the Abbey had collected *"a few hundred pounds,"* as Lady Gregory put it, and they decided to go on tour in America. Here there were more riots—in Boston, New York, Chicago and Philadelphia—over the *Playboy* and other dramas which did not show Ireland as the Irish-Americans wanted to imagine it. In Philadelphia the whole cast of *The Playboy* was arrested! The case was dismissed after some exciting scenes in

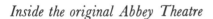

Inside the original Abbey Theatre

court, and Lady Gregory wrote a book about their experiences: *Our Irish Theatre*. As well as her theatrical work at this time she had begun writing books for children. The first one, *The Kiltartan History Book* (1909) was illustrated by her son Robert. *The Kiltartan Wonder Book* appeared the next year. She was also trying to help her nephew Hugh Lane in his efforts to create a Dublin Gallery of Modern Art.

In Dublin's Municipal Gallery may be seen some of the beautiful "Lane Pictures" which were collected by Sir Hugh Lane and left in his will to the City of Dublin *"provided that a suitable building is provided for them within five years of my death . . . the sole trustee in this question is to be my aunt, Lady Gregory."* This was written in 1915, three months before the *Lusitania*, the ship on which he was

Lady Gregory by Jack Yeats The Elder

returning from America, was torpedoed and sunk off the Old Head of Kinsale. Lane was drowned, and it was discovered that his signature on the Codicil to his will had not been witnessed! So, legally the pictures still belonged to the London National Gallery, even though Sir Hugh Lane clearly wanted them to go to Ireland. This started a battle between the two countries which lasted for many years, and Lady Gregory did her very best—without any success—to make the British give them up. She went on working for their return for the rest of her life.

The Easter Rising in 1916 saw the beginning of the Anglo-Irish war, and Lady Gregory, at Coole, was in one of the places which suffered most from the attacks of the Black and Tans. She wrote a series of articles for the

The Tree at Coole with the autographs of Synge, Shaw, J. B. Yeats and his brother W. B. Yeats, AE and Lady Gregory

English paper *The Nation* describing their outrages, but did not sign her name as she did not want Coole to be burnt down in revenge. Her son, Robert, had been killed flying in Italy in 1916, but she wanted to keep the house for her grandson. In the Civil War she favoured the Republican side, though she was never active in politics. She was far more concerned all through this difficult time with the fortunes of her theatre and with trying to bring her nephew's pictures to Ireland where she believed they belonged.

The 1920's saw the rise of one of the Abbey's finest playwrights—Sean O'Casey. Lady Gregory encouraged and helped him from the start, and when *Juno and the Paycock* was produced on March 8th, 1924, many people could not get seats. *"This is one of the evenings at the Abbey which make me glad to have been born,"* Lady Gregory said to W. B. Yeats. O'Casey was invited to stay at Coole. *"He is very happy walking in the woods and dipping into the books in the library,"* Lady Gregory wrote in her diary. A few years later, in 1928, the Abbey rejected O'Casey's play *The Silver Tassie*. *"I had a bad night and early morning thinking of the disappointment and shock he will feel,"* she said on this occasion. O'Casey broke with her and the Abbey for good. It was indeed a sad day for the theatre and for herself.

Lady Gregory had a serious operation in 1926, and knew that she had not much longer to live. She thought calmly of death: *"So much easier to face than another operation,"* she said in 1931. She died on May 22nd, 1932, at her beloved Coole, since pulled down and destroyed. *"I sometimes think my life has been a series of enthusiasms,"* she wrote in her *Journal*. We should be grateful that Augusta Gregory was so enthusiastic about so many worthwhile things.

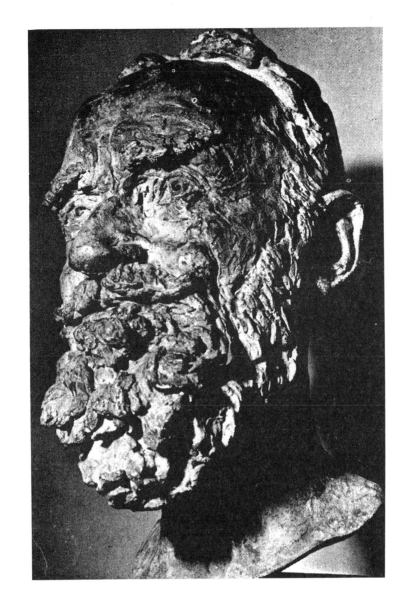

George Bernard Shaw
1856-1950

"What a man Bernard Shaw was for sending his blasts and benedictions everywhere, falling over the land like the thistledown from a blown-out dandelion," said his fellow-dramatist Sean O'Casey. Shaw, who has been called the greatest playwright in the English language since Shakespeare, not only wrote a huge number of plays, some of them of very great length, but he was also a music critic, a drama critic, a political writer and speaker, a producer of his own plays, and a writer of letters to everybody and anybody. Like James Joyce, he left Ireland when he was a young man and lived the rest of his life abroad; and like Joyce he never forgot his own country. *"England had conquered Ireland; so there was nothing for it but to come over and conquer England,"* he said. He conquered England by becoming the most important playwright of his time; by upsetting the English with his unusual opinions, his politics and his Irish sense of humour. He had enough energy for ten men, and set out to see the world at the age of seventy-five. He was a striking-looking figure. The English novelist H. G. Wells described him as a *"raw, aggressive Dubliner, with a thin, flame-coloured beard beneath his white, illuminated face."* Later in life his beard turned white, but he never stopped being aggressive, attacking anybody, no matter how famous or important, whose ideas he thought

Shaw's birthplace

foolish. He often said that he was a coward, and that he would hide under the nearest bed if anyone started to fight, but he was brave in other ways, never afraid of writing something that would make him unpopular, or even hated, if he thought it right. Not all his plays were perfect, of course—some of them he wrote in a great hurry, and some just for his special friends to act. But the musical *My Fair Lady* is based on his *Pygmalion*, and plays like *St. Joan, The Doctor's Dilemma, Arms and the Man,* and *Caesar and Cleopatra* are performed all over the world.

George Bernard Shaw (he hated the name George and never used it) was born on July 26th, 1856, in Dublin, at what is now 33 Synge Street. His father was a businessman, but not a very good one, and his mother a singer. He was brought up surrounded by music and never lost his love for it. He also started reading at a very early age, and used to spend hours by himself looking at the paintings in the National Gallery. His father, though pretending to disapprove strongly of alcohol, gradually took to drink, and this probably made Shaw decide never to taste it. It was not a very happy household. Shaw hated school (he was sent to Wesley College, then on St. Stephen's Green), and what he saw of life in the Dublin slums also gave him a lifelong hatred of poverty and the miserable way in which some people had to spend their days.

The family moved to Dalkey (Shaw's cottage can still be seen there), and he spent his happiest days as a boy wandering over Killiney Hill. Once he and some friends set the gorse alight, but he went to the owner of the land and confessed what he had done in a long speech which sounded very funny coming from a boy of twelve. About this time his father gave up drinking for good and his mother went with his sisters to London, where she hoped to become a teacher of singing. Shaw and his father left Dalkey and went to live in lodgings in Harcourt Street, Dublin. They were very poor and so, before long, the young boy was working as a clerk in a land agent's office at a salary of 4s. a week. He was later promoted to cashier—though he was only sixteen—and his pay increased to 18s. a week. He stayed with the firm, hating every minute of it, until suddenly at the age of twenty he decided to go to London. He explained it in this way: *"London was the literary centre for the English language, and for such artistic culture as the realm of the English language (in which I proposed to be king) could afford. There was no Gaelic League in those days nor any sense that Ireland had in herself the seed of culture."* He also said that *"like all Irishmen, I dislike the Irish,"* and *"I showed my own appreciation of my native land in the usual Irish way by getting out of it as soon as I possibly could."*

Shaw had decided to conquer England, but it was quite a long time before anyone paid him any attention. For nine years, 1876–1885, he lived at his mother's house, out of the proceeds of a legacy which he had received, writing books which nobody would publish. In 1884 he joined the Fabian Society, a group of people who wanted to introduce the new socialist ideas to England, and his political career began. Shaw did not believe in one law for the rich and another for the poor, and he was very enthusiastic about some of the writings

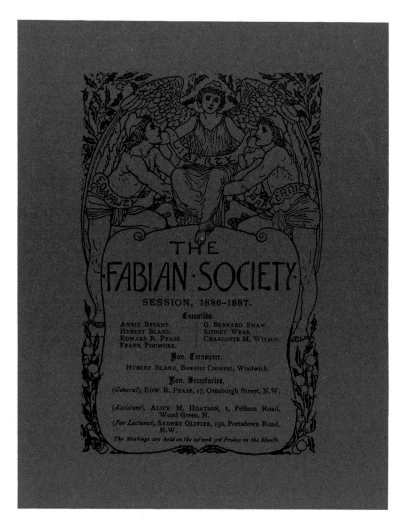

of Karl Marx, the founder of modern Communism. Though he was naturally very shy, he forced himself to speak at public meetings and gradually became a successful orator. He went on writing, however, and found a job as a music critic on an evening paper at two guineas a week, and later as a drama critic on *The Saturday Review*. He began writing plays. The first ones he

George Bernard Shaw

called *Plays Unpleasant* because they shocked the audiences who first saw them. English plays at this time were all much of the same kind, with the same unexciting plots and characters. Shaw started putting real, live people on to the stage, not all of them respectable—just ordinary men and women. *"I write plays because I like it, and because I cannot remember any period in my life when I could help inventing people and scenes."* For a long time he made very little money from his writing, as all his plays were produced in small theatres and did not attract very many people. Nobody understood *Arms and the Man* when it came out in 1894, even though it is now one of his most popular works. Shaw married Charlotte Payne-Townsend in 1898 and she nursed him through a serious illness during which he wrote *Caesar and Cleopatra*. His famous *Man and Superman* was written between 1901 and 1903. It was not until 1904, however, that success really came to him, and a whole series of his plays was put on at the Court Theatre by an actor named Granville Barker, Shaw himself being the producer. After that his fame grew, and he went on writing plays until 1949, a year before he died. *The Shewing up of Blanco Posnet* was

Shaw the motorist

first produced by Lady Gregory at the Abbey Theatre in 1909 because the British Lord Chamberlain thought it was blasphemous and banned it. When Shaw came back on a visit to Ireland after being away nearly thirty years, he said, *"It was not until I went to Ireland as a tourist that I perceived that the charm of my country was quite independent of the accident of my having been born in it, and that it could fascinate a Spaniard or an Englishman more powerfully than an Irishman. . . ."* He wrote *John Bull's Other Island* in 1905 because W. B. Yeats asked him for something for the Irish Literary Theatre. He did not, however, feel himself to be part of the Celtic Revival, as he found the ideas of Yeats and Synge too vague and misty for him.

During the war of 1914 to 1918 he found himself in trouble in London because he wrote about the war in a way which offended many people, even though what he said was usually true. He explained what happened: *"The English are all right, but they don't realise that I am a foreigner and have an inherited hate of what they call patriotism. I am intensely and quite unreasonably proud of being Irish."* He tried to explain to the English that the war was being run badly, that thousands of men were being needlessly killed because of muddle and inefficiency. Afterwards many people agreed with him, but at the time there were those who would have been glad to have seen him shot. At this time he wrote a speech for Roger Casement, who had been arrested in 1916 for his part in the Rising, and hoped Casement would use it at his trial. He refused and *"lost the greatest chance in history,"* as Shaw said, to tell the world of Ireland and her wrongs.

As Bernard Shaw's fame grew he was offered many honours—a knighthood, a seat in the House of Lords—but he refused them all. He won the Nobel Prize, and used the money to finance an Anglo-Swedish foundation for translations from the Swedish. He was not interested in titles and decorations, but when he was ninety he did accept the freedom of the City of Dublin. He had many peculiar ideas: he thought Shakespeare very over-rated and was always attacking him; he also thought English spelling was a hopeless mess and left money in his will to pay for the invention of a new alphabet. He loved driving motor cars and taking photographs. Most of all he loved talking—expressing his unusual opinions on everything under the sun. His ideas are still exciting because, for all his clever political theories, he loved ordinary people and understood them. His humorous plays will last because he was never afraid to laugh at himself.

Bernard Shaw was, indeed, a remarkable person. When

he was nearly sixty he purchased his first motor-bicycle, rode it 77 miles from the factory, then crashed it going too quickly around a corner.

He usually enjoyed excellent health, which he attributed to the fact that he was a vegetarian and teetotaller all his adult life, never eating any meat and never tasting alcohol. He wrote as a joke: *"My will contains directions for my funeral, which will be followed not by mourning coaches, but by herds of oxen, sheep, swine, flocks of poultry and a small travelling aquarium of live fish, all wearing white scarves in honour of the man who perished rather than eat his fellow-creatures."* It was hard to know when Shaw was being funny or serious, and this was one of the things that made his plays so successful and so entertaining. He lived to be ninety-four and even then his death was partially the result of an accident, when he slipped and fell in his garden while pruning the roses which he loved to cultivate.

Shaw's new alphabet

William Butler Yeats
1865-1939

In the year 1890 W. B. Yeats was living with his family in London. He hated the city and longed for the countryside of Sligo where he had spent many years as a child. He remembered a little island in a lake which he knew well, and he wrote a poem about it:

> I will arise and go now, and go to Innisfree,
> And a small cabin build there, of clay and wattles
>   made:
> Nine bean-rows will I have there, a hive for the
>   honey-bee,
> And live alone in the bee-loud glade.

This is probably his best-known poem (there are two more verses), and it tells of the very deep love Yeats had for his own country. He wrote many poems about Ireland and Irish people. At first they were mostly about fairies and magic, and the old Celtic gods and heroes; then he became interested in politics and the struggle for Irish independence. His poetry was about things that were happening around him. Later still he wrote of the important Irish people of the past—Swift, Goldsmith, Parnell, and the philosopher George Berkeley. He was thought by many people to be the best poet writing in English in the last hundred years, and in the year 1923 he was awarded the Nobel Prize for Literature, the most important literary prize in the world.

The Isle of Innisfree

William Butler Yeats was the son of a painter, John B. Yeats, whose pictures can be seen in the Dublin galleries and in other places. He was born in Sandymount, Dublin, on June 13th, 1865, but two years later the family moved to London because his father thought he could get more work there painting portraits. Yeats did not like London at all and came home very often to Sligo where his grandfather lived; in 1880 the whole family moved back to Ireland again and took a house at Howth. He went to the High School in Harcourt Street, Dublin, and later to the School of Art, because his father thought he might become a painter like himself. W. B.

John B. Yeats, Sr.

soon found out, however, that he wanted to be a writer and composed his first poems, some of which were published in the *Dublin University Review*, in 1885. He was still going to Sligo for his holidays and the beautiful Sligo countryside began to appear in his poems:

> Where the wandering water gushes
> From the hills above Glen-Car
> In pools among the rushes
> That scarce could bathe a star
> We seek for slumbering trout
> And whispering in their ears
> Give them unquiet dreams . . .

His father was a nationalist, and soon W. B. met the old Fenian John O'Leary who taught him more about the aim of national independence. In 1887 he published an article on James Clarence Mangan in a paper called *The Irish Fireside*. Then the family moved again to London. W. B. was soon back in Ireland on a visit, during which he went to Sligo and brought out a book of Irish poetry called *Poems and Ballads of Young Ireland,* which contained work by Katherine Tynan and Douglas Hyde as well as by himself. Back in London he went on writing and thinking about a long poem he was planning, to be called *The Wanderings of Oisin*. He was still very interested in what has been called *"The Celtic Twilight"* and his romantic ideas were encouraged by the English poet and artist William Morris, whom he met at this time. He also had his first meeting with George Bernard Shaw and did not like him. Yeats was a shy, retiring young man, not at all like Shaw, and a friend wrote at the time: *"a very pale, exceedingly thin young man with a raven lock over his forehead, his face so narrow that there was hardly any room for his luminous black eyes . . ."* His most important meeting, though, was with Maud Gonne, a

Maud Gonne

beautiful Irish girl with whom he fell in love, and who was the most important person in his life for many years afterwards. Maud Gonne was working secretly for Irish freedom, travelling between Ireland, England and France. Although she liked Yeats very much and was a good friend to him, she did not want to marry him.

W. B.'s first play, *The Countess Cathleen* (1892), was written with her in mind.

All this time Yeats was becoming more and more interested in the future of Ireland, and of Irish literature in particular. *"No great literature without nationality, no great nationality without literature,"* he wrote, and started a London Irish Literary Society and a National Literary Society in Dublin, out of which grew the Gaelic League. In 1893 he published a book of essays, *The Celtic Twilight,* and in 1894 he paid his first visit to Paris, going back later in the year to Sligo. In 1895 came another volume of poems, and the next year he went again to Sligo, to the Aran Islands, and from there to Paris where he met J. M. Synge and suggested to him that he should write plays set in the West of Ireland. These were busy years, but Yeats, though writing a great deal, found it hard to make a livelihood from his books.

The year 1895 was a turning-point in the poet's life: he met Lady Gregory, who had a big house at Coole. *"A new friend Lady Gregory called and invited me to stay at Coole and even before I arrived began collecting for me stories of*

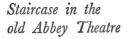

Staircase in the old Abbey Theatre

fairy belief," he wrote. Lady Gregory was to remain his friend until her death, and she was also to join with Yeats and Edward Martyn in the creation of a national theatre movement from which the Abbey Theatre was born. Yeats was not very well, and found Coole Park a wonderful place in which to relax and work. He had annoyed many of his friends in Dublin with his nationalist ideas, which were not popular with the wealthier and Anglo-Irish people at the time, and he wanted somewhere he could be by himself to think and write. He went to Coole again and again, and often wrote about it:

> Under my window-ledge the waters race,
> Otters below and moor-hens on the top,
> Run for a mile undimmed in Heaven's face
> Then darkening through 'dark' Raftery's 'cellar'
>   drop,
> Run underground, rise in a rocky place
> In Coole demesne, and there to finish up
> Spread to a lake and drop into a hole.
> What's water but the generated soul?

Lady Gregory at Coole

That last line may seem hard to understand, but all his life Yeats was interested in magic, in spiritualism, in trying to talk to beings from another world, and in the kinds of religion which prevailed before Christianity. That is why he wrote so much about ancient Ireland, and about the stories which country people tell of the fairies, the pookas, and the *beansidhe*.

On May 8th, 1899, the Irish Literary Theatre gave its first performance in the Ancient Concert Rooms, Pearse Street, Dublin. In 1902 the Irish National Dramatic Society was formed, with Yeats as President, and for several years after this he was concerned with its theatrical affairs. He went to America in 1903, and again in 1911 with the Abbey players, but the most important part of his life was still his poetry.

The Rising of 1916 took him by surprise, but he was quick to realise how important it was for Ireland. In his famous poem *Easter 1916* he wrote that *"a terrible beauty"* had been born. He knew many of the executed leaders well and he knew that by their deaths Ireland had been changed for all time to come.

Throughout these years Yeats had been living both in Ireland and England, but in June, 1917, he bought an old tower at Ballylee, near Gort, in County Galway, and

Ballylee Tower

went to live and write there. He had married earlier in the year, and discovered that his wife was a medium; that is, she had a gift of being able to receive messages from the spirit world. He used these messages in his poems. He went on a lecture tour in America in 1920, and in 1922 became a Senator of the Irish Free State. He enjoyed being a *"smiling public man,"* as he described himself, and was especially interested in improving the standard of education. He did not agree with censorship and made many speeches against it. He was chairman of the committee which chose the designs for the first Irish Free State coins. He was a Senator until 1928, and his last years were spent in travelling, in struggling with illness, and in the writing of his most important poems. His poetry for the most part became very difficult to understand, but there is nothing hard about *Under Ben Bulben* which he wrote a few months before he died:

> Under bare Ben Bulben's head
> In Drumcliff churchyard Yeats is laid.
> An ancestor was rector there
> Long years ago, a church stands near,
> By the road an ancient cross.
> No marble, no conventional phrase;
> On limestone quarried near the spot
> By his command these words are cut:
>> Cast a cold eye
>> On life, on death.
>> Horseman, pass by!

Those words can be read today in Drumcliff churchyard. W. B. Yeats died at Cap Martin on the French Riviera on January 28th, 1939, and was buried in nearby Rocquebrune. But, after the Second World War, on September 17th, 1948, his body was brought back to Ireland on board a corvette of *An Sluagh Mhuiri*, the Irish Navy. As the *Irish Times* wrote of him on that day: *"He believed earnestly in the cause of Irish independence; and around the struggle . . . he made a body of verse that blazes with the vital fire of revolutionary patriotism. A grave has been prepared for him in his own country; and he has come over the sea to claim it."*

John Millington Synge
1871-1909

"A thin, dark-haired, gloomy-eyed young man, with not very much to say for himself"—that is how some people who were at college with him remembered J. M. Synge, who died in Dublin when he was only 38 years old. He had suffered from bad health all his life, and seemed to know that he would not live very long. Although he died young, he has left us some of the finest plays ever to be acted in the Abbey Theatre.

John Synge was born at Rathfarnham near Dublin on April 16th, 1871, the youngest of a family of eight. His father, who was a barrister, died when John was still a boy, and his mother moved to Orwell Park, Rathgar, where the family remained until they moved again, to Dun Laoghaire, in 1890. John Synge was never very strong, and learnt most of his lessons at home. *"My childhood was a long series of coughs and colds, with plenty of amusement in the intervals and summer visits to the sea-side which were delightful,"* he tells us. As a boy he was very interested in nature. He used to collect birds' eggs and go for long walks by himself in the country. He and a friend kept rabbits, pigeons, guinea pigs, canaries and dogs—which must have taken a lot of looking after. *"On wet days we used to draw animals from Vere Foster's copy books,"* he says.

After working at home for the entrance examination, Synge went to Trinity College in Dublin. He did not take much part in the student life, as he was a quiet, rather shy person who was more interested in reading and in music. For a long time he wanted to earn his living as a musician, and in College he played the violin with an orchestra. When he had graduated from Trinity he spent some time studying music seriously, but then, like Oliver Goldsmith, set off to wander around Europe, seeing different people and places. He had a small amount of money—about £60 a year, which at that time was just about enough for one person to live on—and he finally settled down in a small room in Paris and started trying to become a writer. He had decided he was not good enough to earn money from music. At this time he did not think very much about Ireland—he was more interested in French literature and the French writers.

Then in 1898 something very important happened. W. B. Yeats came on a visit to Paris and met Synge. He suggested that the young writer should go home to Ireland and write about his own country. *"Why not go to the Aran Islands and learn Irish?"* said Yeats.

Synge liked the idea, and in 1902 he returned to Ireland for good (though he often visited the Continent),

W. B. Yeats

spending a long time on both Inis Mór and Inis Mean. He listened to the stories of life in the islands, of the danger of the sea in which so many of the fishermen had been drowned, and little by little he learned enough Irish to be able to talk to the people in their own language. So when he began to write his plays he wrote in a language which was neither English nor Irish but a mixture of the two. A knowledge of both languages makes Synge easier to understand, though of course his plays are acted in America, England and Australia where hardly anyone speaks Irish. One of his most famous plays is called *Riders to the Sea,* and it tells of a mother who has had all four of her sons drowned.

Synge's cottage on Inis Mean

"A man who is not afraid of the sea will soon be drownded," an islandman told him, *"for he will be going out on a day he shouldn't. But we do be afraid of the sea and we do only be drowned now and again."* He described a trip in a curragh: *"As we worked out into the sound we began to meet another class of waves, that could be seen for some distance towering above the rest. When one of these came into sight, the first effort was to get beyond its reach. The steersman began to cry out in Gaelic 'Siúl, siúl . . .' and sometimes, when the mass was*

gliding towards us with horrible speed, his voice rose to a shriek. Then the rowers themselves took up the cry, and the curragh seemed to leap and quiver with the frantic terror of a beast till the wave passed behind it or fell with a crash beside the stern . . ." Synge put this terror and all the power of the sea into his play.

It was here, too, on Inis Mean, that he may have first thought about the plot of *The Playboy of the Western World*, for he writes in his book *The Aran Islands* about an old man who told him stories of things that used to happen on the island in the old days. *"He often tells me about a Connaught man who killed his father with the blow of a spade when he was in a passion, and then fled to this island and threw himself on the mercy of some of the natives with whom he was said to be related. They hid him in a hole—which the old man has shown me—and kept him safe for weeks, though the police came and searched for him, and he could hear their boots grinding in the stones over his head."*

An early production of "The Playboy of the Western World"

Synge did not spend all his time in Aran. He was very fond of Wicklow, Kerry and the glens and the mountain roads, and the first play he wrote was called *The Shadow of the Glen*. Here is a poem of Synge's called *Glencullen,* in which he tells us about the way he used to rob nests when he was a boy:

Thrush, linnet, stare and wren,
Brown lark beside the sun,
Take thought of kestrel, sparrow-hawk,
Birdlime and roving gun.

You great-great-grandchildren
Of birds I've listened to,
I think I robbed your ancestors
When I was young as you.

The Shadow of the Glen was first produced on October
8th, 1903, in the Molesworth Hall, Dublin. In 1904
Synge became a director of the Abbey Theatre and all
the rest of his plays were put on there. His most famous
one, The Playboy of the Western World, was first acted on
January 26th, 1907, and there were riots in the theatre
at the performance. This was because some of the
audience thought that the play was insulting to Irish

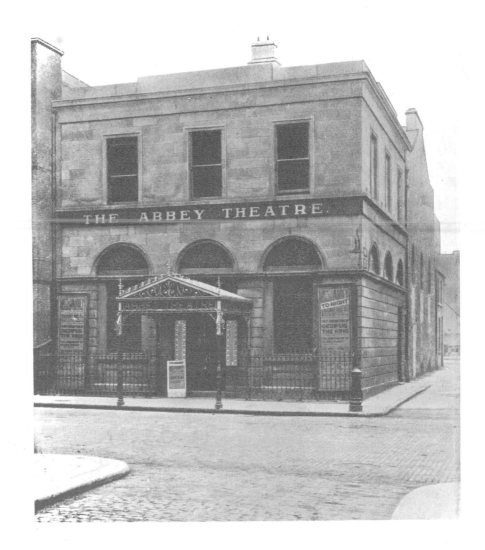

people, because it showed them as not always behaving in the best possible way. Synge tried to write about things the way they really are, about bad people as well as good people, but the Dubliners of 1907 thought he had gone too far. Here is what was said by a Dublin newspaper about the first night of *The Playboy*:

> "*Remarkable scenes were witnessed last evening at the Abbey Theatre during the production of Mr. J. M. Synge's comedy* The Playboy of the Western World . . . *On its initial production unfavourable comments were passed on it and at least two of the Dublin critics expressed the opinion that its production was not desirable. The author and management proceeded with the comedy last evening in the presence of an audience of about 300 . . . At the rise of the curtain there was still no indication that trouble was brewing, but the performance had not proceeded for more than ten minutes when it was obvious that the house was not disposed to a favourable reception of the piece . . .*"

Sara Allgood, Barry Fitzgerald and Arthur Shields in "The Playboy of the Western World"

There were shouts of *"Kill the author"*, and there were fights among the audience. Synge, who was at the performance, was asked to speak but wisely refused. A short time later the play was produced in Britain with great success and again at the Abbey in 1909, where this time very few people complained about it. When the Abbey company went on tour to America, however, they ran into trouble with it all over again and were nearly put into jail for acting Synge's masterpiece.

John Synge was upset by the way people objected to his plays, but he went on writing as hard as he could. He was in the middle of a play called *Deirdre of the Sorrows*, based on the old Irish legend, when he died on March

24th, 1909. To give you an idea of the way the language of his plays sounds, here is an extract from *Deirdre*. Its effect can best be judged by reading it aloud:

"I thought to stay your hand with my stories till Fergus would come to be beside them, the way I'd saved yourself, Conchubor, and Naisi and Emain Macha; but I'll walk up now into your halls, and I'll say it's here nettles will be growing, and beyond thistles and docks. I'll go into your high chambers, where you've been figuring yourself stretching out your neck for the kisses of a queen of women; and I'll say it's here and there'll be deer stirring and goats scratching, and sheep waking and coughing when there is a great wind from the north. I'm going, surely. In a short space I'll be sitting up with many listening to the flames crackling, and the beams breaking, and I looking on the great blaze will be the end of Emain."

Jack B. Yeats
1871-1957

In the year 1923 Jack Yeats made a speech to a meeting of the Celtic Peoples of Europe which was held in Paris. In it he said that the most exciting sights one could see were a man ploughing and a ship on the sea. He was not thinking of a farmer on a tractor or of a nuclear submarine, but of a man of the West of Ireland walking behind a horse, and of a Galway hooker beating up the Connemara coastline in a strong wind, or something very like them. Perhaps these things do not seem very exciting compared to a man landing on the moon or a ride in a big jet plane; but there were none of these things in 1923. Even if there had been, Jack Yeats would still have chosen his ploughman and his ship, because he loved people—ordinary people doing ordinary jobs in the way they had been done for centuries. Nowadays people push buttons, change gears, fasten seat belts and machines do the rest; but when Jack Yeats was a young man most things were done by hand, and most Irishmen and women knew how to enjoy themselves without radio or television or stereograms. Jack Yeats's earlier pictures show many scenes and ways of life that can still be seen; but there are others that have disappeared forever. He loved his country and particularly the ordinary people: not the cabinet ministers or the businessmen or big industrialists but the tinkers, the circus people, sailors, fishermen, farmers—men one would see at a fair arguing over the price of a cow. He lived among them and he watched them; he drew and painted them as no one had ever done before.

There were wonderful artists and craftsmen in Celtic and early Christian times, but the names of the monks who drew the Book of Kells, or of the stonemasons who carved the high crosses, are not known. When their skills died out there was a gap of hundreds of years until visual arts (as we call painting, sculpture and drawing) were important again in Ireland, and when some good artists did appear in the eighteenth and nineteenth centuries they were mostly content to copy British and European "fashionable" painters, and produce pictures of important people, their big houses, and scenes taken from the kind of lives they led. Few of them thought of

"An Island Horseman"

depicting the lives of the ordinary people—probably because no one at that time would have bought the pictures, and artists, like everyone else, have to earn enough money to live.

This is why Jack Yeats is so important to us. He painted the men and women of the country, not of the city, and he painted pictures of life as it was lived in the West of Ireland—a life very different from that in Dublin or London or Paris. For the first time for centuries, there was a really Irish artist, and one who has been recognised since his death as among the best in the world.

Jack Yeats was a brother of the poet W. B. Yeats, and was born in London, where his father had taken the family, on August 29th, 1871. John Butler Yeats, Jack's father, was a brilliant portrait painter—though his pictures were of the kind that other artists were painting at the time. From 1879 to 1887 young Jack spent most of his time with his relatives in County Sligo, and came to love the wild and beautiful landscape as much as his brother did. But where W. B. Yeats thought and wrote of the legends and the magic of the west, Jack was more fascinated by the real people—the circuses he used to see, the country race meetings, the tinkers and the beggars. Back in London in 1888 he went to Westminster School and began doing drawings and watercolours. In the next two or three years he held several exhibitions in London. He was the first Irishman to be given one-man showings in both the Tate and the National Gallery, London. In 1894 he was married to Mary Cottenham White. They visited Venice in 1898 and his subsequent work was influenced by the brighter, deeper colours which he noticed there. About the year 1900 Jack Yeats returned to Ireland, where he was to live until his death in 1957.

The drawings he was doing at this time were very simple and not difficult to understand, because most of them have a story to them—it can be seen exactly what the people are doing and why. Yeats enjoyed drawing pictures for books, and he made some fine illustrations for J. M. Synge's works, *Life in the West of Ireland* and *In Wicklow and West Kerry*. He admired Synge's writings very much. He also made illustrations for the broadsheets (poems printed very beautifully on one side of a single sheet of paper)' which were being published by his brother and sister at the Cuala Press in Dublin. In this way he gradually became known to the public, though he was always a modest man who said that the only thing anyone should want to know about an artist was the work he did; his private life did not matter. In 1913 some pictures by Jack Yeats were chosen for the Armory Show

...f", painted in 1951, when Yeats was eighty years old.

in New York, an exhibition which included the most important painters of the time, among them Picasso and Matisse. At this time hardly anyone in America had seen Picasso's strange pictures, and the show nearly caused a riot among people who just could not understand what it was all about. In the same year Jack Yeats took part in an exhibition of Irish Art in the Whitechapel Gallery, London. He had only been painting in oils for a few years—until then he had been doing drawings and water-colours—but from now on he worked all the time in this material and the look of his pictures gradually changed.

There is not much that can be said about Jack Yeats's life in Ireland from the early years of the century until his death. He lived quietly, holding exhibitions in Dublin and London from time to time when he had collected enough paintings, and he sold enough of them to live quite comfortably. The subjects of his paintings were

277

nearly all Irish, and many of them tell of what was going on at the time. He painted pictures of the Anglo-Irish war and of the Civil War, and a picture of men and women at Seán Heuston Station in Dublin going off to pay their respects to Wolfe Tone's grave at Bodenstown. He painted horses and he painted people; he painted the Dublin quays as well as the western coastline; and in nearly all his pictures there is a feeling of joy, a feeling of fun, and a feeling of excitement, because Jack Yeats really enjoyed life. Although things like the coming of the world war in 1939 made him sad, he was never a gloomy man.

You can see the happiness in his pictures from the colours he uses and the way he puts on the paint. In some of the canvases he painted towards the end of his life, it is rather difficult to see just what he is drawing—they seem to be nothing but splotches and streaks of colour, all mixed up together. But after a while the picture gradually comes to life: there is a horse, and that squiggle in the corner is a man leading it. Soon there is a complete scene evident, with real people, real horses, and real roads and fields, but the way in which Jack Yeats paints them makes them somehow more real than real. He paints the excitement of people as well as the people

NO. I.

A BROADSIDE
FOR JUNE, 1908.
PUBLISHED MONTHLY BY THE DUN EMER PRESS, DUNDRUM, COUNTY DUBLIN. SUBSCRIPTION TWELVE SHILLINGS A YEAR POST FREE.

Printed at the Cuala Press with illustration by J. B. Yeats

CAMPEACHY PICTURE
The sloop's sails glow in the sun; the far sky burns,
Over the palm tree tops wanders the dusk,
About the bows a chuckling ripple churns;
The land wind from the marshes smells of musk.
A star comes out: the moon is a pale husk;
Now, from the galley door, as supper nears,
Comes a sharp scent of meat and Spanish rusk
Fried in a pan. Far aft, where the lamp blears,
A seaman in a red shirt eyes the sails and steers.

300 copies only

278

themselves, so that the picture is alive and not just a dead copy like a photograph. To do this he put on his paint very thickly, and not only with the brush but with the palette knife and even with the end of the paint tube! Some modern paintings are very difficult to understand —they are made up of shapes and patterns of shapes and have no "story." Jack Yeat's paintings always have a story—they are full of real people and real places, but they have to be looked for, and looked for carefully.

An illustration from " The Turf-cutters Donkey"

As he grew older Yeats's fame as a painter grew and his pictures were sought for exhibitions all over the world. In 1948 there was an exhibition of his work at the Tate Gallery in London, and in 1951 and 1952 another big collection of his work toured various galleries in the United States and Canada. In 1955 he held his last one-man exhibition at the Victor Waddington Galleries in Dublin. By this time everybody had realised what a good artist he was and the prices of his pictures had gone up and up. Nowadays they fetch much more than those of any other Irish artist.

In 1950 Jack Yeats was invested an *Officier de la Légion d'Honneur,* a high French decoration which showed how much people thought of him abroad. He died in Dublin on March 28th, 1957, and in 1962 a special exhibition of his work, representing Ireland, was put on at the Venice Biennale, one of the most important art shows in the world. His work put Ireland back "on the map" in the art world, and it helped many young Irish men and women who wanted to be artists themselves to follow in his footsteps, so that now Irish art is becoming as well-known overseas as it was in the days of Columbanus and Colmcille.

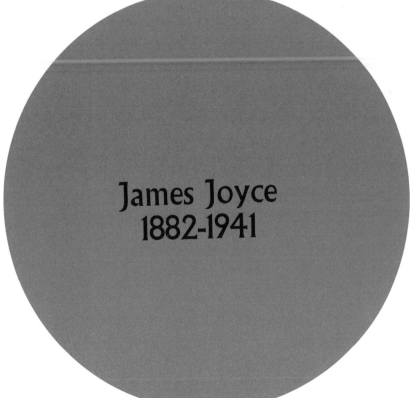

James Joyce
1882-1941

Bloom's House in Eccles Street

On June 16th, 1904, a Dublin Jew named Leopold Bloom left his house in Eccles Street, Dublin, at the beginning of what was going to be a very busy day. At about the same time, but on the other side of Dublin, Stephen Dedalus was having breakfast with some friends with whom he was staying in the Martello Tower at Sandycove. Later on in the day the two men met, but before that they had each had many adventures. June 16th, 1904, is remembered every year by people who gather in Dublin and follow the route of Stephen and Leopold Bloom in their wanderings around the city. They are famous all over the world, and very many books have been written about them, the people they met and the city they lived in. But neither of them really existed! They are only characters in James Joyce's most famous book, *Ulysses*.

Ulysses is the story of one day in the life of a large number of Dubliners, the friends and acquaintances—and enemies—of Stephen and Bloom. It is a very long book, and it is written in a way that is often very difficult to read, because Joyce liked to play tricks with language, to imitate the way other people wrote, and to try to write stories as if people were thinking them—which can seem very muddled at times. When the book first came out there were many people who did not like it because they found some of the things Joyce wrote rather shocking. Nowadays, however, this big book is thought of as one of the most interesting novels ever written, and its author—James Joyce—as one of the most important writers of this century.

Joyce's Tower, Sandycove

James Joyce was born at 41 Brighton Square, Rathgar, Dublin, on February 2nd, 1882. His father was from Cork and his mother from Longford, and he was the eldest of their ten children. Joyce's father had a job in the Tax Office in Dublin and had inherited some money from his family, but in spite of this the family gradually became poorer and poorer. This meant that they had to keep moving from one house to another. James lived in both Bray and Blackrock and finally on the north side of Dublin in 1893. This was the year John Stanislaus Joyce—the father—lost his job, and he never found another one. James knew what it was to go hungry and not to have enough money for the books he was so fond of—for even when he was still a boy he was very interested in writing. His first poem, on Charles Stuart Parnell, was printed when he was only nine.

In 1888, when James was only six, his father sent him as a boarder to Clongowes Wood College at Sallins, County Kildare. He was quite happy at school, though

O'Connell Street in Joyce's time

he was bullied by some of the bigger boys, but he had to leave in 1891 because his father had not enough money to pay the fees. In 1893, when the family had moved to the north side of the city, he went to Belvedere College which, like Clongowes, is run by the Jesuits. Here he was a very good student, and won several prizes, the money from which helped to keep the family. For two terms he was prefect of the Sodality of the Blessed Virgin Mary, but at about this time he began to lose his faith. In 1898 he left Belvedere and was enrolled in University College, Dublin, where he studied languages, and by the time he left with a degree in 1902, he could read Italian, French, German and Norwegian, as well as Latin. He learned Norwegian so that he could read the plays of Ibsen, and he wrote an article about them which was published in the British paper *Fortnightly Review*. Ibsen wrote and thanked him for it. Joyce also published an essay on James Clarence Mangan in the university magazine, and had really begun on his career as a writer.

When he left College, Joyce had ideas about studying medicine, and decided to go to Paris. On the way he met W. B. Yeats in London and the poet gave him some good advice and persuaded the Dublin *Daily Express* to let him review some books. He had to come home from Paris because there was no money to pay the medical school fees, but he went back again in 1902 and met J. M. Synge. He went on with his writing, but again he had to come back to Dublin when he received a telegram from his father telling him that his mother was dying.

Mrs. Joyce died in 1903, and from then until October, 1904, James stayed in Dublin looking for a job, writing poems and stories, and singing. He was always very fond of music, and had a good voice—so good that it won him a Medal for second place in the 1904 Feis Ceoil. Joyce was very disappointed at only being second, but the winner that year was a young man called John McCormack! In this year Joyce taught at Clifton School, Dalkey, for a short while, and lived with his friend Oliver St. John Gogarty in a Martello Tower. Both these experiences found their way into *Ulysses*, which is modelled on the people and places Joyce himself knew. He put in his friends and his enemies, and everything he could find about all the parts of Dublin he had lived in. He had a wonderful memory, and years afterwards could describe every shop and building in the Dublin streets about which he was writing, even though he had not set foot in the city for many years.

In 1904 Joyce left Dublin and never lived in Ireland again. He felt that the city was too dead for him, and that he would only be able to write properly abroad. He had become friendly with a Galway girl named Nora Barnacle, who later became his wife, and together they went to live in Switzerland and Italy. They had very little money, and Joyce found work teaching English in the Berlitz schools in Pola and in Zurich. At this time he was finishing his book *Dubliners,* though some of the stories had already been printed in magazines. He was also writing *A Portrait of the Artist as a Young Man,* which was really a story about his own school and university days.

In 1909 Joyce went back to Ireland for a short visit and had the idea of opening up a cinema—the first in Dublin. It was called the Volta and was in Mary Street, but it was not a success. He also managed to arrange to be the agent for Donegal tweeds in Trieste, where he was then living—one of our first export representatives! This did not bring him in very much money, though, and since he now had two children he found it very difficult to make ends meet and to go on with his writing. He visited Ireland for the last time in 1912, taking Nora and the children to Galway. But he had an argument with his Dublin publishers over his book *Dubliners* and he left, never to return. Most of the rest of his life, however, he spent thinking about Dublin, writing about Dublin, and talking about Dublin to anyone from Ireland who visited him.

After *Dubliners* and *A Portrait of the Artist,* he spent his time on two very long books—*Ulysses* and *Finnegans Wake.* Here is Joyce in *Ulysses* describing the way Mr. Bloom feels just after he has had his lunch:

Belvedere College

The Volta Cinema

"*I wanted that badly. Felt so off colour. His eyes hungrily saw shelves of tins, sardines, gaudy lobsters' claws. All the odd things people pick up for food. Out of shells, periwinkles with a pin, off trees, snails out of the ground the French eat, out of the sea with bait on a hook.*

Silly fish learn nothing in a thousand years. If you didn't know risky putting anything into your mouth. Poisonous berries. Johnny Magories. Roundness you think good. Gaudy colour warns you off. One fellow told another and so on. Try it on the dog first. Led on by the smell or the look. Tempting fruit. Ice cones. Cream. Instinct. Orange groves for instance. Need artificial irrigation . . ."

It is not very easy to understand at first, but *Ulysses* is a complete picture of the Dublin of 1904, and a little study makes it enjoyable reading. It is more difficult to enjoy reading *Finnegans Wake,* because it is written in a language Joyce invented himself, borrowing bits from all kinds of languages and putting them together. People are still arguing over what it all means—and if Joyce were still here he would probably be having a good laugh at them, because he was a man with a great sense of humour. Even though he was very bitter about Dublin and the fact that he had to leave it to make his way in the world, he loved his city and its people more than anything else—the good and the bad, the rich and the poor, the beautiful and the ugly.

Joyce gradually became known as an important writer and the publication of *Ulysses* made him famous. As he grew older he had more and more trouble with his eyesight, and several times very nearly became blind. He worked hard, and was very fond of sitting up till all hours in cafes talking to friends and noting down for use in his books all kinds of things they said. He would ask visitors from Ireland very careful questions about Dublin to make sure that he had his facts right. Towards the end of his life he lived much of the time in Paris, but when the Second World War started and France was invaded, he went to Switzerland, where he died in Zurich on the 13th of January, 1941. He was buried in a cemetery near the Zoo, and his wife Nora said: *"He was awfully fond of the lions—I like to think of him lying there and listening to them roar."*

Robert Boyle
1627-1691

We are so used to the wonders of modern science—
trips to the moon, television, heart-transplants—that it is
easy to forget that only a few centuries ago men were
more interested in magic than in molecules or atoms,
and chemists (or alchemists as they were called then)
spent most of their time trying to find a way to turn
ordinary metal into gold—and so make themselves rich!
In working out a scientific experiment, all the facts and
figures must be checked out and must be right. One of
the first scientists to understand the importance of this
accuracy was Robert Boyle, who was born in Lismore
Castle, County Waterford, on January 23rd, 1627. He
was the seventh son and the fourteenth child of Richard
Boyle, the great Earl of Cork, and when he was eight
years old he could read Latin and Greek as well as he
could read English, so his parents sent him to school at
Eton in England. He must have been by far the youngest
boy there, but he was already showing signs of great
interest in scientific matters. He read the Latin author
Quintus Curtius and recalled later that it *"conjured up
for him that unsatisfied appetite for knowledge that is yet as
greedy as when it first was raised,"* He stayed at Eton College
for three years, and was then taught privately by the
clergyman at Stalbridge in Dorsetshire, where his father
had just gone to live.

At this time wealthy people used to send their sons to different places on the Continent to continue with their education, and Robert Boyle was sent to France, Switzerland and Italy in 1638, when he was only eleven! Travelling with him were his elder brother and his tutor, who came from Geneva in Switzerland. They first went to Paris and Lyons, and then spent almost two years in Geneva where young Robert learned French, dancing, fencing and tennis. He had always been devoted to religion, but it was in Geneva that it really made a strong impression upon him. He remained a firm Christian for the rest of his life.

While he was in Florence in 1641–2, Robert Boyle studied the work of Galileo, the famous Italian scientist who had just died; and he also learned Italian while he was there. But one day came bad news. Funds of £250 (a very large sum in those days) which his father had sent him had disappeared, and he, his brother and his tutor were now penniless. They went back to the tutor's home in Geneva, where they lived on credit for two years until they were able to get enough money to return home. Robert Boyle returned to England in 1644 to discover that his father had just died, leaving him his house at Stalbridge and his estates in Ireland. Robert spent quite a lot of time in the next few years looking after these. But he was really only interested in science and soon began to do experiments and to write scientific books. He did, however, find time to visit his estates in Ireland in 1652 and 1653. The country was in a very disturbed state after the rising of 1641. Robert found it *"a barbarous country, where chemical spirits were so misunderstood, and chemical instruments so unprocurable, that it was hard to have any hermetic thoughts in it."* He turned his attention to medicine instead. Before returning to England he had conducted several important experiments on the circulation of the blood. He went to live in Oxford, which was the centre of scientific ideas at the time, and set up a laboratory in his lodgings near University College.

There were very few real scientists in England in those days, and it was important for them to meet one another and talk about what they were doing. As there was a lot of political trouble at the time, they met secretly so that the Government would not become suspicious of their experiments. When things improved, however, they came out into the open and formed themselves into *"The Royal Society of London for Improving Natural Knowledge,"* or The Royal Society, as it is usually called. It became very famous and still is today. Robert Boyle was one of its first members and its first President, though he soon

Lismore Castle

resigned in favour of Sir Christopher Wren. He was a rather quiet and retiring man who never married and did not want to be mixed up in politics or anything else except science. His only other interest was religion; he wrote many religious books and in 1685 he paid £700 to have the Old Testament printed in Irish for the first time. He himself learned Hebrew, Greek, Syriac and Chaldee so that he could read the Scriptures in the original, even though he did not care for languages! His friends told him he should take holy orders, but he refused because he felt that he had no true vocation. This lost him the position of Provost of his old school, Eton, which was always held by a clergyman. He also refused a title, and was almost the only member of his large family without one! Robert Boyle was a very serious man in everything he did—so serious, in fact, that some people could not resist playing jokes on him. He wrote a book called *Occasional Reflexions on Several Subjects* and Jonathan Swift produced a skit based on it called *A Pious Meditation upon a Broomstick*. He seems to have been very good company, though he was nearly always in poor health and was never very strong. He suffered from weak eyes, which made reading very difficult, and he also had a very bad memory, so it was remarkable that he was able to conduct so many important experiments. He was not a dull man, however; his friends found him witty and he loved meeting people and writing letters to other scientists like Isaac Newton. Three Kings of England were his friends.

In 1654 when Robert Boyle moved to Oxford he began a long series of experiments in physics. He was interested in the air-pump, which had been invented in Germany about 1654 by Otto von Guericke, and he succeeded in making one which worked much better. An air-pump is not like a bicycle pump: it pumps air *out* of something instead of into it and so creates a *vacuum*, which is very useful for all kinds of experiments in science. Boyle's air-pump was so good that for a long time every air pump was called a *Machina Boyleana*, which is the Latin for *"Boyle's Machine."* Air-pumps are still used and are still important: electric light bulbs, for instance, need a vacuum inside them before they will work.

Perhaps you have heard of *Boyle's Law: "If the temperature and quantity of a gas remain constant, the volume varies inversely with the pressure"*—that means that air is "squashed down" when you press it, when you pump it into a bicycle tyre, for example. This does not sound a very exciting discovery, but in the seventeenth century people knew very little about air—what it was and how it behaved. Boyle's Law was important to them because it set them on the right path to make many more discoveries. His other experiments included one showing the difference between a *mixture* and a *compound*, another separating hydrogen from air (though he did not recognise what it was), and another in which he tried to weigh light!

His health began to fail under the pressure of all this work, and about 1661 he decided to keep visitors away for parts of four days a week *"to recover his spirits, to arrange his papers, and to take some care of his affairs in Ireland,"* which, as he put it, *"are very much disordered, and have their face often changed by public calamities there."*

Though Robert Boyle was a very "modern" scientist, he was still interested in the old ideas of alchemy, and spent quite a lot of time trying to find a way to make gold from other metals. In 1668 he moved to London and this gave him more chances to meet his fellow-scientists of the Royal Society and to exchange ideas with them. He was a very methodical and patient man, and would spend days checking experiments to make sure that his answers were correct. He still kept up his strong religious

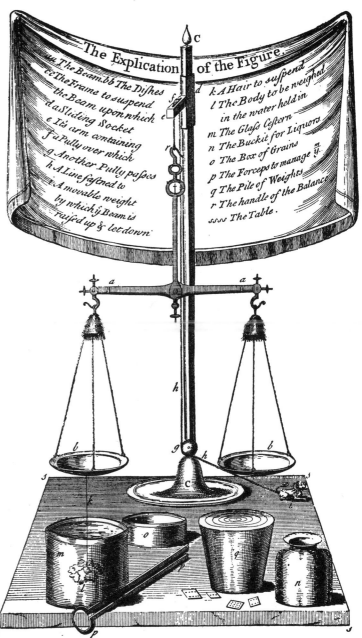

The Explication of the Figure.

a a The Beam. b b The Dishes
c c The Frame to suspend
the Beam upon which
d a Sliding Socket
e It's arm containing
f a Pully over which
g Another Pully passes
h A Line fastned to
i A movable weight
by which ij Beam is
raised up & let down

k A Hair to suspend
l The Body to be weighed
in the water held in
m The Glass Cestern
n The Buckit for Liquors
o The Box of Grains
p The Forceps to manage y.
q The Pile of Weights
r The handle of the Balance
s s s s The Table.

295

beliefs, too, and paid for translations of the Bible into several other languages, including Welsh, Malay and Turkish.

Lady Ranelagh, his sister, kept house for him in London, and they lived happily until about 1688, when his health began to get much worse. He stopped writing for the *Philosophical Transactions* of the Royal Society (in which new discoveries were published) and put a notice in the papers to say that he was no longer well enough to have any visitors at all. He went on with his experiments, however, until 1691, when he became very ill. His sister died on the 23rd of December, and Robert Boyle followed her on the 30th. He was buried in the church of St. Martin in the Fields, Westminster. Though none of his discoveries was of the highest importance, he was the first really methodical modern scientist, and many who followed him were grateful for what he had begun.

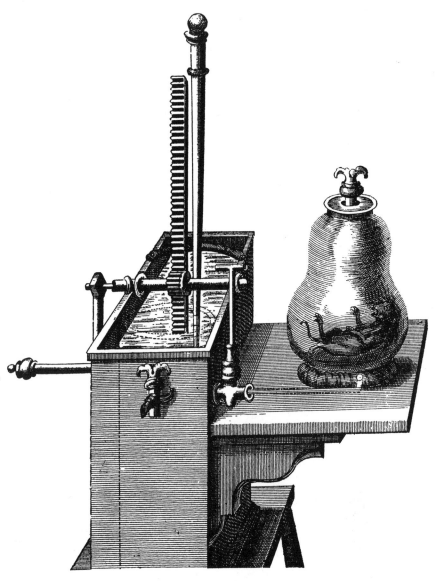

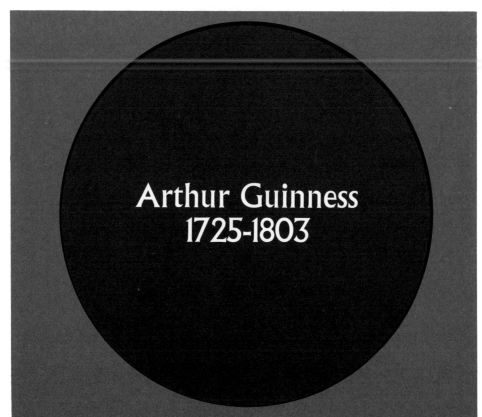

Arthur Guinness
1725-1803

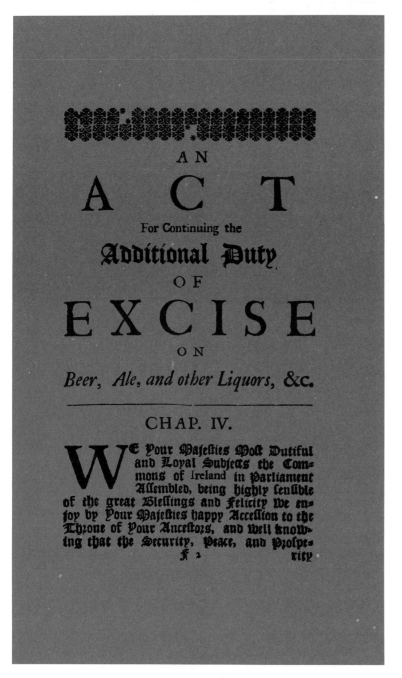

AN

A C T

For Continuing the

Additional Duty

OF

EXCISE

ON

Beer, Ale, and other Liquors, &c.

CHAP. IV.

WE Your Majesties Most Dutiful and Loyal Subjects the Commons of Ireland in Parliament Assembled, being highly sensible of the great Blessings and Felicity We enjoy by Your Majesties happy Accession to the Throne of Your Ancestors, and well knowing that the Security, Peace, and Prosperity

F 2 rity

In the year 1773 the many small breweries which up till then had flourished in Dublin were finding it difficult to stay in business. Porter was being brought in from England and sold at a lower price than that at which Irish brews were available. One of the brewers, Arthur Guinness, was thinking of emigrating and setting up a brewery in Wales, at Caernarvon or Holyhead. Luckily the tax on Irish beer was reduced in 1775 and things began to improve for the brewers. Ireland might be very different today if Arthur Guinness had really decided to leave Dublin.

Arthur Guinness was the eldest son of Richard Guinness of Celbridge, County Kildare, who was the

An 18th century Brewery

agent for the Church of Ireland Archbishop of Cashel, Dr. Price. We know very little of Arthur's early life, but when Dr. Price died in 1752, he left him £100, which probably helped him to start in business. In the year 1756 he was running a brewery in Leixlip, and three years later he moved to St. James' Gate in Dublin, and started the business that has remained in his family ever since.

Nowadays a brewery is usually a huge, factory-like place employing hundreds of people. In the eighteenth century, however, breweries were small, and you could find one in nearly every town in the country. Many brewers kept an inn or public house as well, and sold their own beer. Most beer was drunk close to where it

was made: Dublin beer in Dublin, Cork beer in Cork, and so on. Of course there were no railways, no good roads and no canals, so it was very difficult to carry heavy items like barrels of beer from one place to another. In 1798 Arthur started sending his stout to Athy, down the newly-constructed Grand Canal, and his brewery began to grow into a really large firm supplying the whole country, and many places abroad.

Almost forty years earlier, on the 31st of December, 1759, Arthur Guinness signed the lease for premises at St. James Gate. There had been a brewery there before and the whole area was popular with brewers and all kinds of manufacturers because it was near to the City Water Course, which brought water down from the mountains. Plenty of good water is needed to make good beer, and although the old brewery which Mr. Guinness was buying was in very bad shape, he must have felt it was worth the money for the water supply. He was right! The lease itself is an interesting document, though it is full of difficult lawyers' language. These are some of the *"bits and pieces"* which Arthur Guinness

An Irish Brewery

bought together with the land and the buildings: *"Three Marble Chimney Pieces; One Kitchen Grate Rack and Shelves; Two small fixed Grates; Eleven Troughs; One float very bad; One Kieve very bad and two Brass Cocks; One underbank quite decayed; One Copper; seventy barrels with a large brass Cock; Two Underbank Pumps; Two old Coolers quite decayed; One Tunn; Six Oars; One Shute; One Horse Mill; One Hopper and pair of stoves; Box of Drawers and Desk in the Office."*

When Arthur Guinness started brewing, he made beer *and* stout. The derivation of these words is of some interest. *Porter* is a dark beer which was at first drunk by the porters in the markets in London. The brewers then started making a stronger porter which they called *stouter porter*—and this soon became known as *stout*. So *beer* came to mean the light-coloured drink, which is called *ale*.

In Dublin in the early 1700's people drank ale as well as gin and whiskey—stout was not yet very popular. The government tried to persuade people to drink more ale and stout by charging duty on spirits. The government was greedy, too, and sought to tax the brewers as well as the distillers (whiskey is *distilled*) and so made the beer almost too expensive for ordinary people to buy. It used to be about 4d a quart—not very much by our standards, but at that time a man's weekly wage might be only ten shillings. In the 1790's there was a big debate in the Irish House of Commons in College Green, Dublin (the building now houses the Bank of Ireland) about the taxes on the brewers and all the government rules and regulations which made life and business very hard for them. Arthur Guinness was called in to tell the Parliament what he thought about the issue. He said that he had been a brewer for 30 years and had never known the trade to be in a worse state than it was at that time. He blamed it on too much spirit drinking, too much beer imported from England, and

The Chapel at St. James's Gate

301

the high price of malt, which is needed in making beer and stout. He had a good friend in the parliament— Henry Grattan, who was a relation of his by marriage and one of the best speakers of his day. Grattan managed to persuade the government to change their minds about the duty on beer, and in 1795 it was abolished. This made a big difference to the Irish brewers, and particularly to Arthur Guinness. In 1799 he wrote in one of his brewing books: *"Today April 1st 1799 was brewed the last ale brew."* He had decided that Irishmen would in future prefer stout to ale.

What kind of person was this first Arthur Guinness? He seems to have been a kind and generous man, a religious man, and a citizen of Dublin who was very interested in how the city and the country were run. He married Olivia Whitmore in 1761 in St. Mary's Church in Mary's Street, Dublin, and they had twenty-one children, of whom ten lived. In 1764 he bought a country house at Beaumont, County Dublin; he had already made so much money that he could live like a gentleman. He built extensions to his brewery and by 1767 had been made Master of the Corporation of Brewers, which was a guild or kind of trade union which looked after the affairs of all the brewers. He was very keen on making sure that Parliament should know of the complaints of the brewers about taxes and other things, and went to speak in College Green about them, as we have seen. In 1789 and 1790 he built flour mills, and was interested in many other businesses besides brewing. He became Governor of the Meath Hospital and tried to make things better for the prisoners in Ireland's jails.

This was a difficult time for Catholics in Ireland. They were still not allowed to stand for Parliament or to own land, though this was changed in 1793. Arthur Guinness believed that everybody should be treated equally, no matter what his religion, and he stood up and said so at the meetings of the Dublin City Council. He was a strong supporter of his own church, and particularly of St. Patrick's Cathedral and its school. He started the first Sunday School in Ireland in 1786. He once tried to persuade the Aldermen of Dublin not to hold a big banquet they were planning and to use the money for charity instead, but the City Fathers were too fond of eating and drinking and would not listen to him. He had had trouble with the Corporation before. In 1775 they had tried to interfere with his water supply—the argument went on for ten years, with Guinness finally winning, though at one time he had to grab a pick-axe from a workman who was starting to block up the water course. He could be very fierce and determined when he had to be.

Arthur Guinness went on looking after his brewing business until he was very old. Luckily he had his sons Benjamin and Arthur to help him, because by this time the brewery was one of the biggest concerns in Dublin. He retired to Beaumont for the last years of his life and died in 1803 at the age of seventy-eight. He was buried at Oughterard, near Kill, County Kildare. He left his son, Arthur, in charge of one of the busiest and most important industries in Ireland, and one which was to grow and grow to be the biggest brewery in Europe and the biggest exporter of stout in the world. Dublin and Ireland owe a great deal to the hard-working, generous and high-principled brewer who changed his mind about emigrating and bought the old brewery at St. James's Gate instead.

The Second Arthur Guinness

Charles Bianconi
1786-1875

Charles Bianconi as a boy

It may seem surprising to find someone with a name like Bianconi in a book about famous Irish people. It certainly is not a Gaelic name—but then neither is Pearse, nor Davis, nor Wadding, nor de Valera! Charles Bianconi was born in Italy, where he was christened Carlo, but spent most of his life in Ireland, where he became mayor of Clonmel and one of the most important men in the country. In those days one could not become a naturalised Irishman because Ireland was still controlled from London, but he did the next best thing—he became a citizen of the United Kingdom of Great Britain and Ireland. He was a friend of the Liberator Daniel O'Connell, of Father Mathew, and of Edmund Ignatius Rice. He started with a shilling a day and ended his life a wealthy man, with a big house in the country and friends among all the important people. But he is chiefly remembered because he gave Ireland her first complete transport system, and in doing so he changed people's lives.

Joachim Carlo Giuseppe Bianconi was born on the 24th of September, 1786, at a place called Tregolo in the north of Italy, not very far from Lake Como. His grandmother, who was a fierce old lady, wanted him to become a priest, but Carlo, as he was always called, preferred horses to books and was very bad at his studies. He left school when he was 15, and the next year, in 1802, he crossed the Saint Bernard Pass into Switzerland with three young friends, apprenticed to a man named Faroni, who was taking them to England to seek their fortune. Faroni changed his mind, however, and in the autumn of 1802 young Bianconi found himself in lodgings in Temple Bar, Dublin. He had no English, and knew nothing at all about the country he had come to live in. Faroni decided to set up as a print seller, because he found out that all the big houses in the city were very short of pictures. After he had made some special lead frames, he sent Bianconi and his young friends out into the streets to sell the little engravings he had brought with him from the Continent. The rich ladies took a fancy to Carlo, and he did so well that Faroni soon sent him off into the country for a week at a time with a stock of prints to sell. So at the age of seventeen he became a kind of commercial traveller, wandering the roads of Ireland and often getting into difficulties because he still spoke very little English.

In 1804 he was free to leave Faroni, and he decided to set up on his own as a travelling print seller. He went south from Dublin and soon reached Thurles where a young man named Theobald Mathew, later to become famous as the Apostle of Temperance, rescued him from a fight and they became firm friends. From Thurles he went on down the Suir Valley to Carrick, where he stopped wandering and opened up a shop, but the following year, in 1807, he moved his business to Waterford. Cards which he handed out said: *"Charles Bianconi, Gilder and print-seller, Looking-glass and Picture-Frame Manufacturer, at Mr. Prendergast's opposite the Royal Oak, George Street, Waterford, informs all Ladies and Gentlemen that he executes all kinds of Gilding in oil and burnished gold, equal to any other person in this country, and on moderate terms . . ."* In Waterford he made friends with Edmund Rice, who persuaded him to go back to his studies. He worked hard both at his books and at his trade. In 1809 he decided to move again, this time to Clonmel, where he first took small premises in Dublin Street, and then a much better shop opposite the Main Guard. The people of Clonmel called him Brian Cooney (which is how the Italian name sounded to them) and made him welcome. His business prospered and he made many friends, including Daniel O'Connell, whom he met on one of his trips to Dublin. He had several people working for him, and his corner shop, which sometimes would have a new picture by Edward Hayes (who lodged with him) hanging in the window, nearly always had a crowd around it.

He bought a yellow gig to travel around in, but he was thinking a lot about the very poor state of transport and communication in the country as a whole. Most people had to walk wherever they wanted to go, as very few could afford the stage coaches. There were some boats on rivers and canals, but these were very slow. The roads were very bad and what are now our trunk routes were little more than tracks. Bianconi wondered if anything could be done about this situation. Then in 1814 the Napoleonic wars in Europe ceased, at least for a time, and the price of horses (which all armies used then) began to go down. Bianconi saw his chance, and after Napoleon had finally been defeated at Waterloo, he bought a horse for £10 and a jaunting car. On July 6th, 1815, the first Bianconi car ran from Clonmel to Cahir and back at an average speed of $7\frac{1}{2}$ miles an hour. It carried six passengers at a fare of 2d. a mile.

People were suspicious at first, and preferred to walk and save their money. But gradually the idea caught on, and by the end of the year the route had been extended to Limerick, Cashel and Thurles, and in 1816 Bianconi's cars were covering 226 miles a day. They were soon given the nickname "Bians," and this is what everybody called them after that. Further and further they went, linking towns and villages which had never known any kind of public transport before, employing more and more people as drivers, guards, agents, stable hands and suppliers of the 15 pounds of oats and the 16 pounds of hay that each horse ate each day. Bianconi was a very good businessman, keeping a careful record of everything that was spent and received, and making sure that everybody who worked for him was absolutely honest. He started building his own cars in workshops which he set up specially in Clonmel. They were beautifully turned out in yellow and crimson, with silver plated harness. The names of the towns on the route were shown on the back. By the year 1825 the Bians were covering 1,170 miles every day—as far as Cork, Kilkenny, Wexford, and Portumna. In 1826 Bianconi helped one of Daniel O'Connell's supporters to win an election by

lending him some of the cars, and soon afterwards he joined the Order of Liberators. He moved from the corner shop to new premises near his coaching head-quarters in Dublin Street. In 1827 he married Eliza Hayes (who was no relation to his friend Edward Hayes) whom he had met on one of his trips to Dublin.

In August, 1831, Bianconi became a naturalised citizen, which meant amongst other things that he would now be able to buy land in Ireland. In 1832 his son Charles was born, and in 1833 he went to London to try to get the contract for carrying mails in Ireland (the Irish and British Post Offices had been joined together since 1830). He found that he still did not know enough English to be able to explain the design of his cars to the officials, so he wrote home to ask young Michael Angelo

Hayes, who was the son of his old friend Edward, and a promising artist, to send him some drawings. Later young Hayes did several fine drawings of Bians, and he also designed a symbol in the shape of a wheel which Bianconi put on all his offices and depots. The design of the Bians had changed since 1815; they were now mostly four-wheelers carrying 14 to 19 passengers and pulled by three or four horses. There was a special well or compartment for luggage. The two-wheelers were, however, still used on the shorter and less busy routes.

In 1833 Charles Bianconi bought a house, which he called Silver Spring, about a mile from Clonmel on the Waterford Road. The same year he paid his first visit to Italy since he had left it thirty years before as a boy of sixteen; his father had died and he had inherited some of his money. The year after that the first railway in Ireland, between Dublin and Kingstown, was built by William Dargan. Most people thought this meant the beginning of the end for the coaching business, but Bianconi could see that it would take the railways a long

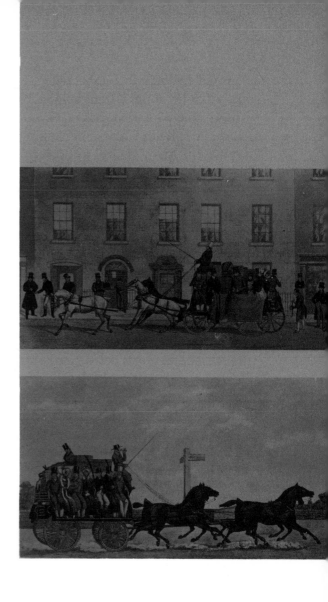

time to cover the country and that even then his cars
could provide "feeder" services in the way that buses do
now. He bought shares in the different lines and became
a director of the Waterford and Limerick Railway Co.
In 1835 Daniel O'Connell founded the National Bank
and Bianconi was made one of its directors. He had
proved himself a good businessman. His cars were still
doing very good business, and in 1836 were running a
daily mileage of 2,234. They had reached as far as Dublin,
where Bianconi established his headquarters in
Clondalkin. In 1843 he was asked to read a paper about
his transport system to the British Association for the
Advancement of Science. In 1844 he was elected mayor
of his adopted town of Clonmel and on the day he was
installed held a banquet in Hearn's Hotel (Hearn had
been working with him in the coaching business from
the beginning) at which 130 people from every political,
religious and social group were present. Bianconi, though
a devout Catholic, had many friends amongst the
Quakers and other Protestants of Clonmel, and was

respected by rich and poor alike.

In 1846 he bought Longfield, a big house that he had wanted since he first passed it as a boy many years before. A splendid mansion, it has recently been taken over by the Irish Georgian Society. During the Famine years of 1846–49 he gave many men and women work on the estate, and taught them how to enjoy macaroni when the potatoes failed! In 1851 he again went to Italy, hoping the change would help one of his daughters who was seriously ill. She died, however, in 1854, and Bianconi came back to Ireland again, where he bought the house at 86 St. Stephen's Green for the new Catholic University that was being founded by John Henry Newman. In 1857 he again spoke to the British Association at a meeting in Dublin at which Dr. Livingstone (the African explorer) and Lord Rosse were present, and told them that he still had over 900 horses and 67 cars, travelling 4,244 miles a day.

During his last years Charles Bianconi gradually sold off his interests in the coaching business, often to people who had worked for him, but in 1864 they still earned him a large income. He was made a Deputy Lieutenant for the County of Tipperary in 1863 and went on taking a keen interest in politics and in business until his death. He died at Longfield on Wednesday, September 22, 1875, and the story goes that phantom horses were heard galloping up the drive as he breathed his last.

Longfield

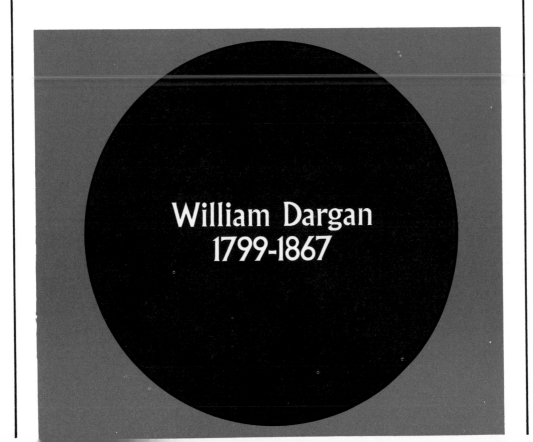

William Dargan
1799-1867

There is a small suburban street between Dun Laoghaire and Dalkey, in County Dublin, called *Atmospheric Road*. It has nothing to do with the atmosphere around us, and it was not named in this strange way because the surroundings were "atmospheric", or particularly attractive. It was called after the Atmospheric Railway that used to run from Kingstown, as Dun Laoghaire was then called, to Dalkey, and which opened on March 29, 1844. The railway worked by compressed air, but was not a success and was converted to steam power in 1855. The man behind this unusual venture, and the man who by 1853 had built more than 600 miles of Ireland's railway network, was William Dargan.

Dargan was born on February 28, 1799, in County Carlow. His father, who was a farmer, sent him to England to be educated, and he served his apprenticeship in a surveyor's office. His first big job, though it was in Britain, was closely connected with Ireland; he helped the famous engineer Thomas Telford build the Holyhead Road, which was designed to give a better transport service to Dublin by allowing the ships to dock in Holyhead harbour rather than at Parkgate near Chester, a port that was troubled by contrary winds. When this big project was finished (as important in its day as constructing a motor expressway would be today), Dargan came back to Ireland and worked as a private contractor on several schemes, including the road from Dublin to Howth harbour. Then he decided to go into

The Atmospheric Railway

the new-fangled railways that were creating such a stir in England. He found several important people to back his idea and on December 17th, 1838, the first train in Ireland left Westland Row Station, in Dublin. The six engines which had been built for the service each had four wheels, tall chimneys and no covering for the driver; and the passengers, at least in the second and third class, were not much more comfortable. But the line was a great success, and the Railway Age in Ireland had begun.

Dargan then turned his attention to Ulster. His Ulster railway, which opened on the 12th of August, 1839, was the first in Ireland to carry both passengers and goods, and it was planned to work closely with the Ulster canal —linking Lough Neagh and the Upper Lough Erne— which he also built between 1834 and 1842. Dargan planned things on a large scale; his trains brought passengers to Portadown where they transferred to his steamers on Lough Neagh to continue their journey. At Belfast itself he made two cuts in the sandbanks in the Lagan River, which opened the port up for large-scale navigation and created the famous Queen's Island—at first known as Dargan's Island—on which the huge shipbuilding works were later constructed. He became the contractor for the railway line to Carrickfergus and Ballymena, and the coastal line towards Bangor, which opened in 1848.

By this time railways were being built all over the country. Some were never finished, because the directors ran out of money, or because they were badly planned or built. William Dargan, however, went from strength to strength, not only acting as building contractor for the new line, but sometimes, as in the case of the Newry and Warrenpoint Railway, leasing it when it was completed, and running the traffic and collecting the profits himself. At this time successful railways made a great deal of money, for there was no real competition except sometimes from canals and other railways, so Dargan became a rich man. He was responsible for the Dublin and Drogheda railway (the beginnings of the Dublin-Belfast line), the Great Southern and Western, to Cork, and the Midland and Great Western, which served the west. He became almost a millionaire and was always known as a good employer, paying high wages and paying them on time, and looking after his workers. He was what we would call a tycoon, but he was a modest one who did not go about boasting of wealth. He was full of ideas—big ideas—and his whole excitement in life

A train leaving Westland Row Station, Dubli,
(now Pearse Station)

seems to have come from seeing his ideas become reality.

In 1851 there was a big international exhibition in London, a kind of World's Fair. William Dargan decided that what London could do, Dublin could do better. He formed a committee composed of the city's leading citizens and gave them £30,000 to spend on the arrangements. This was afterwards increased to £100,000—all out of Dargan's own pocket. The Crystal Palace exhibition in London had been devoted to "*The Arts and Industry*," but had shown very few good pictures. Dargan decided that his exhibition should have a really large section devoted to painting, and he sent the Secretary of his Committee, Sir Cusack Roney, to Europe to arrange for the loan of famous masterpieces. He also collected, from country houses in Ireland, many fine paintings which were later to hang in the new National Gallery.

On May 12th, 1853, the Exhibition was opened by the Viceroy in Merrion Square behind Leinster House (now Dáil Éireann), which was then the headquarters of the Royal Dublin Society. The exhibition building was 300 feet long and the main hall was 100 feet high. A Dublin firm built a huge organ specially for the occasion and there were cast iron fountains driven by a 40 h.p. steam engine. William Dargan must have been very pleased with the success of his idea, even though he lost £20,000 altogether. He had built himself a large house in what was then the countryside—Mount Anville, in Dundrum —and on August 29th, 1853, he and his wife were visited there by Queen Victoria, who had come over to Ireland for the Exhibition. The Queen offered to

The opening of The Exhibition

The Queen visits Dargan at Mount Anville

make William Dargan a Baron, but he refused the title, which rather upset his royal visitor. His idea of fame and success was not in honours but in enterprises—and he already had more ideas in his mind for new projects.

When he had first collected his pictures for the Exhibition he had thought only of how they would look in the big temporary building in Merrion Square, but he began now to see them as the start of a national collection. Such a collection needed a permanent home, and Dargan began to plan—and to pay for—a National Gallery. This was opened, again by the Viceroy, in 1864. A statue in front of the fine building in Merrion Square commemorates the man who was responsible for giving the nation a magnificent new home for its art treasures, but Dargan himself was so modest and retiring that he probably did not even attend the opening ceremony. He did, however, have his portrait painted by the Gallery's first director, George Mulvany.

In the years between the Exhibition and the opening of the Gallery, William Dargan had been investing his money and his ideas in several other enterprises. He tried to develop the growing of flax, and he established a number of mills in the Dublin area. Neither of these projects was successful however, and for the first time in his life he began to lose money. He was still interested in railways, and became Chairman of the Dublin-Kingstown line he had pioneered in 1831. His own private coach—a very splendid affair—can now be seen in the Belfast Transport Museum. Dargan had always

Dargan's statue outside the National Gallery

controlled all his affairs himself—he did not believe in employing secretaries and other helpers—so that when he fell from his horse in 1866 and was badly injured there was no one who could take control of his many business interests and save them from going from bad to worse. He had to sell his splendid mansion in Dundrum, but kept his town house, at 2 Fitzwilliam Square. It was here that he died on February 2nd, 1867. *"His affairs became disordered and his health and spirit were undermined,"* said a writer at the time. He was thought to be bankrupt, but even though his financial situation was not quite as bad as that, he had certainly lost a great deal of the fortune he had made and spent so generously. He was buried in Glasnevin in a tomb which, like his statue outside the National Gallery, carries the one word DARGAN.

Perhaps because William Dargan was a retiring, modest man, his work for his country has not been fully appreciated. He tried long before anyone else to industrialise Ireland, to make her able to rely on her own manufactures. He opened up the country both to business and to tourists, and he founded what has grown to be one of the finest art galleries in Europe.

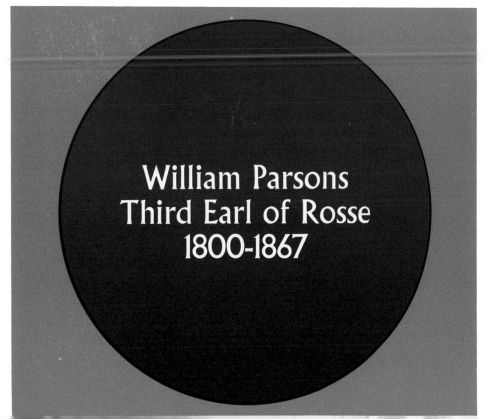

William Parsons
Third Earl of Rosse
1800-1867

The town of Birr, in County Offaly, used to be called Parsonstown. The Parsons family came to Birr at the end of the sixteenth century, and have been living there ever since. Many of them have been famous in different ways, but perhaps the cleverest of them all was William Parsons, who became the third Earl of Rosse. He was born in June, 1800, in York, where his parents were on a visit, but he spent nearly all his life in Birr, in the fine castle which is the family home. His father, Sir Laurence Parsons, as he was when his eldest son was born, was a member of the Irish Parliament, first of all representing Dublin University, but later elected for his own county of Offaly. In the year 1800 the Act of Union put an end to the Dublin Parliament, and Sir Laurence was so upset by this that he took no further part in politics, though many British politicians wanted him to take his seat at Westminster. He was still the member for Offaly, or King's County as it was called then, and when he became the Second Earl of Rosse he had a seat in the House of Lords, but he hardly ever bothered to attend and retired to Birr, where he spent his time replanning and rebuilding the town; he gave land from his estate for the building of both a Catholic church and a Protestant church.

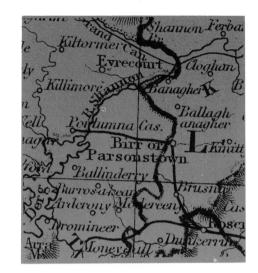

William had two brothers, John and Laurence, and two sisters Alicia and Jane. They were all taught at home by their parents, both of whom were very clever, and by special tutors, so that when William went to Trinity College, Dublin, in January, 1819, he was already well educated. His brother John went to Trinity with him, and they did so well that their father decided to send them to Magdalen College, Oxford. William graduated with first-class honours in mathematics in 1822, and at about the same time was elected M.P. for King's County, the seat formerly held by his father. He remained in Parliament until 1834, taking a particular interest in Catholic Emancipation. He had always been more interested in science than politics, however, and when he gave up his parliamentary seat he went back to Birr to continue with the experiments he had begun while still a student.

Nowadays, photographs of the stars and planets, taken through huge telescopes, are commonplace. There are maps of the moon and of galaxies millions of millions of miles out in space. In William Parsons' time, however, very little was known about such things because there were no telescopes sufficiently powerful to bring them *near* enough for detailed study. Viewed through a telescope, an object appears larger than to the naked eye, and this *magnification,* as it is called, is brought about in two different ways—either by refraction or by reflection. Refraction makes use of lenses, as in a toy telescope, or the kind sometimes found on a pier at the seaside. But the kind of telescope William Parsons was interested in was a reflecting telescope, which uses a mirror to help make the stars look nearer. The diagrams will help explain the difference.

Mirrors are made by silvering a piece of glass to make it reflect. This silvering process was not discovered until 1850, so that before then mirrors had to be made of something else: usually bright, shiny metal, very well polished. It is easy enough to take a small sheet of flat metal, such as tin, and make it shiny enough to reflect a face; but it is much more difficult to make the kind of mirror that is needed for an astronomical telescope. This has to be very large, the larger the better; and it has to be curved in a special way to reflect the light properly. This was the first problem William Parsons had to solve: how to make a really big mirror, or *speculum* as it is called when it is

The Great Telescope

used in a telescope, and to polish it really well. It was an engineering as well as astronomical problem, and he had no one in Birr to help him. He had to make his own tools, his own furnaces, and try out many ideas until he found the right one. He discovered that the best metal to use for the speculum was a mixture of four parts of copper to one of tin, and in 1839 he succeeded in producing one three feet in diameter.

In 1836 William had married a Yorkshire heiress, Mary Field, who greatly encouraged his scientific experiments. She was particularly interested in photography, which at that time was only beginning, and she became one of the first members of the Irish Photographic Society. It was she who—using her husband's forge for the purpose—arranged for the construction of the great cast-iron gates which can still be seen at the entrance to Birr Castle.

The three foot telescope was a great success, but William Parsons was far from satisfied with it. The speculum of this instrument was not solid but mounted on a framework, and he realised that he would have to make a solid one if he was to obtain the best results. He cast a solid three-foot speculum in 1840, and in 1843 produced a reflector six feet in diameter, which was more than half as big again as any other that had ever been made. Of course a mirror is only a part of a telescope, and such a big mirror needs a very solid structure to hold it up and move it into position. The Earl of Rosse, as he now was (he had inherited the title when his father died in 1841), built two solid stone walls 70 feet long and 50 feet high in the grounds of Birr Castle, between which there was a huge tube 58 feet long. At the bottom of this tube he placed the 6 foot reflector— and the biggest and most powerful telescope in the world was complete.

Birr Castle

The Great Telescope as it is today

People came from all over the world to see it, and to
observe the heavens through it, but though it was ready
for use in 1845 it was not until 1848 that regular
observations were made. This was because of the Great
Famine, which brought misery, starvation and ruin to so
many people in Ireland. Lord and Lady Rosse spent
nearly all their time and a great deal of their money
helping people around them who were starving, and
so the scientific work had to wait. When he was at last

able to get back to his great telescope, Lord Rosse spent most of his time studying misty-looking patches in the sky called *nebulae*. He discovered to his surprise that some of these patches were in fact spiral in shape, and spinning round and round like catherine wheels. It is now known that these nebulae are separate galaxies which contain millions and millions of suns and planets like our own. Lord Rosse did not understand exactly what he had discovered, but he was a very good artist as well as a scientist, and he was able to make drawings of everything he saw so that other scientists could take part in guessing the riddles of the heavens. When, many years later, astronomers were able to take photographs of what Rosse had seen, they discovered that his drawings were almost completely true to life—sometimes they were even better than the photographs!

Rosse became very famous because of his giant telescope. He was President of the Royal Society from 1848 to 1854, and Chancellor of the University of Dublin from 1862 until he died. He was made a member of the Imperial Academy of St. Petersburg in Russia in 1853 (St. Petersburg is now called Leningrad) and when he went to Paris in 1855 was made a Knight of the Legion of Honour by Napoleon III. He had been a member of the Royal Irish Academy since he was a young man. In spite of all these honours and distinctions, he was a kindly, simple man who seemed to get on as well with the workmen who built his big stone walls as with the famous professors who came to make use of his telescope.

The Third Earl was only sixty-five when his health began to break down, and though he moved to Monkstown, County Dublin, to enjoy the sea air, he died there on October 31st 1867. He is buried in the parish church at Birr, and a memorial there tells of a man who *"revealed to mankind by the unrivalled creation of his genius a wider vision of the glory of God."*

His son Laurence, who became just as interested in astronomy as Rosse himself, was born in Birr in 1840, went to Trinity, and after his father's death used the great telescope to study the moon; the last time it was pointed at the sky was in the year in which Laurence died, 1908.

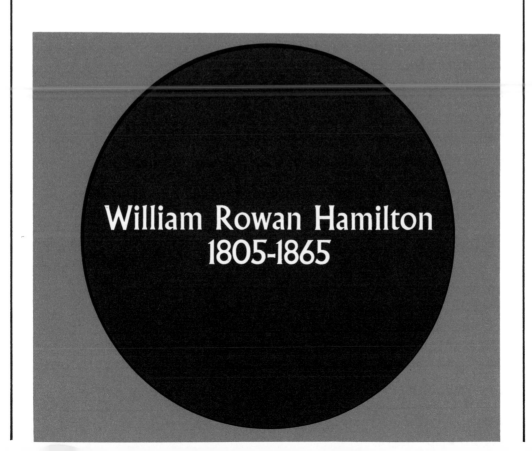

William Rowan Hamilton
1805-1865

A *quarternion* is defined as: *"The quotient of two vectors, or the operator which changes one vector into another, so called as depending on four geometrical elements, and capable of being expressed by the quadrinomial formula*

$$w + xi + yj + zk,$$

in which w, x, y, z are scalars and i, j, k are mutually perpendicular vectors whose squares are −1." Anyone who understands that must be very good at mathematics, but when Rowan Hamilton first discovered quaternions in 1843, there were many clever people who had no idea what he was talking about.

Rowan Hamilton was born at 29 Dominick Street, Dublin, on August 4th, 1805. His father was an attorney, and gave him the name Rowan after Hamilton Rowan, one of the leaders of 1798. When he was seven years old he knew nine languages, including Hebrew, and by the time he was thirteen he had mastered Persian, Arabic, Sanskrit, Hindustani and Malay. When a new ambassador from Persia arrived in Dublin, Rowan Hamilton wrote him a letter of welcome in perfect Persian. He was then only fourteen years old!

It was clear to everybody that this young boy was a genius, particularly when he started teaching himself mathematics by reading Euclid in Greek. Dr. Brinkley, who was the Astronomer Royal of Ireland at the time, said of him: *"This young man, I do not say will be, but is, the first mathematician of the age,"* and this was before Rowan Hamilton was twenty. He entered Trinity College, Dublin, in 1823, taking his B.A. in 1827, but while he was still a student, Dr. Brinkley, who was giving up his position at Dunsink Observatory, suggested that Rowan was the man to take his place. So at the age of twenty-two, in 1827, Rowan Hamilton became not only Astronomer Royal of Ireland but also Professor of Astronomy at Trinity—the two posts went together.

The Astronomer Royal naturally had to live at Dunsink Observatory, and in those days this was quite a journey from Dublin. Hamilton moved out to the country in 1827 and stayed there for the rest of his life, coming into Dublin only to give lectures in Trinity—about twelve a year—and to attend meetings of the Royal Irish Academy. It must have been a lonely life, particularly since he enjoyed company and spending an evening talking and drinking with friends, but he wrote letters to a great many people all over Europe discussing his mathematical and scientific ideas. He did have a

Here as he walked by
on the 16th of October 1843
Sir William Rowan Hamilton
in a flash of genius discovered
the fundamental formula for
quaternion multiplication
$$i^2 = j^2 = k^2 = ijk = -1$$
& cut it on a stone of this bridge

great deal of peace, moreover, to develop new theories. His son later wrote about what he was like at home: *"He used to carry on long trains of algebraical and arithmetical calculations in his mind, during which he was unconscious of the earthly necessity of eating; we used to bring in a snack and leave it in his study, but a brief nod of recognition of the intrusion of the chop or cutlet was often the only result, and his thoughts went soaring upwards."*

Rowan Hamilton was not a man who wanted to be famous, but he was very patriotic and thought that he could put Ireland "on the map" in the world of science. At this time mathematical studies were strong in Europe but very weak in Britain, and when Hamilton went over to a meeting of the British Association for the Advancement of Science in 1831, he stood out as one of the most important people there. He became one of the leaders of the mathematics and physics sections, and once said *"At the beginning of the century people read French mathematics, but by the end of it they will be reading Irish mathematics."* He was not far wrong.

Though Hamilton was one of the leading scientists of his day he had many other interests besides mathematics. As already stated he was extremely good at languages when he was young and kept up this interest throughout his life. He used to say that though he was a mathematician, he really wanted to be a poet, and he wrote some sonnets (14-line poems). He was a friend of the English poet William Wordsworth. He was also interested in religion and philosophy. Since he had much time to himself, he read many books on these and other subjects. One thing he was not very interested in was astronomy!—at least not the part of it that involves looking through telescopes and noting down the movements of the heavenly bodies.

The Four Courts in Hamilton's time

One day Rowan Hamilton was walking into the centre of Dublin with his wife. It was the 16th of October, 1843. They were passing one of the bridges on the canal —Broom Bridge—when he began to behave in a strange way. Passers-by suddenly saw him pull a penknife out of his pocket, dash over to the stone parapet of the bridge and start to carve something on it. Those who went up later to look at what he scratched saw a row of queer looking letters and numbers which they could not understand. This was not surprising because what he had carved on the canal bridge was the formula for quaternions, a problem he had been working on for many years. He had suddenly worked out this formula in his head and was so excited that he scratched it on the stone just like a schoolboy. That was the beginning of one of the most important discoveries in mathematics in the nineteenth century and one which is still important today.

What, then, *are* quaternions? Can the ordinary person understand what they are about? First of all, the name reminds us that Hamilton was equally at home with classics and languages as he was with mathematics.

Commemorative stamp

The word quaternion means *"four,"* and it is found both in the Bible and in the works of the poet John Milton. Hamilton used it to stand for a set of four numbers which could be used in several ways. We are used to thinking of three dimensions: length, breadth and height. This is adequate for a simple calculation such as finding the volume of a cube, but some years before Hamilton's theory, mathematicians had been trying to find some way of introducing another idea into geometry—motion. So instead of thinking of a line as having only a size, of being "frozen" like a photograph, they thought of it as having direction or movement. Then of course to think of movement is to think of time—the time it takes to make that movement. So we have the idea of time as the fourth dimension—an idea which Einstein took much further in his relativity theory. Rowan Hamilton wrote a poem about his idea of four dimensions in which he put it like this:

And how the One of Time, of Space the Three
Might in the chain of Symbol girded be.

Portrait of Hamilton

Quaternions, though they are hard to understand in theory, were very useful in practice. Not only were they used to solve problems in astronomy, engineering and electricity: they were also a great help to the builders of Irish railways in working out just how to design an awkward bridge or viaduct. One of Hamilton's friends, a Scottish mathematician called Tait, compared them to an elephant's trunk, *"ready at any moment to do anything, be it to pick up a crumb or a field gun, to strangle a tiger, or uproot a tree; portable in the extreme, applicable anywhere and adapting itself to work."* They are no longer much used in practice, however, having been superseded by tensor calculus.

After his great discovery Rowan Hamilton went on working at the theory of quaternions for the rest of his life. He thought that they held the clue to the whole of the physical universe, and could be used to explain all the difficult problems that were puzzling scientists. This was not so, and some people have felt it a pity that he spent so much time on this one discovery. He also made great advances in optics and in higher dynamics and it is on his discoveries in these sciences that his fame really

The Library, Trinity College

rests. Hamilton, however, was not out to prove himself the best mathematician in the world, even though he became President of the Royal Irish Academy in 1837 and was also made a Corresponding Member of the Academy of St. Petersburg. He was a true genius, but he found many things in life to enjoy and to interest him.

A transit circle in use at Dunsink in 1800

Saint Colmcille
521-597

[...] pro diebus quibus nos h[...]

annis quibus uidimus mala ÷

Et respice in seruos tuos et in opera tua 48

Et dirige filios eorum

Et sit splendor domini dei nostri super nos

÷ Et opera manuum nostrarum dirige super nos

Et opus manuum nostrarum dirige

XC

Qui habitat in adiutorio altissimi

in protectione dei caeli commorabitur

Dicet domino susceptor meus es tu

Et refugium meum deus meus sperabo in eum

quoniam ipse liberauit me de laqueo

uenantium et a uerbo aspero

In scapulis suis obumbrauit te

Et sub pinnis eius sperabis

Scuto circumdabit te ueritas eius

non timebis a timore nocturno

a sagitta uolante in die

a negotio perambulante in tenebris

ab incursu et demonio meridiano: cadent a latere tuo mille

et decem milia a dextris tuis

Sometime in the year 563 A.D. thirteen men set out in a currach—probably from the Inishowen peninsula in County Donegal—and sailed to Iona, a remote island off the Scottish coast. One of them looked back with great sadness because he believed that he would never see Ireland again. There is an ancient Irish poem in which he is said to have expressed his thoughts:

> There is a grey eye
> That will look back upon Erin.
> It shall never see again
> The men of Erin nor her women.
>
> I stretch my glance across the brine
> From the firm oaken planks:
> Many are the tears of my bright soft grey eye
> As I look back upon Erin.

The man was Colmcille, and he was going into exile with his twelve companions because he had been blamed by a synod of the Irish Church for starting a battle in which, so the story says, 3,000 men were killed. Some say that he was sent, as a penance, to convert 3,000 men to Christianity, others that he had set himself the penance of exile—it is very difficult to be certain about things that happened so long ago. But we do know that at the age of forty-two this big and sometimes bad-tempered priest landed on the Scottish island of Iona and founded a monastery which was to become famous as the place from which most of the Highlands of Scotland were converted to the new faith.

Colm (he was not called Colm of the Churches until later) was born on the 7th of December, 521, at Gartan in County Donegal, the son of Fedhlimidh who was of royal blood; through his mother Eithne he was related to the great Niall of the Nine Hostages, High King from 380 to 495. It seemed that he was likely to become a king himself, because kings were chosen from all descendants of the royal house, but he went to study with Saint Finnian at Clonard, where he learned Latin, history and poetry, and decided to devote his life to God. According to Adomnan, who wrote the story of Colmcille's life a hundred years or so later, he was *"devoted even from boyhood to the Christian novitiate and the study of philosophy. . . . he showed himself, though placed on earth, ready for the life in heaven, for he was angelic in aspect, refined in speech, holy in work, excellent in ability, great in counsel."* It is hard to

St. Colmcille's house at Kells.

believe everything that was written about Colmcille because many stories grew up around him long after he was dead, but the story of his ordination sounds as if it might be true. Saint Finnian decided to make Colmcille a bishop (which, in those days, was not as important an office as it is now) and sent him to a bishop nearby for consecration. For some reason a mistake was made and Colmcille came back ordained as a priest. He took this as a sign from God. He remained a simple priest all his life, though when he became Abbot of Iona he was really much more important than any bishop.

Monasteries in Ireland at this time were more like universities, and many subjects were studied there which had nothing to do with the religious life. Colmcille went from Clonard to Glasnevin, near Dublin, but the Abbot there, Saint Mobhí, died of yellow fever, and in the year 546 Colmcille returned north again and founded a church at Derry on a piece of land given to him by some of his relations. For the next few years he travelled all over Ireland. About 552, he founded Durrow, County Offaly, the most important of all his monasteries in Ireland. There are many churches which claim to have been

founded by the saint, but it is very difficult now to prove these claims. *"A hundred churches which the wave frequents is the number of churches he had on the margin of the sea,"* says Adomnan, but some of these may have been founded by his pupils. Certainly the most famous were Derry and Durrow; the English historian Bede, who was born about a hundred years later, had heard of Durrow and wrote about it.

The battle of Culdremhne, which was to make such an important change in Colmcille's life, took place in the year 561. The story goes that when he was staying with another Finnian, at Moville, he borrowed a copy of St. Jerome's Latin translation of the Bible—the only one in Ireland—and took it secretly to the library every evening to make a copy of it. Books in those days were very rare and beautiful, as can be seen by looking at the *Book of Kells* or any of the famous Irish manuscripts. Saint Finnian found Colmcille at work one night and told him that the copy belonged to him—he was claiming what

Page from the Book of Durrow.

would now be called in legal language *"copyright"*. Colmcille did not agree, and the two men asked the High King of Ireland, Diarmuid, to be the judge of who was right and who was wrong. The King's verdict has become very famous: *"To every cow her calf, to every book its copy,"* meaning that Finnian had won. This verdict made Colmcille furious, and he called on his relations, the O'Neills, to make war on the High King and avenge him. Another story says that Colmcille gave shelter to a political refugee whom the High King was trying to catch and then Diarmuid declared war on *him*. Whatever the truth of it, the battle of Culdremhne, near Ben Bulben in County Sligo, certainly took place, and so many were killed there that Colmcille was horrified by what happened and set out in his boat for Scotland and exile.

There had been an Irish colony called Dalriada, in Scotland for about fifty years and there were close connections between the Celtic people of the two countries. Recently this settlement had been attacked by the Picts, who then occupied most of the north of the country, and so Colmcille decided to found his monastery on an island, which would be harder to attack. He first built a church of wood and reeds (all the heavy timber had to be brought from the mainland), and several years passed before he felt he was ready to go out and begin his great work—the conversion of the Picts.

Not all the Scots at this time were attached to older beliefs, though how many were Christian is something still argued about. Saint Ninian, a Pict who had been trained in Rome, had converted some of them about two hundred years before Colmcille arrived, but there was still plenty of work for the Irishman to do. First he had to build his monastery on the island that a cousin of his, Conall, had given him. Then he and his followers had to plant corn, put up farm buildings, build their church, their huts, and a guest house for visitors from home. With only twelve of them working, all this took time. Then there was the religious work of the monastery —prayer and fasting, and copying manuscripts. No wonder it was several years before Colmcille set sail for the mainland to begin his great mission.

There are many wonderful stories told about this. Brude, the king of the Picts, lived in a palace at Inverness, surrounded by magicians who tried to use their magic powers to stop Colmcille from getting through the huge gates. But the saint made the sign of the cross, knocked, and the doors opened by themselves. Later the chief magician tried, with noise, to drown out the Mass which was being celebrated in front of the palace but Colmcille's voice sounded louder than thunder and a fanfare of trumpets put together, so that it could be heard for miles around. The king was converted and his people with him. Iona became the training college for young Scottish priests and its Abbot was primate of the whole Church in Scotland, which Colmcille organised in monasteries according to the Irish system. He was now a very important person, and when King Conall of Dalriada died, the same king who had granted him Iona, he was asked to crown his successor. There are many stories about him during his time in Scotland— about his kindness to animals, his miracles, and even one about his meeting with the Loch Ness monster! Yet all the time he was making long journeys to distant parts of Scotland and its islands, his thoughts were never very far away from Derry and all the places in Ireland he knew so well.

St. Martin's Cross, Iona.

In 575 Colmcille returned to Ireland for what we would now call a top-level conference which was summoned at Drumceat by the High King, to discuss whether the colony at Dalriada should still be governed from Ireland. Why did he go back when he had vowed never to return? This is impossible to answer, but it is said that he kept his eyes covered for the whole year he was in Ireland to avoid breaking his promise. It was a long conference, but at the end of it Colmcille went back to Iona with a promise of home rule for the Scottish colony, which after that did not have to pay taxes to the lords and kings in Ireland. When he was at home Colmcille went to visit his monastery at Durrow and several other places which he knew well, and is said to have performed miraculous cures on many sick people who came to see him at Drumceat where the conference was held.

Colmcille's last years were spent at Iona, continuing the work he had begun so well that he was now head of a large and growing Church in Scotland. He was a famous man. According to Adomnan he was known throughout Ireland and Britain and *"as far as three-cornered Spain, and Gaul, and Italy situated beyond the Pennine Alps, also the Roman city itself which is the chief of all cities."* In the summer of 597 he knew that he was near death and one of his monks helped him to the top of a little hill near the monastery so that he could give his last blessing. He sank down in front of the altar in the middle of his evening devotions on the night of June 8th. His was a peaceful death after a long and busy life.

St. Mary's Cathedral, Iona.

Saint Columbanus
543(?)-615

In the sixth century it used to take about a year to travel from Ireland to Rome. News travelled just as slowly, and it might take two years to get an answer to a letter on an important subject—on matters of Church organisation, for example. Rome, though the headquarters of the Catholic Church, had not very much control over Churches in other countries, which had grown up in their own ways. In Ireland especially there were big differences, not in the faith itself but in the way things were organised. The Irish celebrated Easter on a different day, preferred monasteries and abbots to bishops and dioceses, and used private instead of public confession. These differences were to cause St. Columbanus a great deal of trouble when he left Ireland for France to found monasteries and teach Christianity in his own way.

We know very little about his early days, because no one thought about writing down his place of birth, his parents, or even the exact year in which he was born. He was brought up somewhere in Leinster, and seems to have had a good education, so he was probably one of a noble family. We do know that when he decided to enter the monastic life he went to Bangor, which was then under the control of St. Comgall and one of the most important centres of learning in the whole country. He must have spent several years there, because it is not until the year 585 or 590 that we hear of him deciding to leave Ireland with twelve companions and travel to the Continent. He reached the north coast of what is now Brittany in the following year and set out for the court of King Childebert II of Burgundy.

France at this time was ruled by the Franks, who had invaded it from Germany, and was divided into several smaller kingdoms which spent most of their time fighting and quarrelling amongst themselves. Childebert ruled over most of what is now the eastern part of France, and his lands included what is now Switzerland. These kings and rulers had become Christian about a century before, but many of them had lapsed and the worship of the old Roman gods (though the Roman Empire was almost finished as a great power, its influence was still very strong) went on side by side with the new faith. The person who held the real power in Burgundy was Brunhild, King Childebert's mother, and though the King welcomed Columbanus, she was to cause the Irish monk and his followers serious trouble later on.

An Irish ecclesiastic

At first everything went well. Columbanus stayed for some time at the court and then went out into the mountains, to the part of the kingdom called Neustria, taking with him many local men who had heard his preaching and wanted to become his followers. He founded his first monastery at a place called Anegrates, now called Anegray, in the Vosges mountains in Alsace, a very wild part of the country in which wolves and bears still roamed. There was a castle there which had been built by the Romans long ago, and he used the stones from this to build his monastery. Soon, however, he had to move on, not that there was anything wrong with the

Irish monk holding book

site except that it had grown too small for the huge
numbers of followers which kept arriving to join them.
The monks moved eight miles to Luxeuil, which had
once been a Roman spa. Some of the buildings could
still be used to house the 600 people whom Columbanus
was now leading, but there was very little food and they
were surrounded by hostile tribes, the Suevians, who
stole from the fields the crops they were trying to grow.
Life was hard, and it was made even harder by the very
strict rules which the community had to obey. The
smallest punishment for breaking them was the recital of
three psalms, but for more serious offences there was
beating with a leather strap, fasting on bread and water,
and expulsion. On the other hand the Irish came to be
respected throughout the kingdom for their honesty,
their devotion to the spiritual life, and their hard work.
The monks toiled all day for very little food but they

Pages from a manuscript in the library of St. Gall

seemed to be quite happy. All things were shared amongst them and all work divided up between them. Columbanus seems to have been a very striking man indeed: stern and unbending, sometimes bad-tempered, full of enthusiasm for religion, proud of being Irish and of the devotion of his country to Christianity. He criticised adversely the behaviour of the King and his Court and was never afraid to speak out about what he thought was an unChristian way of life. And, of course, this kind of plain speaking did not make him popular with everybody.

His views about the date of Easter and the other ways in which the Irish Church was different from the Church of the Continent made the local bishops angry with him. Many of these were men who had been appointed for political rather than religious reasons. It is hard for us now to understand why people could lose their tempers over something like the date on which Easter should be held, but this is what happened, and Columbanus was at last driven to write a rather angry letter to Pope Gregory in or about the year 600. In this letter he not only argues that he is right about the Easter date, but asks the Pope many more questions about things that are bothering him. The Pope, who could see himself becoming involved in a long argument, did not reply. He knew the Irish monks were doing good work, but he could not support them without annoying the native clergy. So he put Columbanus under the protection of the Abbot of the monastery at Lérins, and probably hoped that he would have no more trouble from the awkward Irishman who could boast: *"We Irish, living at the edge of the world, followers of Saints Peter and Paul—there has never been a heretic or a schismatic among us."*

King Childebert died in 595, and his kingdom was divided between his two sons—Theudebert II, who ruled the part called Austrasia, and Theodorik II, who was king over Burgundy. Theudebert, who was only twenty when he came to the throne, respected Columbanus and his monks as much as his father had done and visited him at Luxeuil. But Brunhild, the King's grandmother, who was now living at his court, did not like the power that the Irishman seemed to possess over her grandson, or the way in which he criticised the court. She persuaded the local bishops, who were jealous of Columbanus, to take sides against him, and in the year 612 soldiers arrived at the monastery to turn the monks out. They said that only the Irish must go—that they must go back to their own country. So the small group of old men—Columbanus was now nearly seventy— sadly set off on the long journey, crossing France until they reached the river Loire and then travelling down that long waterway towards Nantes. There is a rowing chorus which is thought to be by Columbanus, though it probably was written for a later journey up the Rhine:

> The tempests howl, the storms dismay,
> But skill and strength can win the day.
> **Heave, lads, and let the echoes ring!**

When he reached Nantes and was waiting for a boat to take him to Ireland, he wrote to the monks he had left behind him at Luxeuil: *"Now as I write a messenger has reached me, saying that the ship is ready for me, in which I shall be borne unwilling to my country; but if I escape, there is no guard to prevent it; for they seem to desire this, that I should escape."* He did, in fact, escape. The ship was blown

back to land—some said by a miracle—and Columbanus and his friends were free to go, not back to Burgundy, but to the court of Lothair II, King of Neustria. From there he decided to try to reach Rome and see the Eternal City before he died.

It was a hard journey. The little band reached Switzerland and decided to stay there, but again Brunhild made this impossible and they had to move on over the Alps. One old Irish monk, Gall, who had been with Columbanus since his days in Bangor, felt too weak to make the journey. Columbanus, who could not understand weakness, was furious, but Gall stayed in Switzerland, recovered from his sickness, and built a monastery which is still there in the town of St. Gall, together with a library containing some beautiful Irish illuminated manuscripts.

Columbanus and his followers pressed on over the Alpine passes and at last arrived on the plains of Lombardy. The Lombards at this time were Christians but followers of the Arian heresy, which meant that they disagreed with the Church's teaching on the Trinity. Their King Agilulf welcomed the Irish to his capital near Milan, because he had heard about their teachings. Columbanus set about trying to heal the breach between the Arians and the Catholics. Forty miles from Pavia, the capital, the old monks set about building yet another monastery, with money sent by King Lothair of Neustria. This was at a place called Bobbio, where St. Peter is said to have founded a church. The monastery grew and grew, attracting many to join it, as Luxeuil had done, and Columbanus helped to build the extensions with his own hands. He continued preaching in his fiery and furious manner, trying to heal the differences between Arians and Catholics, and amongst the Catholics themselves. The King was an Arian, but his wife was a Catholic, and Columbanus was allowed to continue his preaching in peace. Even though he was a long way from home, the Abbot still kept in touch with Ireland, and two manuscripts from Bangor found their way out to Bobbio, probably soon after it was opened.

On November 23rd, 615, Columbanus died. He left poems and other writings in Latin, and a tradition of Irish Christianity and scholarship on the Continent which was to grow into full flower in the centuries ahead. His disciples founded monasteries all over Europe, bringing light and learning to many people. Whilst the Continental clergy and bishops were fighting over the kingdoms of earth, he spoke and taught of nothing but the kingdom of heaven. Robert Schuman, who in our own time tried to bring the peoples of Europe together, called Columbanus *"The patron saint of those who seek to construct a united Europe."*

The tomb of St. Columbanus

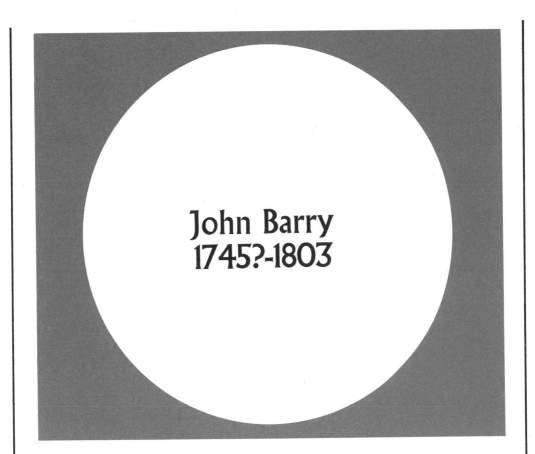

John Barry
1745?-1803

Tacumshane windmill

Irishmen have played an important part in the early history of several of the navies of the world: Argentina, Chile, Ecuador, Russia, Venezuela and the United States of America. Since the invention of aeroplanes, naval fleets have not been as important as they were in the past, but in the eighteenth and nineteenth centuries every large country, and many small ones, needed men-of-war to protect their trading vessels from the attacks of enemies and the many pirate craft that roamed the seas.

America's navy is as old as that country itself, for the first fleet of eight ships was formed in the same year as the Declaration of Independence, 1776. Until then, much of North America, so far as it was settled by white men, had been a colony of Great Britain. The American navy was formed to help the colonists in their struggle against King George III and his Government, and one of the men who was in the thick of the fray and fought many famous battles was John Barry, from Tacumshane, County Wexford. We do not know much about his parents or his family, for like many young, adventurous lads of his time he went to sea at an early age as a cabin boy, and almost lost touch with his native country. Both his parents were dead by 1785, but by that time John Barry had been fifteen years in America, where he made the city of Philadelphia his home.

He rose steadily in his profession, and in 1760 was given his first command, a schooner trading from his home port to the West Indies, a route on which he sailed for eight years. He was then made commander of the *Black Prince,* a 200-ton ship, but he had made only two voyages, to Great Britain and back, before she was taken over by what was then known as the Continental Navy (the navy of the American colonists) and given a new name, the *Alfred.* This was in November, 1775, about six

George Washington and Governor Clinton of New York

months after the first shots had been fired in what was to be known as the Revolutionary War, in which George Washington, Thomas Jefferson, John Adams and other brave and determined men became the founders of a new nation that was to grow into the richest power in the world.

It was a very complicated war, at least in the beginning, because at first all that the colonists wanted was freedom to run their own affairs while still remaining subjects of the English king. The British Government, however, tried to impose *"taxation without representation"* and made one foolish mistake after another which drove even the most loyal and law-abiding colonists further and further towards a desire for independence. The British made the same blunders that they made over and over again in Ireland, both before and after this date, and the American Parliaments (there were several in different areas or states) thought of themselves rather in the way the Irish Parliament did at the time: they would have been quite happy to recognise the King if they had been left alone to govern their country in their own way.

So, when John Barry's ship was taken over, he did not have to wait long for another, because he was asked to help in getting the first ships of the Continental Navy ready to sail out and fight. In March, 1776, he was commissioned Captain and put in command of the *Lexington*, a brig armed with sixteen 4-pounder guns, which sailed under a flag of thirteen stripes with a Union Jack in the corner. The *Lexington* was a small ship, but in April it captured the British ship *Edward* and sent her as a prize to Philadelphia, the first capture by a properly commissioned ship of the new American navy. John Barry at once became a national hero, and in June of the same year was named as captain of one of the four frigates which the Government planned to build. She was to be called the *Effingham* and mount twenty-eight guns, but before she could be completed the British captured Philadelphia and discovered the half-finished vessel (which had been moved up the river) and burned her. Captain Barry was very angry and complained to

The British fleet leave New York 1783

'The Alliance' in action (right)

Congress that a bad mistake had been made. He was a good seaman, but he seems to have had a very hot temper.

In 1777 John Barry married for the second time, his first wife, whom he had married in 1767, having died. The second Mrs. Barry was Sarah Austin, a member of a wealthy family, but all her property was seized by the American Government because her brother had declared himself pro-British, and Captain Barry went to a lot of trouble to try to get it back. He was now without a ship again, but made himself useful bringing some small boats across the Delaware River, past the occupied city, and joining up with an American brigadier who was carrying on guerilla warfare against the British. He then captured an armed schooner and two other ships that were unsuspectingly making their way up the river, and from the cargo they were carrying he sent a present of some oysters and pickled onions to General Washington, who thanked him very politely. Then in May, 1778, the Wexfordman was given the command of the *Raleigh*, a thirty-two gun frigate. The ship was not ready for sea until the 25th of September, and then ran into trouble

357

almost at once from two British ships, which disabled her and forced Barry to run ashore, where the *Raleigh* was captured and towed away by the enemy. Barry and most of his crew escaped, but the loss of his ship meant the end of his sea-going career for a time, since the navy had no other vessel to give him. In January, 1779, he asked Congress for permission to sail on another trading voyage to the West Indies, since he had back pay owing to him and needed some money. He made two trips, on one of which he captured a British sloop, so he was thinking of taking to privateering or raiding enemy supply vessels, when he was offered the command of a large ship which was being built. He was unlucky, however, because the Government had no money to finish her, or to pay her future captain! John Barry had to sail for the West Indies again, and when he returned he was given a new command at last: the thirty-two gun frigate *Alliance*,

George III

John Paul Jones

358

La Fayette (left) meets Washington

which had been one of a squadron led by John Paul Jones, the great naval hero of the Revolution. Before this he presided at the court-martial of Pierre Landais, a Frenchman who had been in command of the *Alliance* but had turned traitor.

The Americans were, at this time, being helped by the French in their struggle against Britain, and now John Barry found himself making long voyages to Europe on important missions. He sailed on February 11th, 1781, with one of George Washington's officers on board, and after a mutiny and a couple of sea fights he reached France safely, delivered his important passenger, and started out again for home, again having to deal with a mutiny. On May 27th he sighted two British ships, the *Atlanta* and the *Trepassey*, and, after a very hard battle in which Barry was wounded, his ship, the *Alliance*, forced them to surrender. The American Congress congratulated him on his voyage when he reached Boston on June 6th. His next important passenger was the Marquis de La Fayette, whose full name was Paul Yves Gilbert du Motier, and who had served with distinction in Washington's armies, being present at the siege of

Yorktown and the British surrender on October 19th, 1781. On Christmas Day in that year he left Boston for France on the *Alliance,* and since Captain Barry had such an important passenger he did not look for enemy ships but sailed as fast as possible and landed the Marquis at l'Orient on January 17th, 1782.

The war was drawing to a close, and John Barry returned from a voyage to the West Indies, during which he fought a battle with the British frigate *Sybill,* to discover that his adopted country was once more at peace. This meant the end of his eight-year naval service, because the new Republic was not in favour of keeping up military strength and soon sold their ships of war. John Barry turned to politics, taking an interest in the future of the many ex-servicemen and war veterans and supporting Washington who was trying to create a strong central government. Then he was given command of a ship which was setting off on a trade mission to China. In 1791 he was again called to the colours, this time to take action against pirates from Algeria who were crippling American sea trade. After a great deal of delay, it was decided to build three ships, and in his Eighth Annual Address to Congress on December 12th, 1798, President Washington spoke of how important it was to build up a navy for use both in peace and in war. On February 22nd, 1797, John Barry was commissioned *"Captain of the Navy of the United States and Commander of the frigate called* The United States, *to take rank from the fourth day of June, one thousand seven hundred and ninety-four."* He sailed for the West Indies in July, 1798, and his last years were spent in this service and in organising the new American navy, of which he was the first Captain. This was the highest rank granted at the time, though Barry was often known by the courtesy title of Commodore.

John Barry, who in his later life had suffered badly from asthma, died on September 13th, 1803, and was buried in the graveyard of St. Mary's Church in Philadelphia. He was a big man, a good-looking man, a natural leader and a fine seaman. Though he had little or no education he could hold his own with people like Washington and La Fayette in conversation and good manners, and in 1956 the American Government, to show how proud they were of him, erected the monument to him that stands today in Wexford town.

Commemorative stamp

William Brown
1777-1857

There are many stories of Irish brigades fighting with foreign armies but from the time of Brian Boru to the present day, no fleet of ships has sailed under the Irish colours. The many Irishmen who felt the call of the sea had to serve in foreign ships and under foreign flags, but this did not prevent them winning fame for both themselves and their country. One of the finest sailors ever to come out of Ireland was Admiral William Brown, who was born in Foxford, County Mayo, on June 23rd, 1777.

William Brown emigrated to America with his family in 1786, and when his father died shortly after this, he was left without anything to live on. He signed on as a cabin boy on a merchant ship and learned his seamanship the hard way, because in 1796 he was press-ganged into the British navy. At this time most of the recruiting for the navy was done in this way—young men were captured when wandering around a port and found themselves on board a man-of-war as part of the crew. William Brown served in the navy for several years; he must have been a good seaman, because soon after he

left he was given command of an English merchant ship. He was therefore a fully-qualified sea captain when he reached Buenos Aires with his family in 1812, intending to settle down there.

He found himself at the beginning of the great struggle for independence between Spain and her colonies in South America. Irish people had been emigrating to these colonies for some years, and many more were to follow during the time of the Great Famine, so that Irish names appear many times in the history of these countries at this period, and particularly in the story of the fight for freedom. In the year 1776 the Spaniards set up a separate Viceroyalty (a governor representing the King of Spain) in Buenos Aires, which was the most important town on the eastern side of South America, with control over what are now Uruguay, Paraguay and Bolivia, as well as Argentina. The Spaniards tried to stop all trade between their American colonies and anyone else except themselves, but the people of Buenos Aires imported books which described the French

Revolution, the American War of Independence, and
other struggles for independence throughout the world.
Then in 1806, during the wars between England and
Spain, a British force invaded Buenos Aires and occupied
it, though they were forced to surrender after a month.
They tried again in 1808 and again the citizens fought
them off, though they could get no help from Spain
and had to rely on their own efforts. Shortly after this
Napoleon in Europe overthrew the Spanish monarchy,
deposing Ferdinand VII and putting Joseph Bonaparte
on the throne, and this gave the people of Buenos
Aires the chance they were waiting for. On July 19th,
1809, a new Viceroy, Cisneros, was appointed to rule
in the name of Ferdinand. Having opened the trade of
the country to foreign nations, on the 25th of May,
1810, he agreed to a council being formed with the
title of the Provisional Government of the Provinces of
the Rio de la Plata. He retired to Montevideo, across the
river in what is now Uruguay, and continued to support
Spain by blockading Buenos Aires and by stopping the
bringing in of supplies by sea.

Top: Decoration awarded to Brown following the Battle of Juncal 1827

Bottom: Medal struck in the Argentine 1919

This was the situation when William Brown reached Buenos Aires. The revolutionary leaders soon discovered how good a seaman he was, and after their first flotilla of ships had been defeated by the Spaniards in 1811, they were not long in calling upon him to build up another one and to take command of the navy of the United Provinces. He was appointed on March 1st, 1814, with the rather strange rank of Naval Lieutenant-Colonel. A committee had been formed to work out the best way to build up the navy, but it had not the support of all the revolutionaries, some of whom thought it would be better to strengthen the army. Amongst these was the famous Liberator, San Martin, who was at this time helping the Chileans in their fight for independence. It was largely due to the military governor of Buenos Aires, General Alvear, that William Brown was allowed to go ahead with his assignment. He was helped by a Captain Baxter, who was also probably from Ireland, and together they collected a force of two corvettes, three brigs, a brigantine, a schooner and some smaller vessels, all of them merchant ships which had been armed and turned into warships. By March 8th he had three ships ready: his flagship *Hercules*, the *Nancy*, and the *Céfiro*, which was to be put under the command of another Irishman, John Santiago King.

The Spaniards at this time had a base at the island of Martin Garcia which they supplied from Montevideo. When Brown set out with his small flotilla he found a convoy on its way there, and decided to attack it. He waited until he was joined by some more of his ships from Buenos Aires, and then attacked the enemy, which was still much stronger than he was, and had anchored near Martin Garcia under the protection of a shore battery. William Brown sailed into the attack, but his quartermaster on the *Hercules* was killed and the flagship went aground. The ship continued firing, however, until nightfall, and during the hours of darkness Brown succeeded in getting *Hercules* afloat again and visited every vessel in his flotilla to plan a landing on the island in the early morning. The crews went ashore at 4 a.m., captured the Spanish battery and turned it on the Spanish ships. The Spaniards were very lucky; a favourable wind blew them clear of the guns and up the river to Uruguay, but Brown captured a supply vessel which he sent back to Buenos Aires with the request that another ship, the *Belfast*, be sent out to help him. He also annoyed a number of people in the town by asking rather rudely for more supplies of clothes, shoes and other things for his crews.

A model of Hercules *Brown's flagship at Martin Garcia and Montevideo 1814*

Leaving a few ships to watch the Spanish fleet which had been forced up the river, Brown sailed down again to Montevideo, which held the main Spanish forces, and blockaded it, so that they were forced to come out and fight to keep their supply lines open. Their ships, commanded by Captain Sierra, numbered 13, as against Brown's force of only 8, but the Mayo man lured them out into deep water where by brilliant seamanship and tactics he broke their line and captured three vessels. This was on the night of May 16th, 1814. The next morning he forced three more ships ashore. The power of Spain was broken, and a few months later the patriot forces under General Alvear captured Montevideo, seizing eighteen warships and more than 80 merchant ships. The military stores which were captured helped San Martin to equip his army across the Andes and to win the struggle for independence in Chile.

After the victory of Montevideo the fleet was disbanded, so William Brown set off in the *Hercules* to round Cape Horn and attack the Spanish outposts on the Pacific coast of South America. He blockaded the port

The Press Gang

San Martin

of Callao and captured a Spanish frigate which he renamed *La Argentina*. He still held the rank of Naval Colonel, though when he returned to Buenos Aires about three years later he found that there was nothing left for him to command. He therefore retired from the sea and it looked as if his active days were over, until December, 1825, when Brazil declared war on the United Provinces, who now found themselves completely without a navy. William Brown was once more called upon and on January 13th, 1826, he hoisted his flag as Admiral in the brigantine *Balcarce*. Though outnumbered by the enemy he immediately began a series of battles which led to the victory of Juncal, in which the Brazilian blockade of Buenos Aires was broken. News of this victory reached Buenos Aires on February 10th, 1827, and on March 2nd William Brown was awarded 20,000 pesos out of the public funds *"as a gift which might perpetuate the gains of his merit."* On the 9th of April he was in action again, and this time was badly wounded.

The war against Brazil was followed by a civil war in the United Provinces, and for five months in 1828

Admiral Brown served as Delegate Governor of Buenos Aires. In his first speech as Governor he said, *"He who has the honour of presiding over you will know how to respect your rights and guard the glory and renown of the great Argentine people."* When he heard of the appointment San Martin said: *"I have not the honour of knowing him, but as a son of the country he will merit from her an everlasting recognition for the distinguished services he has given her."*

In the years 1842–45 Admiral Brown was again in command of the Buenos Aires fleet in another outbreak of civil war, but after that he retired to a small property near the city and took no further part in political affairs. He died on May 3rd, 1857, and a decree which was immediately issued by the Governor of Buenos Aires paid tribute to the name of the man who had been described as *"the living monument of our naval glories."* Everyone who knew him spoke of his generous heart and his deep political wisdom, as well as his courage and very great skill as a seaman and commander.

Bernardo O'Higgins
1778-1842

Chile is a long, thin country on the west coast of South America. Until the opening of the Panama Canal in 1914 the only way to get to it from Ireland was around the stormy Cape Horn, or across South America from Buenos Aires. In spite of this there were a great many Irishmen in Chile when she set out to win her independence from Spain, in 1810, by establishing her own Parliament. And the man who led them in all the important battles which finally succeeded in making Chile an independent republic was Bernardo O'Higgins.

The Spaniards had, of course, been ruling most of South America for more than two centuries, and Bernardo's father, Don Ambrosio, was a Spanish government official who reached the rank of Viceroy of Peru, which meant that he was Spain's most important man on the whole continent. In spite of his very Spanish-sounding Christian name, Don Ambrosio was born in either County Sligo or County Meath—nobody is really certain. He may have been born in Ballinarry, County Sligo, and brought up in Summerhill, County Meath: certainly in later years when he was asked by the Spanish Government to choose a title of nobility he decided to call himself Baron Vallenar (as Ballinarry is spelled in Spanish), and he even wrote to Ireland to get a document saying that he was descended from Sean Dubh O'Higgins, an ancient nobleman. His son Bernardo was born in the small Chilean town of Chillan (pronounced *cheel-yan*) and was sent to school first of all in Peru, which was the headquarters of the Spanish Government in South America, and later on in Spain and England. In Europe he met many men, some of them Irishmen, who were planning to fight for the independence of Chile, and when he got home again in 1802 after some exciting adventures, he quickly joined the revolutionary movement.

His father had died while Bernardo was away, and so he was able to go and live on a very large estate farm called *Las Canteras* which the Viceroy had left him in his will. Don Ambrosio, though he worked in the service of Spain, never forgot that he was an Irishman and was also very fond of the country of Chile where he had settled down. He hoped to persuade Irish emigrants to come to Chile instead of North America, and his son Bernardo wanted to do this also. Ambrosio did many things to improve the country—building roads and towns —and even the Chileans who wanted to get rid of Spanish rule and run their own affairs admired him. Bernardo always admired his father, too, even though he

on Ambrosio O'Higgins

did not agree with his political ideas, and he thought of himself as both a Chilean and an Irishman.

When he went back to Chile, Bernardo O'Higgins had not had much practice at being a soldier, but after only three years he was commander-in-chief of the army the Chileans had gathered to fight the Spaniards! At first the fighting did not go very well; the Chileans had not enough guns and food, and they were always arguing about who should run things, so that in 1814 they were beaten by the Royalist Troops (as the Spanish were called) at the battle of Rancagua, and forced to retreat to Mendoza. The Andes here are over 12,000 feet high, so they had quite a march! Most of the army's food and guns were carried on mules, and these poor animals would very often slip and fall over precipices because there was no proper road, only a rough track.

The Chileans remained based at Mendoza for three years and joined with an Argentinian general called San

Martin, who had led his own country to independence. O'Higgins and San Martin gradually got together a very big army which they called the Army of the Andes, and in 1816 they set off across the mountains again to try to beat the Spaniards in Chile. This time they had nine thousand mules. They managed to take the Spaniards by surprise, and chased them out of the whole of the north of Chile so that when San Martin and O'Higgins reached the capital, Santiago, they were welcomed as heroes.

On the 15th of February, 1817, the most important

citizens were called together to elect a new head of state or President. Most of the people wanted the Commander-in-Chief of the Army of the Andes, who was San Martin. But he was an Argentinian, and did not think it was a good idea that he should rule someone else's country, so everyone quickly chose Bernardo O'Higgins, who was appointed Supreme Director and began to try to make the new Republic into a rich and peaceful country. The Royalists were not finished, though; in the south they had made friends with the Araucanians who used to live there long before the Spaniards ever arrived. At the battle of Cancha Rayada, O'Higgins was badly wounded in the arm, and the Patriots, as the Republicans were called, had to retreat. But soon after that the battle of Maipo put paid to the Royalist armies once and for all.

From 1817 until 1823 Bernardo O'Higgins was Director of Chile. He himself preferred the soldier's life, and he never really enjoyed all the professional political squabbles that went on around him. There were other men in Chile who thought that they should be leading the country, and O'Higgins had many enemies who thought of him as a foreigner (perhaps because he could

Avenida O'Higgins

speak English as well as he could Spanish) and who wanted him to resign. Some people felt he was too much of a dictator, keeping all the power for himself and running the country on his own. But all Bernardo O'Higgins really wanted for Chile was to see her becoming a real nation with enough food and work for all her citizens. He also wanted to help rid Peru of the Spaniards, because as long as they were there in South America, they could send another army south to attack Chile. So O'Higgins set about building up a Chilean navy, and found a very good English sailor, Admiral Cochrane, to command it. The admiral's flagship was named the *O'Higgins* and in 1821 it headed a large fleet which took the Chilean Expeditionary Force northwards to try to end Spanish rule in Peru. The commander of the expedition was again General San Martin.

Things did not go very well, however, and the people at home began to blame O'Higgins. In January, 1823, a meeting of the chief citizens of Santiago called on him to resign, but he said that unless he could hand over his office to someone who had been properly elected by the whole country, he would not do so. It was a very noisy meeting, and at last three men were elected to make plans for a national assembly. O'Higgins took off his sash of office, and put it down on the table. *"Now I am a simple citizen,"* he said. *"Now you may speak freely. Let my accusers make themselves known! I want to know the evils I have caused, and the tears I have made to flow! Wreak upon me what vengeance you will, I will not resist! Here is my breast!"* And tearing his coat he bared himself before them all.

At that the whole assembly cried out, *"We have nothing against General O'Higgins! Long live O'Higgins!"* And Bernardo was once more the hero of the great battles that had won them their independence.

O'Higgins still had many enemies, even though he had retired with honour from the post of Director, and because of them he had to spend the last years of his life in exile in Peru, which had been liberated from the Spaniards by the great patriot Simon Bolivar, after whom Bolivia is named. When he left Chile, Bernardo was making plans to come to Ireland to see his distant relatives; perhaps if he had arrived then, he would have taken up arms again in the cause of liberty. But he changed his mind, probably because he wanted to stay as near to his friends in Chile as possible, and perhaps because he hoped that the Chileans would ask him back to lead them once again, or at least help them in the running of the country. After O'Higgins left, however, things went from bad to worse in Chile, with civil wars, bandits and robbers terrorising the countryside, and all the leaders fighting among themselves. O'Higgins decided to take no more part in Chilean politics, but he was on his way back in 1842 when he had a heart attack and knew that he would never see his beloved country again. He died on October 23rd, 1842, and is now buried under a monument in Santiago which records the great things he did for Chile.

Bernardo O'Higgins was a brave soldier, a great leader, and a patriot who was always proud of his Irish blood. He fought for the freedom of a small nation and for justice for all its citizens. The main street in Santiago is called Avenida O'Higgins and he—and his father Ambrosio—will always be remembered as founders of the nation.

Robert O'Hara Burke
1820-1861

Though the first European settlers landed in Australia in 1788, it was many years before the huge continent was fully explored. Until very recently it was possible to come across tribes of aborigines who had never seen a white man, and there are still vast areas of the interior of the country which are completely uninhabited. In the early days of settlement people stayed close to the coastline, and this is where the big cities of Australia are located today. But there were adventurous men who wanted to know what the rest of the continent looked like, who wanted to be the first to discover new lakes and mountains and perhaps an inland sea, and to be the first to travel from one coast to another. Many of their expeditions ended in failure or disaster, because the *"outback,"* as it is sometimes called, is unfriendly country for travellers unless they are very well equipped. The distances are very great, the heat is intense, and there is hardly any water. Even today people travelling in cars sometimes get lost or, if their cars break down, die of thirst before help can reach them. In the time of Robert O'Hara Burke, the only way of travel was by horse and camel; there were no roads, no settlements, no one to help if anything went wrong. And for Burke and his companion William John Wills things went very wrong indeed.

Robert Burke was born in 1820 at St. Cleran, Co. Galway, a townland half-way between Craughwell and Loughrea. He was the second son of John Hardiman Burke, an army officer. After receiving his education in Belgium, Robert decided to follow the same profession. In 1840 he joined the Austrian army and quickly rose to the rank of Captain. Eight years later he returned to Ireland and became a member of the Irish Constabulary, the police force. He seemed to find it hard to settle down, however, for in 1853 he left home again, this time for Australia. He went first to Tasmania and then to the State of Victoria where he became a district inspector of police, stationed at Castlemaine.

Burke appears to have been popular with all sections of the people in Victoria—a brave, dashing individual who seemed to be the ideal man to head an exploring expedition. In fact, though he had been an army officer, he had had no experience in this kind of work and of course he was new to Australian conditions. When, however, the State decided to equip an expedition to

Burke sets off

cross the continent from south to north, he was chosen to command it. The plan was to reach the sea on the Gulf of Carpentaria. Funds were raised—£1,000 from the government of the State of Victoria and £12,000 from public subscription (exploring was very popular at the time)—and some camels were specially imported from India at a cost of £5,500. The expedition was to collect information about plants, rocks, and other matters of scientific interest, but its real aim was to be the first to cross the continent. Other expeditions were known to be preparing and the race was on.

The Victorian Exploration Expedition left Melbourne on August 20th, 1860, and headed north. Burke quarrelled with one of the members, the camel expert G. J. Landells, before they had left the inhabited areas,

379

Burke, Wills and King at Cooper's Creek

and Landells left the party before they reached Menindee, on the river Darling, on October 19th. On November 11th an advance party under Burke arrived at Cooper's Creek, where they were to wait for the others to catch them up. Ahead of them lay 500 miles of unexplored country, not a great distance by Australian standards, and Burke was anxious to make a start. He began to show signs of impatience and rashness, though no one doubted his courage. On the 16th of December he decided to push ahead, even though the rest of the expedition had not yet caught up with him, and set out on the last lap. This is how Wills, the second in command, recorded the departure in his Field Book: *"SUNDAY, DEC. 16, 1860. The two horses having been shod, and our reports finished, we started at forty minutes past six a.m. for Eyre's Creek, the party consisting of Mr. Burke, myself, King, and Charley (Gray), having with us six camels, one horse and three months' provisions. We followed down the creek to the point where the sandstone ranges cross the creek, and were accompanied to that place by Brahe, who would return to take charge of the depôt."* Brahe had been told to wait three months for them and then to head for home. Burke had left behind him all the scientific part of the expedition and its equipment; he thereafter had no means of gathering any information that would be useful to geologists and botanists. What was worse, neither he nor his companions had any experience in bush-craft, or travelling safely through such difficult and dangerous country.

It was now the height of summer but Burke was lucky in that it was a comparatively wet season and there was plenty of water in the creeks and lagoons. They made good speed, and Wills recorded in his diary: *"MONDAY, DEC. 24th. We took a day of rest on Gray's Creek, to celebrate Christmas. This was doubly pleasant, as we had never in our most sanguine moments anticipated finding such a delightful oasis in the desert."* They crossed the northern dividing range without any difficulty and, following the Cloncurry and Flinders rivers, came within sight of the sea. They did not actually reach the shores of the Gulf of Carpentaria, but found salt water. Satisfied with this, they turned south again.

The journey back was not nearly as pleasant as the journey out. On March 5th Wills wrote: *"Started at 2 a.m. on a S.S.W. course, but had soon to turn in on the creek, as Mr. Burke felt very unwell, having been attacked by dysentry*

On the way to Cooper's Creek

since eating the snake (caught the day before)." Soon Gray
became ill, too. He was caught taking extra flour from
the rations and for this Burke thrashed him. He started
to complain that he could not walk, and on April 17th,
he died. On April 21st the small party, badly weakened,
reached the depôt at Cooper's Creek: *"Arrived at the
depôt this evening,"* wrote Wills, *"just in time to find it
deserted. A note left in the plant by Brahe communicates the
pleasing information that they have started today for the Darling:
their camels and horses all well and in condition. We and our
camels being just done up, and scarcely able to reach the depot,
have very little chance of overtaking them."*

It was here that Burke made two mistakes. He decided
that they could not overtake Brahe's party (he could not
have known that they were camped only 14 miles away),
and that instead of following the route to Menindee, the
way they had come, they should head down the creek
to Mount Hopeless in South Australia, in the hopes of
reaching some settlement. There was plenty of food and
equipment at the depôt, and had they remained there

The death of Wills

they would, in time, have been rescued. But Burke's impatience was his downfall. The party set out again after five days' rest to follow the creek southwards, leaving no sign or message that they had passed through the camp. After they had gone Brahe returned, but finding no trace of them, decided that they were still on the way back from Carpentaria.

The small group did not get far. On April 28th one of their remaining two camels became bogged and had to be shot. They dried the flesh in the sun for food. On May 10th the last camel was killed, and they had to abandon most of their remaining equipment. They fell in with some tribesmen who gave them food, but then left them to fend for themselves. The tribe had been living on a plant called nardoo, from which they made a kind of bread, but Burke could not discover where it grew.

"*SATURDAY, MAY 11. Today Mr. Burke and King started down the creek for the blacks' camp, determined to ascertain all the particulars about the nardoo. I have now my turn at the meat jerking, and must devise some means for trapping the birds and rats, which is a pleasant prospect after our dashing trip to Carpentaria, having to hang about Cooper's Creek, living like the blacks.*"

They existed like this for a few weeks longer, returning to the depôt on May 30th to leave their records of the journey, but getting steadily weaker. They left on June 26th, and on that day the entries in Wills's journal come to a stop. Robert Burke, the leader of the expedition, did not last much longer. Two days later he had to give up from utter weakness, and the next morning when King tried to wake him he found that Burke had died. He had written in his diary: "*I hope we shall be done justice to. We have fulfilled our task but have been aban . . . We have not been followed up as we expected, and the depôt party abandoned their post . . . King has behaved nobly. He has stayed with me to the last, and placed the pistol in my hand, leaving me lying on the surface as I had wished.*"

King was found several months later, living with a group of natives who had looked after him, but he was extremely weak. The bodies of Burke and Wills were taken back to Melbourne where a public funeral was held and a statue of Robert Burke erected in one of the main streets. He had been the wrong man doing the wrong job, killed by a series of misfortunes, misjudgments and misunderstandings, but his expedition paved the way for the opening up of communications across some of the most difficult and dangerous country in the world.

The last entry in Burke's diary

Thomas Francis Meagher
1823-1867

Addressing a political meeting

"*Be it for defence, or be it for the assertion of a nation's liberty, I look upon the sword as a sacred weapon.*" There was a terrible disturbance in the Conciliation Hall in Dublin on July 27th, 1846, when Thomas Francis Meagher said these words. He and his friends were asked to leave by the supporters of Daniel O'Connell, who did not believe in taking up arms, even to gain a nation's liberty. This speech marked a big change in Irish political thought and paved the way for the Rising of 1848.

Thomas Francis Meagher was at this time only twenty-three, but he was already a fine public speaker and anxious to serve his country's cause. "*We walked out together towards my house in Upper Leeson Street,*" John Mitchel wrote, remembering their first meeting, "*through College Green, Grafton Street, Harcourt Street, and out almost into the country near Donnybrook. What talk! What eloquence of talk was his! How fresh, clear and strong!*" In the next few years Meagher was to make many fighting speeches, earning himself the title *Meagher of the Sword* from the English writer William Makepeace Thackeray; and he went on to prove that his bravery was a match for his words.

Thomas Francis Meagher was born in Waterford on August 3rd, 1823. His father, who was Mayor of Waterford and for a time Member of Parliament for the city in the British House of Commons, sent him first to the Jesuits at Clongowes, and then to Stonyhurst in England to complete his education. He was back in Ireland in 1843 and immediately flung himself into the Young Ireland movement, headed by Thomas Davis. Davis died in 1845, but Meagher, Mitchel, Smith O'Brien and their friends went on preparing for a rising. On January 13th, 1847, Meagher became a founder member of the Irish Confederation, which was set up to plan the action, and in 1848 he stood for Parliament in Waterford but was defeated. In the same year he said in a speech: *"If you do not give us a Parliament in which to state our wrongs we shall state them by arms and force."* The British authorities did not like this and Meagher was arrested for sedition. He was released and went to France to take the greetings of the Irish Confederation to the new French Republic which had just been set up. He came back with a tricolour as a present to the citizens of Dublin, the same green, white and orange standard that was to become the national flag nearly seventy years later.

Smith O'Brien

Meanwhile, the Great Famine had struck the country. There was no spirit left in the people for rebellion and on August 5th, 1848, Smith O'Brien's rising at Ballingarry, County Tipperary, was easily put down. On August 13th Meagher was arrested for treason and lodged in Clonmel jail to await trial. He was brought before the court in December with Smith O'Brien, Terence Bellew McManus and Patrick O'Donoghue and sentenced to be hanged, drawn and quartered. He was twenty-five years old. In his speech from the dock he said: *"I do not despair of my old country, her peace, her glory, her liberty! For that country I can do no more than bid her hope. To lift this island up —to make her a benefactor to humanity instead of being the meanest beggar in the world—to restore her to her native power and her ancient constitution—this has been my ambition, and my ambition has been my crime."* The sentence of death was not carried out; instead, Meagher was sentenced to be transported to Tasmania, where convicts were often sent at this time, and sailed on July 27th, 1849, on the *Swift* for Hobart town, a voyage of four months via the Cape of Good Hope.

In Van Diemen's Land, as Tasmania was then called, Meagher was a "ticket of leave man", which meant that he was allowed to live more or less as a free man provided he did not try to escape. Whilst in the colony he was married to Catherine Bennett, on February 22nd, 1851. He lived quietly in a little cottage up in the mountains, paid for by his father in Waterford, and went riding and shooting with his dog. He had to report once a month to the police, but they did not know that a group of Irishmen in America were planning to help him escape. On January 3rd, 1852, Meagher wrote a letter to the magistrate telling him that he was taking back his promise not to escape. As the police came to arrest him, he dashed off into the bush on horseback with four friends, heading for the coast. Two fishermen took him out to the uninhabited Waterhouse Island where he had to wait for a week, living on sea birds' eggs and shellfish, before Captain Bates on the barque _Elizabeth Thompson_ picked him up and took him to Pernambuco in Brazil. There he was transferred to the brig _Acorn,_ which sailed with a cargo of sugar on April 23rd, 1852.

Meagher reached New York at the end of May, 1852, and was given a public reception on the 10th of June. He started giving lectures on his life in Tasmania and

then on the affairs of Ireland. They were very popular and he travelled all over the country. In 1852 he published a book in New York, *The Legislative Independence of Ireland,* which was a collection of his speeches, and in 1854 he started a newspaper, *The Citizen,* with John Mitchel, who had also managed to escape from Van Diemen's Land. The next year he was admitted to the New York Bar and became a lawyer. In this year also he set off on an expedition to Costa Rica in Central America which he afterwards wrote about in *Harper's Magazine.* He was full of energy and ideas, and only waiting for some great cause to follow.

He did not have very long to wait. On April 12th, 1861, guns of the Confederate army opened fire on Fort Sumter, which was on an island in the harbour of Charleston, South Carolina, and was held by Union forces. The American Civil War had begun. On April 11th, President Abraham Lincoln called for 75,000 volunteers to join the armies of the North. Thomas Francis Meagher raised a company for the Sixty-ninth Regiment of the New York State Militia, and, having been elected its captain, set off to join the regiment, which was stationed near Washington, the capital. The *Fighting 69th* was made up mostly of Irishmen, and Meagher's

company, which was also very largely Irish, was to grow into the famous Irish Brigade which played such a large part in the earlier battles of the war.

At first things did not go at all well for the Northern forces. The Confederates defeated the Union forces at the battle of Bull Run (July 12th, 1861) and again at the same place in 1862. Meanwhile, Meagher had returned from the front to raise an Irish Brigade, and he left New York for Washington on November 18th, 1861, with the first regiment, carrying colours with the proud motto *"No Defeat."* He was made a Brigadier-General on February 3rd, 1862, and put in command of a unit which he was to lead with great bravery through many terrible battles.

The Civil War was, like all civil wars, a very bitter one, because brother often fought against brother and father against son. The Irish Brigade was ordered to Virginia, where it fought its first battle on June 1st, 1862—the

Battle of Fair Oaks. *"The chivalry of Virginia met its match in the chivalry of Tipperary,"* Meagher wrote. There followed the battles of Mechanicsville and Gaines Mill, which forced the Union forces to retreat. These conflicts and those that followed became known as the *"Seven Days' Battles;"* and one writer describing the battle of Glendale said, *"Meagher's Irish Brigade rendered itself very conspicuous by the gallantry with which it rushed, with cheers that made the welkin ring, upon the swarming rebels."* When the withdrawal was complete, Meagher went to New York to look for more recruits for his regiments, but found this very difficult, as several commanders were in the city looking for men. The next important battle in which the Irish Brigade took part was Antietam, which was described as the *"bloodiest single day of the war"*— September 17th, 1862. The battle lasted fourteen hours and nearly 120,000 men fought in it. The Confederate army under General Robert E. Lee was forced to retreat and the invasion was stopped.

Banner of the Irish Brigade

The Brigade's last battle was Chancellorsville, on May 2nd, 1863. It had already suffered severe losses in the fighting of the earlier months of the year, but after this battle Meagher wrote to the Assistant Adjutant-General of the Army: *"I beg most respectfully to tender you, and through you to the proper authorities, my resignation as Brigadier-General commanding what was once known as the Irish Brigade. That Brigade no longer exists."* His resignation was accepted, and he was sent by the government westwards to Chattanuga in Tennessee, to take command of the Etowah district. The history of the Irish brigade had been short, but it had covered itself with glory and Meagher had become a national hero.

Meagher did not stay long in Chattanuga. In 1865 he was appointed to the Secretaryship of the Territory of Montana, even further west and hardly settled by white men. The Indians were still dangerous (*"fiendishly ferocious,"* Meagher called them), but he looked forward to the job and wrote from Virginia City on October 6th that he had arrived and was *"Acting Governor of the richest territory of the Union."* He was soon involved in local politics, which he found very tiring and complicated after a soldier's life. On July 1st, 1867, he went to Fort Benton to begin trying to raise a local militia to protect the people from Indian attacks. There was nowhere for him to stay, so he spent the night on an old Missouri steamer which was waiting to set off down the river. About nine o'clock he went for a walk on deck, slipped on a coil of rope and fell overboard. All efforts to save him failed, and his body was never found.

Meagher's life, though a short one, captured the imagination of both the Irish and the Americans through his bravery and devotion to high ideals. Proud of his descent from a second century king of Munster, he believed passionately in his country's right to independence and set an example to many who came after him.

Peter Lalor
1823-1889

Early on Sunday morning, December 3rd, 1854, a small band of gold-diggers at Ballarat in the Australian state of Victoria opened fire from inside a wooden stockade on a force of two hundred and ninety soldiers advancing under cover of darkness. The military fired back and within fifteen minutes the battle of Eureka Stockade was over. Of the thirty-two miners who were killed or wounded many were emigrants from Ireland; and their leader, who escaped with a price of £200 on his head, was Peter Lalor, who had been in Australia only two years.

Peter Lalor was born in Tinakill, in County Laois in 1827. His father, Patrick, was a farmer, and in 1831 he organised what would now be called a "civil rights" campaign against the tithe system. There was fighting between the farmers with their pikes and pitchforks and the tithe-collectors, backed up by the military, and of course the military usually won in the end. But the campaign was a success. Seven years later, in 1838, the British Parliament passed the Tithe Commutation Act, and a great burden was lifted from the ordinary people of Ireland. The tithe system was unfair, because it meant that the Catholic population—and the Presbyterians—had to pay to support the Established Church and its Ministers, thus further reducing the little they had to pay their rent and feed their families. Patrick Lalor fought hard in every way against this injustice (he was elected M.P. for Laois in 1832) and so did his famous son, James Fintan Lalor, who believed that the land of Ireland should belong to the whole community and not just to a few rich landlords. Fintan was ten years older than Peter, and was dead before his younger brother became famous, 13,000 miles away from Abbeyleix, for waging his own fight against government injustice. Had he been alive he would certainly have been proud of him.

Peter Lalor was sent to Trinity College, Dublin, and took up engineering as a career, but like so many young men of his time he decided to emigrate to a country where there was more work and more money to be made. He arrived in Australia in 1852 with his younger brother Richard, and the two of them set up a business in Melbourne, the capital of Victoria, with another Irishman called Phelan, opening a grocery, wine and spirit shop in Elizabeth Street. Richard went back to Ireland in 1853, and Peter and his partner decided to try their luck in the goldfields. Gold had been discovered in Victoria and New South Wales in 1851, and men from all over the world were hurrying to Australia in the hopes of making fortunes for themselves. Peter Lalor went

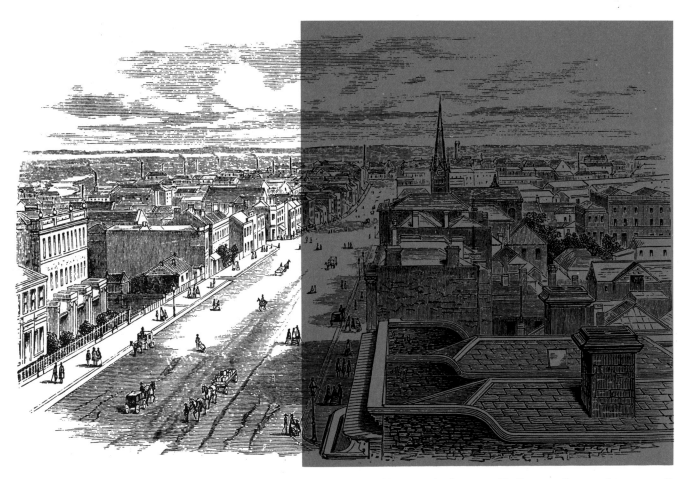

*Melbourne in
Lalor's time*

first to Bendigo and then to Ballarat, formerly a small village of about 70 families which had suddenly become a town of 20,000 people—nearly all of them digging for gold. A prospector's licence cost thirty shillings a month, a large sum in those days, particularly if you were not having any luck with your digging. But then in 1854 the Victorian Government raised it to £3 a month, which was far too much for most of the miners to pay. They felt that they were being very badly treated, because although they had to pay the Government to be allowed to dig for gold, they were not allowed to vote and had no real civil rights. In 1854 a miner called Scobie was murdered, and though everyone knew who had done it, the Government allowed all the suspects to go free. This led to a riot and the burning down of the Eureka Hotel, owned by one of the men who had been mixed up in the murder. The Government acted strongly against the miners and on November 1st, the Ballarat Reform League was formed to fight for equal rights for miners and a fair deal from the Government. On November 28th a detachment of troops was passing the end of one of the mineshafts which was known as *"the fixed headquarters of Young Ireland"* when it was attacked with stones, lumps of wood and broken bottles. The next day there was a huge meeting called by the Reform League at a place called

395

The Rising at Ballarat

Bakery Hill. On this hot summer's day Peter Lalor made a political speech for the first time in his life.

He had been behind the scenes in all the miners' affairs which led up to this meeting, and they had come to recognise him as a natural leader. The meeting decided to burn their licences as a protest against the Government's action and not to take out any more. The next day, November 30th, the Gold Fields Commission sent their representatives to ask the miners to show their licences. What happened is best told in Peter Lalor's own words:

"I was working in a shaft at the Eureka 140 feet deep. Mr. Hayes was at the windlass, and the diggers were employed as usual . . . Suddenly the news was spread that the diggers were being fired on at the Gravel Pits. 'To arms' was the cry, and all that could muster arms moved forward in great confusion toward the Gravel Pits. When we reached Barker and Hunt's store on Specimen Hill, we perceived that the military had taken up a position behind some logs on Bakery Hill. We did not interfere with them. The 'Southern Cross' was procured and hoisted on the flagstaff belonging to Barker and Hunt; but it was almost immediately hauled down, and we moved down to the holes on the Gravel Pits Flat. These holes lie near the road, between the camp and the position which the soldiers occupied. As soon as we commenced moving towards the holes, the bugles of the military sounded a retreat, and the detachment withdrew to the camp."

Another meeting was called for that evening on Bakery Hill. Again Peter Lalor spoke. *"I looked around me,"* he said. *"I saw brave and honest men, who had come thousands of miles to labour for independence. I knew that hundreds were in great poverty, who would possess wealth and happiness if allowed to cultivate the wilderness which surrounded us. The grievances under which we had long suffered, and the brutal attack of that day, flashed across my mind; and, with the burning feelings of an injured man, I mounted the stump and proclaimed 'Liberty'."*

Lalor called for volunteers, and hundreds of men answered his call. There were very few weapons and no one with any real knowledge of warfare, but the men were divided into groups and marched off to wait for the licence inspectors. There was no attack, however, and so a small "inner group" of the volunteers met in a room at the back of a store run by John Diamond, from County Clare, and elected Peter Lalor commander-in-chief by eleven votes to one. Later in the evening all the volunteers went back to Bakery Hill for another meeting. Peter Lalor stood under a pole from which floated the Southern Cross, a silken flag six feet by eight feet, navy blue with a huge white cross emblazoned on it. *"It is my duty now,"* he said, *"to swear you in, and to take, with you, the oath to be faithful to the Southern Cross."* About 500 miners knelt and took the oath with him. Later in the day he wrote to his fiancée, Alicia Dunn: *"Should I fall, shed but a single tear on the grave of one who has died in the cause of honour and liberty, and then forget me until we meet in heaven."*

The next two days, Friday and Saturday, were spent in drilling and preparing for an attack. On Saturday morning they occupied the stockade, a piece of ground at Eureka around which they had built a wall of

398

wooden slabs. *"On Saturday evening there were about 1,500 men within the enclosure, ready and willing to use their arms in defence of their rights,"* said Peter Lalor. *"We had scouts and sentries throughout the diggings, for the purpose of giving us information of any movement on the part of the force at the camp, so that we might have it in our power to rearrange our movements. About twelve o'clock I retired to bed, leaving Mr. McGill in charge; at this time the majority of the men were still in the enclosure. Shortly after this a false alarm was given, which was soon succeeded by another. On the third and real alarm being given, only about 120 men were present in the enclosure."*

Why had so many left? Perhaps because they had decided that there was not going to be an attack after all. When the attack came *"there were about seventy men possessing guns, twenty with pikes, and thirty with pistols, but many of those men with fire-arms had no more than one or two rounds of ammunition,"* said Lalor. No wonder the fight was over so quickly. Many of those killed were shot by the military after they had surrendered. Some managed to escape, including Peter Lalor, who had had his arm shot off at the shoulder. He was hidden in the bush, and later in the presbytery of Father Smyth, an Irish priest who was ministering in Ballarat and who had tried to persuade the miners not to fight. When he was well enough to be moved, he was taken to the home of his fiancée in Geelong.

Thirteen men were arrested and tried for their part in the Eureka affair, many of them Irish. The password had

Trial of the leaders of the Ballarat rising

been "*Vinegar Hill*", and if the revolt had succeeded, perhaps they would have tried to carry on the fight until they had made the state of Victoria an independent republic. Lalor said afterwards that he was only fighting for the miners' rights, but there were men with him who felt they were fighting Britain just as much as the Government of Victoria. No jury would convict the 13 men, and they were all released. The miners raised a subscription for Lalor to help him buy 160 acres of good land within ten miles of Ballarat. In 1855 he was elected to represent the goldfield in the Victoria Parliament, and became Inspector of Railways. He later became Commissioner for Customs (1875), Postmaster General (1878) and Speaker of the House (1880–88). He died on February 9th, 1889, and is buried in Melbourne General Cemetery. Most Australians now think of Peter Lalor as one of the founders of their democracy. He and his fellow Irishmen carried the tradition of '98 halfway across the world, and though they lost the battle, they won the fight—the fight for equal rights and a fair deal for all.

Memorial of the rising at Ballarat

John Philip Holland
1841-1914

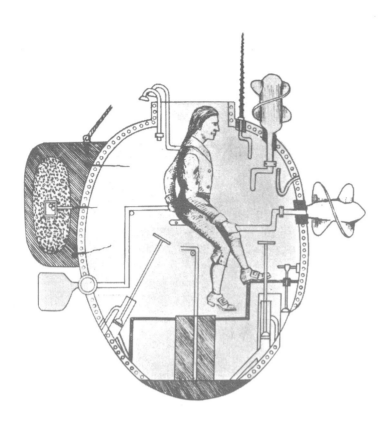

An early American submarine

The seas that beat upon the rugged coastline of County Clare come roaring all the way across the Atlantic, and the turbulent waters that lie under the lee of the cliffs of Moher have been the graveyard of many ships. John Philip Holland was born within sight and sound of these seas, and perhaps their storms and huge waves made him wonder whether it would not be easier and safer to travel under the surface than upon it. Certainly he began sketching ideas for *"submarine boats,"* as they were called then, when he was still a boy at school in Limerick. He had another idea at the back of his mind as he grew to manhood—perhaps such a boat could be used by the Fenians in their fight for independence. He found no one in Ireland to back his idea with money, and without the means himself to turn his ideas into reality he had no choice but to remain a schoolteacher and continue perfecting his plans in his spare time.

John Philip Holland was born in Castle Street, Liscannor, County Clare, on February 24th, 1841. The family name is an English form of the Irish Ó hUallacháin, the name of two septs which spread from Offaly and Thomond into other parts of the country. He went to the Christian Brothers' schools in Ennistymon and Limerick and began teaching in 1858. After the Fenian rising of 1867 he decided, like many others, that there would be more scope for him across the Atlantic, and he emigrated to New Jersey in 1872, taking up a teaching position in the town of Paterson. He was still very interested both in submarines and in the Fenian cause, and, after one of his designs was rejected by the United States navy in 1875, he was given help by the Fenian Society which hoped to be able to sail one of his underwater vessels back across the Atlantic to attack the British navy. Holland built a submarine soon after his arrival in America. It was rather like a big cigar—16 feet long and 2 feet in diameter, and was operated by the one-man crew lying amidships and pedalling it like a bicycle (the pedals turned a propellor at the stern). Holland himself cruised underneath the Passaic River in this strange machine, and it gave him ideas for bigger and better craft.

John Holland was by no means the first man to try to sail under the sea. Experiments had been going on since at least the sixteenth century, and a wooden rowing boat covered with skins was supposed to have sailed under the Thames, carrying King James I of England, sometime

olland's first successful submarine

between 1620 and 1624. Various experimenters tried their hand in the following centuries (including an English clergyman who developed a steam-powered boat in 1879), but when Holland seriously began his experiments there were many problems still to be solved. Most important was the source of power: steam, compressed air, electricity and human power had all been tried, but none had proved completely satisfactory. Then there was the question of control when under the sea—early boats were almost impossible to steer in a straight course because their centre of gravity was wrong. There were other matters, too: strengthening of the hull to stand up to the pressure of the water; supplying the crew with fresh air to breathe; and, since the crafts were to be used in war, designing an efficient method of firing torpedoes. Holland set himself the task of finding the solutions to all of these difficulties, and after many years of experiment and failure he succeeded.

Holland No. 2 was a big advance on *Holland No. 1*. She was a one-man craft with a double hull, fitted with ballast tanks and powered by a 4 h.p. engine. Everything worked well except the engine and John Holland had to try again. His first really successful boat was built in 1881 and was called the *Fenian Ram,* having been paid for by the Fenian Society. She was a 30 foot, three-man craft, driven by a 17 h.p. double-acting oil engine, which gave her the good speed of 7 m.p.h. on the surface. She had both vertical and horizontal rudders, and was armed with a tube in the bow from which dynamite could be fired under water. Holland spent two years experimenting with the *Fenian Ram,* during which he realised that it was very difficult to steer a submarine under water without some means of seeing where you were going. Here was another problem for him to solve!

Although John Holland had a long way to go, he had already discovered and put into practice the most important principles of submarine construction, principles which are still observed today. By the use of small buoyancy chambers to which water was introduced as required, he gave his ships a fixed centre of gravity and stopped them from wandering about all over the ocean. The horizontal rudders kept the submarine's nose pointed downwards, keeping her submerged, and the *trim* of the vessel (the angle at which it lies when under water) was kept the same at all times by letting more water into the ballast tanks to make up for weight lost through fuel or provisions being used up on board.

Cross section of **Holland No. 9**

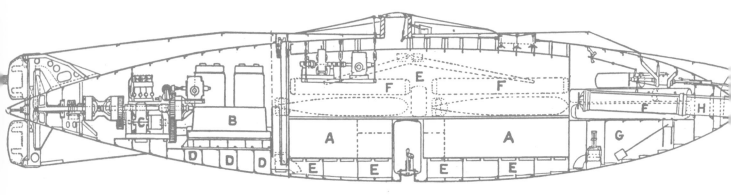

Holland entering his submarine

The United States Government was becoming very interested in submarines, and in 1887 invited people to send them ideas about the best method of building them. John Holland and his rival, an inventor called Nordenfelt, sent in the plans, and it was announced in 1893 that the County Clare man had won a government contract to build a submarine. This vessel, to be called the *Plunger,* was Holland's seventh, but she was never completed. The government thought they knew better than the designer how she should be built and powered, and insisted that she should have two propellers to pull her under the water (an idea of Nordenfelt's). Holland disagreed strongly with this, and he was quite right, but the government would not listen. The *Plunger* was to have been steampowered on the surface, giving her a speed of 15 knots, but the engine power was altered to petrol. There were so many changes in his design that Holland asked to stop work on the vessel and start all over again.

He built the *Holland No. 8* which did not come up to his expectations. Then in 1898 came the *Holland No. 9*. The official report on this submarine said: *"She has shown herself capable of such perfect control in the vertical plane that she may be kept whilst moving within a few inches of any desired depth, and that she may be brought to the surface and submerged again in a very short time."*

John Holland had succeeded. A Navy board headed by Admiral George Dewey studied the *Holland No. 9* and recommended that six more like her should be built. She was 53 feet 10 inches in length and 10 feet 7 inches in diameter, displacing 75 tons on the surface. She was fitted with a petrol engine which gave her a speed of 7 knots on the surface and electric motors moved her at 6 knots submerged. The range of the craft was 1,500 miles on the surface and 50 under water, and she could dive

Holland No. 9 *submerging*

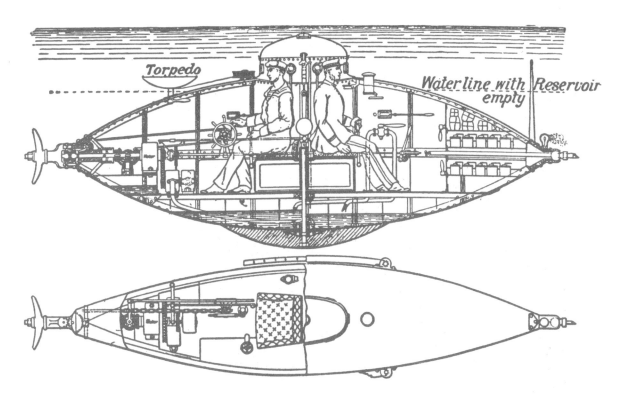

Torpedo

Waterline with Reservoir empty

Section of a French Submarine designed by Goubet

28 feet in 5 seconds. The armament consisted of three tubes—one for torpedoes and two for dynamite shells, which were still popular as undersea weapons. One problem had not been completely solved: no periscope was fitted and the target had to be sighted through portholes in the ship's hull—not a very satisfactory arrangement. But the United States navy was satisfied. *Holland No. 9* became the *U.S.S. Holland,* the first submarine in the American Navy, and she was followed by forty-seven others of the same or improved types. Other governments were interested, too. The *Holland* was commissioned as S.S.1 on October 13th, 1900, and in the following year the British Admiralty ordered five ships of the same type. Soon there were Holland submarines being added to the navies of Russia, Japan, and many other countries all over the world. In America nearly sixty submarines had been built by the time the 1914 war broke out, most of them to John Holland's design.

The Irish inventor should have enjoyed a well-earned success, but it seems that he was a better ship-designer than he was a businessman. The first three submarines for the United States navy were built by the Crescent Shipyards, Elizabeth, New Jersey, which had been set up in 1895. This Company ran into difficulties, however, and though foreign navies ordered Holland's ships or paid him royalties for using his design, John Holland

Holland's submarine in dry dock

spent a great deal of time in the last years of his life
arguing with people to whom he owed money or who
owed him money.

These difficulties did not stop him from inventing,
however. John Holland realised that submarines, by
their very nature, were bound to be dangerous craft to
sail in, and he turned his attentions to the safety of the
crew. In 1904 he built a *respirator,* a device that would
make it possible for men to escape from a submarine
which had been damaged and could not surface. This
idea was used by several navies and saved many lives in
both world wars. Though Holland was a Fenian and a
builder of warships, he was not altogether a blood-
thirsty man; in fact, it was said of him that his idea in
developing the submarine was to make war such a
terrible thing that it would be outlawed. We are still
hoping for that to happen. Nowadays submarines can
circle the earth underwater, and plans for huge submarine oil tankers and passenger ships are being
developed. All these have been made possible by the
genius of John Philip Holland, who had a good idea and
was determined to make it work.

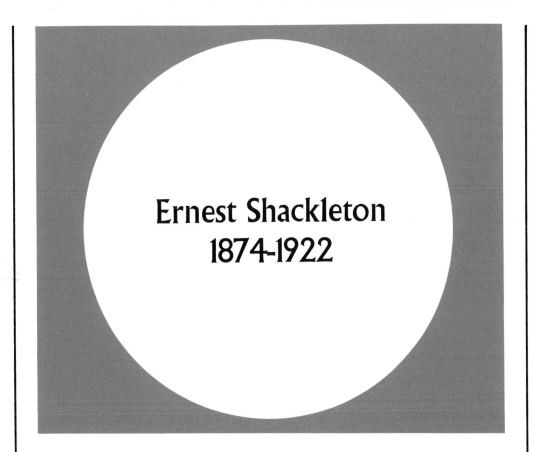

Ernest Shackleton
1874-1922

"*The most pig-headed, obstinate boy I ever came across.*"
That was what the Captain of the *Houghton Tower* said
about Ernest Henry Shackleton after he had completed
his first voyage to South America and back as a boy
apprentice. It was a long voyage, lasting from 30th
April, 1890 till 4th April, 1891, and young Shackleton
was only sixteen when he set out on it. By the time he
came back he had decided there was only one life for him
—sailing to far-away places in search of excitement and
adventure . . . and a fortune.

At the end of the last century there were still many
places in the world waiting to be discovered and it
took weeks rather than days to get to places like China
and Australia. There were two vast areas man had
never explored—the lands and seas around the South
Pole and the lands and seas around the North Pole.
Explorers were racing each other to be the first to
reach the Poles; it was not long before Shackleton
decided to enter the race.

Shackleton's family had been living near Athy,
County Kildare, since the early 1800's, when his
ancestors had emigrated from England. Ernest was
born at Kilkea on 15th February, 1874. His father
Henry, who was educated at Trinity College, Dublin,
was a farmer, and his mother was a member of the Gavan
family from County Cork. He had five brothers and
sisters. In 1880 his father decided to give up farming and
go back to Trinity to study medicine, so the family

Shackleton as a boy

moved to 35 Marlborough Road, Dublin. They stayed there for four years until Mr. Shackleton had finished his studies. Then the whole family moved to London, where Mr. Shackleton took up practice as a doctor and Ernest started going to school. He was called *"Mick"* because of his Irish accent. Ernest may have been pigheaded as a boy, but he turned out to be a good seaman, passing his examination for Second Mate in 1894 and for First Mate in 1896. By then he had travelled the world and was looking for more excitement. He joined the Union Castle line in 1899 and heard not long afterwards about the expedition being organised by Captain Robert Falcon Scott to go to the Antarctic. He decided to do all he could to join it. Thanks to some friends who put in a good word for him, he found himself sailing from England in the *Discovery* on July 31st, 1901, bound for the Southern seas and perhaps the South Pole. His job was to look after the stores and to conduct scientific experiments on the amount of salt in the sea at different places, but what he was really looking forward to was the adventure. *"It is a unique sort of feeling to look on lands that have never been seen by human eyes before,"* he said a little later, as

Trapped by the ice

the ship made its way between the ice-floes off the Antarctic continent. Their destination was McMurdo Sound. On February 9th, 1902, the *Discovery*, tied up and locked in by ice, stopped being a ship and became officially a "shore station". The idea was to use her as a base camp from which to reach the South Pole using dogs and sledges.

Antarctica is not a very homely place. The temperature never rises above freezing point, there are scarcely any plants and the biggest animal is a wingless fly less than half a centimetre long! Scott's expedition had trouble with scurvy, a disease which is caused by a lack of the Vitamin C in fresh food, and with their teams of dogs, which were very unruly. There was also trouble because the expedition was run on naval lines, even though several of the men, including Shackleton, were merchant seamen and not used to the navy way of doing things. In spite of these setbacks, Scott decided to set out for the South Pole. After a winter spent in camp—during which Shackleton edited the *South Polar Times*, the first periodical to be produced in the Antarctic—Scott chose two companions, Dr. Edward Wilson and Ernest Shackleton, to go with him. The three men reached Latitude 82° 16′—further south than anyone had ever been before—but Shackleton became ill and had to be sent back on a relief ship in 1902. Some people think that Scott and Shackleton did not get on very well together on this journey: certainly after this they were rivals rather than friends.

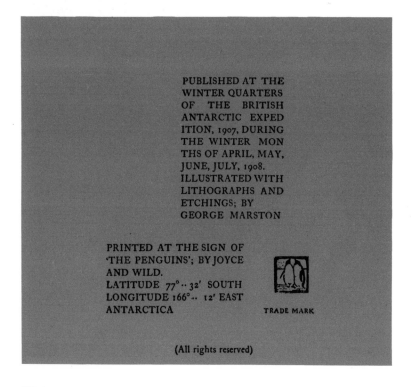

PUBLISHED AT THE WINTER QUARTERS OF THE BRITISH ANTARCTIC EXPEDITION, 1907, DURING THE WINTER MONTHS OF APRIL, MAY, JUNE, JULY, 1908. ILLUSTRATED WITH LITHOGRAPHS AND ETCHINGS; BY GEORGE MARSTON

PRINTED AT THE SIGN OF 'THE PENGUINS'; BY JOYCE AND WILD.
LATITUDE 77°·· 32′ SOUTH
LONGITUDE 166°·· 12′ EAST
ANTARCTICA

TRADE MARK

The crater of Erebus

Shackleton returned to England and tried several different jobs—including journalism and running a cigarette firm. He married in 1904 and stood for parliament for Dundee in 1906, but was not elected. His heart was really set on going back to the Antarctic, this time with his own expedition. Later in 1906 he began raising money to buy a ship and equip it, and in 1907 the British Antarctic Expedition set sail, with Shackleton as the leader. He had promised Scott, who was organising his own expedition, that he would not use his old base at McMurdo Sound, but when he

413

reached the ice he was forced to do so as there was no
other way open to him. He established a camp at Cape
Royds, building a hut with rooms made out of packing
cases and all kinds of bits and pieces, and on February
22nd, 1908, their ship, the *Nimrod,* steamed off and left
them there—they were to be out of touch with civilisation
for a year at least. There were fifteen in the party, and
they had many things to keep them occupied during the
long Antarctic winter, including a printing press on
which they produced a magazine called *Aurora Australia.*
They climbed nearby Mount Erebus, an active volcano
13,200 feet high, and went into training for their journey

towards the South Pole. At last, on October 29th, 1908—
spring in the Southern Hemisphere—Shackleton and
three companions set off with ponies and sledges on the
great journey. The ponies went lame, the weather grew
worse and worse, and food began to run out. They
climbed a huge glacier hoping that it would flatten out

into a plateau, but it went on and on and when they did get to the top they were too weak and short of food to go much further. On January 5th, 1909, they lay in their tent listening to a ninety-mile-an-hour blizzard outside. The temperature was down to minus 30°C. On January 9th, they made one more dash forward, and that night Shackleton wrote in his diary: *The last day out we have shot our bolt and the tale is 88° 23'S. 162°E. . . . Beaten the South Record by 366 miles.* . . . By the time they reached the safety of the *Nimrod*, which had come back on 28th February to pick them up, they had covered 1,725 miles in 126 days.

When Shackleton returned to England he was welcomed as a hero. He was knighted, wrote a book and gave lectures all over Europe about his experiences. He still had his heart set on reaching the South Pole, but in 1912 it was reached by the Norwegian, Amundsen, and then by Captain Scott, who died on the way back. Shackleton next had the idea of trying to cross the Antarctic continent from one side to the other, and his

The James Caird

ship, the *Endurance*, left Plymouth on August 8th, 1914, headed once more for the southern oceans, carrying much new equipment, including propellor-driven sledges. They reached the island of South Georgia in November and sailed south again on December 5th.

Things did not go well, however. By January 27th, 1915, the *Endurance* was stuck fast in the ice. On the 24th February she became a "winter station" and the dogs were unloaded into special "dogloos" that the crew had built for them. As the Antarctic winter wore on, the pressure of the ice on the ship grew greater and greater, until on October 27th they had to abandon her completely and on 21st of November she broke up and sank. The expedition was now stranded thousands of miles from anywhere. There was nothing for it but to make camp, wait for the weather to get better, and get ready for a journey that seemed certain to end in disaster.

The party stayed on the ice near where the ship had gone down until 9th April, 1916, when they launched three of the small boats they had saved from the wreck and set sail for Elephant Island, about 570 miles southeast of Cape Horn. This was completely uninhabited and there was no chance of their being rescued unless someone could go for help. Shackleton picked five of his men and set off in a 20-foot boat, the *James Caird*, to sail 800 miles to South Georgia, the nearest inhabited land, across the roughest, coldest, most dangerous seas in the world. It was a terrible journey—from April 24th to May 10th. This epic voyage proved Shackleton to be one of the bravest commanders and finest leaders in the history of the sea. Even when he reached South Georgia he had to cross mountains and glaciers 10,000 feet high to get to the whaling station at Stromness. It took four attempts to rescue the men he had left on Elephant Island.

In May 1917 Shackleton was back in London. The Great War was still on, and he was given the job of getting military equipment to northern Russia. After the Armistice he was again planning an expedition, and in 1921 went to Norway to buy a boat which he renamed *Quest*. It was on board this small vessel that he died suddenly on January 5th, 1922 at Grytviken, South Georgia, on his way to fight once more against the ice and snow and danger. Shackleton was a leader loved by his men for his bravery, his Irish wit, his ability to plan every detail and foresee almost every danger. His courage showed men the way to developing the Frozen Continent peacefully and for the good of all.

Index